D1559533

THE CANNIBAL WITHIN

EVOLUTIONARY FOUNDATIONS OF HUMAN BEHAVIOR
An Aldine de Gruyter Series of Texts and Monographs
EDITED BY
Monique Borgerhoff Mulder • Marc Hauser

Richard D. Alexander, **The Biology of Moral Systems**

Laura L. Betzig, **Despotism and Differential Reproduction: A Darwinian View of History**

James S. Chisholm, **A Navajo Infancy: An Ethological Study of Child Development**

Russell l. Ciochon and John G. Fleagle (eds.), **Primate Evolution and Human Origins**

G.A. Clark and C.M. Willermet (eds.), **Conceptual Issues in Modern Human Origins Research**

Lee Cronk, Napoleon Chagnon, and William Irons (eds.), **Adaptation and Human Behavior: An Anthropological Perspective**

Martin Daly and Margo Wilson, **Homicide**

Irenäus Eibl-Eibesfeldt, **Human Ethology**

Richard J. Gelles and Jane B. Lancaster (eds.), **Child Abuse and Neglect: Biosocial Dimensions**

Kathleen R. Gibson and Anne C. Petersen (eds.), **Brain Maturation and Cognitive Development: Comparative and Cross-Cultural Perspectives**

Frederick E. Grine (ed.), **Evolutionary History of the "Robust" Australopithecines**

Barry S. Hewlett (ed.), **Father-Child Relations: Cultural and Biosocial Contexts**

Kim Hill and A. Magdalena Hurtado, **Ache Life History: The Ecology and Demography of a Foraging People**

Warren G. Kinzey (ed.), **New World Primates: Ecology, Evolution, and Behavior**

Jane B. Lancaster, Jeanne Altmann, Alice S. Rossi, and Lonnie R. Sherrod (eds.), **Parenting across the Life Span: Biosocial Dimensions**

Jonathan Marks, **Human Biodiversity: Genes, Race, and History**

Lewis Petrinovich, **The Cannibal Within**

Richard B. Potts, **Early Hominid Activities at Olduval**

Eric Alden Smith, **Inujjuamiut Foraging Strategies: Evolutionary Ecology of an Arctic Hunting Economy**

Eric Alden Smith and Bruce Winterhalder (eds.), **Evolutionary Ecology and Human Behavior**

Barbara Boardman Smuts, **Sex and Friendship in Baboons**

Patricia Stuart-Macadam and Susan Kend (eds.), **Diet, Demography, and Disease: Changing Perspectives on Anemia**

Wenda R. Trevathan, **Human Birth: An Evolutionary Perspective**

James W. Wood, **Dynamics of Human Reproduction: Biology, Biometry, Demography**

THE CANNIBAL WITHIN

Lewis Petrinovich

ALDINE DE GRUYTER
New York

About the Author

Lewis Petrinovich is Professor Emeritus, Department of Psychology, University of California, Riverside. Dr. Petrinovich is currently a resident of Berkeley, California.

ALDINE DE GRUYTER
A division of Walter de Gruyter, Inc.
200 Saw Mill River Road
Hawthorne, New York 10532

This publication is printed on acid free paper ∞

Library of Congress Cataloging-in-Publication Data
Petrinovich, Lewis F.
    The cannibal within / Lewis Petrinovich.
        p. cm. — (Evolutionary foundations of human behavior)
    Includes bibliographical references and index.
    ISBN 0-202-02047-9 (cloth : alk. paper) — ISBN 0-202-02048-7 (pbk. : alk. paper)
    1. Cannibalism.   I. Title.   II. Series.
    GN409.P47 2000
    394'.9—dc21   99-057940

Manufactured in the United States of America

10 9 8 7 6 5 4 3 2 1

Contents

Preface

Why is a dedicated Neo-Darwinist writing a book on such an unlikely subject as human cannibalism? The topic has a lurid fascination and provokes at minimum a morbid interest in some, rising to a sense of revulsion in others (particularly when offered as a topic for dinner conversation). My initial interest in cannibalism was aroused when, in a previous book, I considered the question of whether it is morally permissible for people to eat animals of other species. That book, *Darwinian Dominion: Animal Welfare and Human Interests* (Petrinovich, 1999), dealt with moral, scientific, and practical issues regarding the various uses of animals of other species by humans. While thinking through issues regarding the permissibility of eating animals it occurred to me that it would be interesting to consider the question of whether it is ever permissible to eat humans, and if so under what circumstances. As I read about some of the well-known instances of survival cannibalism, and considered the archaeological evidence for cannibalism, I discovered that it has been a common occurrence throughout human history—so common that the subject merits careful review. Because the length of *Darwinian Dominion* was becoming excessive, I eliminated the material on cannibalism, and the present book is the result.

After a cursory examination of the literature, I decided something significant can be revealed about evolved aspects of human morality through an examination of cannibalism. This revelatory significance is sufficient to justify careful inquiry, particularly into survival cannibalism—that done by starving people in order to avoid imminent death. When such starvation occurs the social rules that apply in normal times are no longer relevant, and people revert to more basic survival behaviors. The title of the book reflects my belief that cannibalism is not a pathology that erupts in psychotic individuals, but is a universal adaptive strategy that is evolutionarily sound. The cannibal is within all of us, and cannibals are within all cultures, should the circumstances demand the appearance.

The major instances in which survival cannibalism occurred convinced me that there is a consistent pattern and a uniform regularity in the order in which different kinds of individuals are consumed. In considering who eats whom, when, and under what circumstances, this regularity appears, and it is consistent with what would be expected on the basis of evolutionary theory. I conclude that starvation cannibalism is not a manifestation of the chaotic, psychotic behavior of individuals driven to madness, but reveals underlying characteristics of evolved human nature.

Some are of the opinion that cannibalism has never taken place among "normal" humans, particularly those in "civilized" societies, and questions have been raised as to whether it ever existed, even among "savages" (note that the scare quotes around those words signal that there are definitional and political problems lurking in the wings). I review as much of the extensive literature concerning survival cannibalism as I could find. To address the issues involved in cannibalism more completely I considered instances of ritual cannibalism, and was surprised to find how widespread it has been throughout human history and in most regions of the world. Not being an anthropologist or ethnographer, I made no attempt to determine why and under what circumstances ritual cannibalism is practiced. That task remains a fascinating one for a qualified expert.

I am grateful for the aid and comfort I received from a number of friends and colleagues. I had many discussions regarding the project with my former students and now colleagues A. J. Figueredo, University of Arizona, and Patricia O'Neill, University of Mississippi, both of whom read the manuscript in one form or another. Marc Hauser, Harvard University, encouraged me to begin and complete the book, served as academic editor for Aldine, made me realize that my first attempt was off the mark, headed me in a more profitable direction, and straightened out a major problem in the final draft. His continuing advice was to adopt a consistent voice and not to try to address too many audiences at once—in other words to be less schizophrenic—and I think I was able successfully to bridge the gap between the scholar and the general reader.

I profited greatly from conversations with Tim White, University of California, Berkeley, and Christy Turner, Arizona State University, Tempe. They influenced my thinking about archaeological issues, particularly those concerning the Anasazi.

Curtis Hardyck, University of California, Berkeley, read the first complete draft of the manuscript, flagged a number of unclear and confusing sections, and urged me to lighten up in some of my more pedantic moments. Kim Hill, University of New Mexico, reviewed the entire final manuscript, made numerous helpful suggestions that I took, and provided unpublished material regarding Ache cannibalism, which is included in Chapter 6.

I have had several interesting and informative communications with Richard Koffler, the executive editor for Aldine. He wisely shepherded me and the book throughout the processes of thinking, writing, and production. The production editor, Mai Shaikhanuar-Cota, was a joy to work with; she made the final steps in the process of publication more of a pleasure than a chore.

Bon Appétit!

1

Introduction to People Eating

Cannibalism is one of the primordial mores. It dates from the earliest existence of man on earth. It may reasonably be believed to be a custom which all people have practiced.

—Sumner (1940)

STORY OF THE *FRANCIS MARY*

In 1826, the timber ship *Francis Mary*, with 21 people aboard, crashed en route to Liverpool. As survivors died they were eaten, and some of the living were killed and eaten. This is one of several cases of survival cannibalism to be discussed; it is a real and common phenomenon, rather than a myth as some have claimed. Survival cannibalism is a fact of human nature, and I open this chapter with this case to introduce the essence of cannibalistic events.

The tribulations of the *Francis Mary* began when a severe gale stove in the stern of the ship on February 5, and the crew was able to save only a little bread and cheese (Simpson, 1984). Although the captains of two vessels spoke with the crew of the derelict shortly after the disaster, they offered no assistance because of severe adverse weather conditions. At that time the rule of the sea was that no ship had a legal obligation to aid other vessels in distress. This seemingly heartless behavior was reasonable because rescue activities could jeopardize the safety of the rescuers, and might even leave the rescue ship shorthanded should any disaster occur while part of the crew was taking the victims off—not too far fetched given that commercial sailing vessels of that time carried crews of minimal size to reduce costs. Also, if a number of survivors were rescued, the limited supplies of food and water might not be sufficient to support the increased number of people, particularly if unforeseen delays were encountered. Another tradition of the sea was that if members of the crew

2 Introduction to People Eating

were cast adrift in a lifeboat they had no obligation to obey officers; authority was determined only by the personal qualities of the captain (Simpson, 1984).

For the survivors of the *Francis Mary*, both provisions and water were nearly depleted by February 6. On February 12, a crewman died, followed 10 days later by another. By the time the second sailor died the 18 people still alive had not eaten for 10 days, and had only a biscuit and a half during each of the 6 days before that (Leslie, 1988). The second sailor to die was quartered, hung up for food, cut in slices, and dried. The meat was divided among the survivors, and one survivor described it as a "sweet morsel." The next day another person died and his liver and heart were eaten. In the next few days 7 more died, including the cook, leaving 11 still alive—9 men and both of the women who were on board.

The cook was accompanied by his betrothed, Ann Saunders, and Simpson (1984) wrote that as he was dying (she claimed he was already dead) she cut his throat and claimed prior property rights to his blood. Simpson (1984, p. 126) characterized her as "a particularly tough character" who assumed the duty of cutting up and cleaning the dead bodies thereafter.

Ann Saunders (1827) recounted a similar version in a narrative she published, only she gives her role a slightly better spin. She wrote that as hunger increased, "we eyed each other with mournful and melancholy looks." She acknowledged she did "plead her claim to the greater portion of his [the betrothed cook's] precious blood," but having been reduced to that horrid alternative by hunger and thirst, she did so to preserve her own life. She wrote (p. 101): "Oh, this was a bitter cup, indeed!," and emphasized the importance of her strength of character, which enabled her to unite the group in prayer to prepare their precious souls for eternity. The six survivors rescued on March 7 included the captain, his wife (who had sustained herself on the brains of an apprentice for 2 days), and Ann Saunders.

The lieutenant of the British frigate who was sent to rescue them remarked: "You have yet, I perceive, fresh meat." He was informed: "No, it is part of a man, one of our unfortunate crew." The survivors claimed that all the dead had expired gradually and naturally, usually driven mad by drinking sea water, but it was suspected some may have been killed.

The story of the *Francis Mary* is typical of what is encountered in shipwreck disasters: In the beginning, attention is devoted to securing the vessel and available provisions and tending to the needs of the survivors. Supplies usually are rationed and order prevails until people begin dying from exposure, starvation, and dehydration. At first the dead are buried at sea, but soon their blood is drunk and they are eaten; if there are no dead available for consumption, killing begins. In most survival stories, the survivors attest to the natural death of all who were eaten. When someone is killed for the purpose of being eaten, the survivors almost always swear that a fair lottery was held. However, as we shall find, the loser is usually the obvious choice: a boy (apprentice seaman), a foreigner, or a slave, never an officer and seldom a cook. And who is going to represent the case of the eaten fairly; certainly not the diners. There may be many unreported cases in which cannibalism occurred, but the evidence was thrown overboard and the survivors denied all.

In almost none of the cases of seagoing cannibalism were any charges brought against anyone, and only in the case of the *Mignonette* (discussed fully in Chapter 3) were charges brought against officers for killing a young, dying seaman. These charges were brought only because the officers stated publicly that no lottery had been held. The authorities and general public usually accept the utilitarian argument that it was necessary for one (or a few) to die so that any (or more) could live. The survivors were often hailed as brave heroes who had suffered horribly and should be acclaimed, and they were usually provided with financial support. Such acclaim and support are particularly strong from other seamen.

As I searched the literature, I was struck by the widespread occurrence of cannibalism (the term I will use for all types of anthropophagy—the eating of humans by other humans) throughout prehistory and recorded human history, and became impressed by the wide range of circumstances under which it occurs. Rawson (1992) pointed out that cannibalism is often considered by many writers to be too horrible to mention (and others have described it as unthinkable). Yet there is an immense literature that not only mentions this "unthinkable" aspect of human nature, but dwells on it profusely. Cannibalism is not practiced only by maddened people at the edge of their wits because of starvation or severe mental derangement. As abhorrent as cannibalism seems to many, it is as ubiquitous as other "uncivilized" practices that have characterized human societies throughout their existence, such as torture, murder, incest, infanticide, and war. To a Darwinist, the suggestion that a behavior is universal sparks interest because it might signal unexplored aspects of an evolved human nature, and such universals could place limits on the conceptions of some anthropologists who stress cultural relativism (see Brown, 1991; Cook, 1999).

In this book I will discuss a number of cases of survival cannibalism that have been documented extensively. I sketched this one instance of seafaring cannibalism here to highlight some of the issues that will concern us throughout this book. I will challenge the view that cannibalism is rare; it is not in the realm of mythology and has occurred throughout human history. This discussion introduced the type of events that occurs in such instances; these events exhibit a regularity and patterning consistent with expectations based on evolutionary theory.

When sailing vessels provided the major mode of sea travel, before the development of radio communication, the survivors of a shipwreck often had to spend many days on disabled ships or in lifeboats with little in the way of food or water. On such occasions a decision often had to be made as to whether to throw some individuals overboard because there were inadequate provisions for all. When it was necessary to abandon the ship there often were not enough lifeboats to accommodate all of the crew and passengers. Lifeboats were therefore overloaded and often leaked due to poor construction, inadequate maintenance, or damage during launching. In many instances humans who died were eaten and their blood was drunk; in other instances the survivors killed and ate some of their fellows. These cases will be considered in detail in Chapter 3 because they provide historical instances similar to those involved in the lifeboat fantasy dilemmas we have used in empirical studies of moral intuitions—studies that will be discussed briefly below.

THE CANNIBAL AGENDA

Some have claimed there are almost no tidy historical accounts of people eating people, and there even are disagreements about the derivation of the term *cannibal;* some commentators question both the trustworthiness of accounts of various authorities and observers as well as their motivations in presenting the accounts as they do. There has been disagreement regarding how prevalent cannibalism has been throughout human existence, although there are many myths about its significance throughout recorded time, as well as a lively industry in fictional representations of cannibalism. Lestringant (1997), a French Professor of Renaissance Literature, surveyed the writings of European explorers, intellectuals, and missionaries in order to understand the mythic thinking contained in Western ideas regarding cannibalism. His survey, discussed in Chapter 9, begins with Christopher Columbus, discusses Montaigne's famous essays (Book One published in 1580), and includes discussions of the fictional representations of Dickens, DeFoe, Melville, and Swift, among others. Cannibalism has been the focus of a wide range of writers, and the fascination with cannibalism has occasioned extensive discussions that are more open than many discussions regarding certain human sexual practices.

A few words are in order regarding the origin of the term cannibalism. Strictly speaking, we should use the more neutral, descriptive word *anthropophagy,* derived from a combination of the Greek words *anthropos* (man) and *phagein* (to eat), and broadly defined as the eating of human flesh by human beings. Lestringant (1997) noted that the noun *cannibal* derives from the Arawak *caniba,* which is universally accepted to be a corruption of *cariba,* meaning "bold," the term the Caribbean Indians of the

Lesser Antilles applied to themselves. When used by the neighboring, peace-loving Arawak, the term caniba carried the pejorative connotation of extreme ferocity and barbarity.

Lestringant (1997) credited Christopher Columbus with not only the discovery of America but also with the use of the term cannibal during his voyage of 1492. Columbus noted that his informants told him there were men with only one eye and others with dogs' snouts who are men, and he promoted the use of the insulting name the victim Arawak tribes had bestowed on their cannibalistic neighbors. Natives of many tribes throughout the Americas were construed to be much "like starving wolves" who greedily drank the blood of their enemies. These views led to the demonization of the natives; they were characterized as lacking religion, laws, rulers, and private property and as violating the incest taboo. Lestringant (1997; pp. 28–29) noted that these views represented a shift "back towards savagery and away from the tranquillity of Paradise lost . . . fathers have been seen to eat their wives and children . . . with their ferocious appetites and unrestrained sexuality, [being] the precise opposite of Christian society, as conceived by the Renaissance."

This characterization was used by the Spaniards to mount what they termed to be a just war against the Caribs, and, incidentally, to justify selling Carib prisoners as slaves. The cannibal label was applied to even the most peaceable Indian tribes to justify their enslavement (in the interest of financing expeditions in search of gold) and to permit the annihilation of such savages. The negative connotations of the term *cannibal* continue to the present time, and are used to express horror and indignation whenever acts of anthropophagy take place.

Although I will offer evolutionary interpretations throughout this book, I emphasize that it is not possible to make evolutionary predictions with great certainty regarding who eats whom, when, why, and in what order. There are too many unique exigencies and fortuitous circumstances involved in each particular case. What can be done is to construct an explanation that is consistent with the way evolutionary predispositions are known to affect better understood complex organic systems, and to ask whether the sequence of cannibalistic events can be fitted into the evolutionary mold without making too much of an adaptationist stretch.

In the section "Suspending Societal Norms" we have been successful in empirical attempts to understand moral intuitions—although we have shifted several of our emphases as data accumulated. Now, I have moved toward a more reasonable and parsimonious model than entertained originally. I will offer what I think is a defensible evolutionary interpretation of cannibalism, but I am certain it is wrong in some details. However, the episodes of survival cannibalism add another converging line of evidence regarding the role of evolved processes in the working of human nature.

Concerning an ecological and evolutionary model to understand ritual cannibalism, I hope that far more competent and informed people than I will develop and elaborate it for the many cultures that exhibit such cannibalism.

Finally, I am reminded of one of my favorite quotations from Darwin (1871, p. 909): "False facts are highly injurious to the progress of science, for they often endure: but false views, if supported by some evidence, do little harm, for every one takes a salutary pleasure in proving their falseness; and when this is done one path towards error is closed and the road to truth is often at the same time opened."

TYPES OF CANNIBALISM

Several types of cannibalism have been described in terms of their purpose (Salmon, 1995):

1. to satisfy hunger, provide a supplement to the regular diet (gastronomic cannibalism), or to survive under conditions of extreme starvation (survival cannibalism);
2. to cure or ward off disease (medicinal cannibalism);
3. to maintain continuity with one's dead relatives (mortuary cannibalism);
4. to propitiate gods, enact revenge, or gain the strength of an enemy (sacrificial cannibalism); and
5. to terrify one's neighbors or enemies by ruthlessly and publicly consuming those you capture and kill (political cannibalism).

There is also a general classification used to refer to the relationship between eater and eaten: exocannibalism, when those eaten are outsiders, and endocannibalism, when they are members of the community.

Survival Cannibalism

Survival cannibalism tends to occur when conditions become such that the traditions, rules, and laws that regulate normal day-to-day existence are no longer effective. In these cases people are freed from constraints that have been instilled by the culture within which they have been nurtured, educated, and indoctrinated. Such conditions exist when severe and prolonged disasters drive them to the edge of starvation; then there is an almost universal tendency to engage in cannibalism. It is as though the outer coverings of society have been peeled away to reveal the basic core of human nature. If cannibalism occurs when normal societal rules break down, it has been suggested that these rules are replaced by incoherent, psychotic patterns of behavior. If so, there should be a chaotic pattern to those behaviors that occur, and that will not be seen to be the case.

The patterns of behavior that occur in cases of survival cannibalism are orderly, and make biological sense—they appear to reveal behavioral tendencies that have evolved to forward the ultimate goal of perpetuating one's genes into future generations—an outcome known as reproductive success. I will consider some of the ecological and societal factors that predispose some groups of individuals to engage in cannibalism more readily than others in similar circumstances.

Edmonson (1984) suggested that cannibalism should be examined using an old journalistic adage: When did who do what to whom and where and how and why? This is a sensible suggestion to keep in mind as we wend our way through the literature bearing on the different types of cannibalism.

SUSPENDING SOCIETAL NORMS

One way to glimpse the basic mechanisms that regulate behavior would be to study events that take place when people must survive in times of disaster. When the disaster is severe and continues over a long term, with the survival of many individuals involved, the normal rules of civilization are no longer operable. Behavior during disasters can reveal basic patterns of coping that come into play as victims are forced to devise ways to survive. Such disasters often are those in which people starve because they are isolated and stranded, are under severe conditions of siege in wartime, have suffered shipwreck and are adrift in lifeboats, and have endured times of prolonged famine. Those disasters in which cannibalism did not occur also can be examined to try to understand the constraints that prevented the appearance of a behavior that occurs frequently, although most members of society deplore it.

Another way to peel away the layers of social convention in order to glimpse the structure of people's moral beliefs is to ask them to resolve hypothetical dilemmas (Petrinovich, 1995). I chose to study those dimensions identified by philosophers and biologists as possibly being important factors determining the moral choices people make.

My colleagues and I investigated human moral intuitions by posing dilemmas in which people were asked to make choices between unpalatable alternatives (Petrinovich, O'Neill, & Jorgensen, 1993; Petrinovich & O'Neill, 1996; O'Neill & Petrinovich, 1998). These dilemmas were remote from anything that the respondents would have experienced, or would likely ever experience, in the course of their normal existence; but the choices had to be made, even though all available alternatives were often abhorrent to them. People took this exercise seriously and became involved in the process of choosing; there was consistency in choices, both across individuals and different cultures.

Two fantasy dilemmas are used most often in our studies: the trolley and the lifeboat dilemma. In the trolley dilemma a participant is told to imagine that a trolley is hurtling down a track out of control. If it continues on the track it will kill the beings on the track straight ahead. However, there is a switch that can be thrown to shunt the trolley to a side track, but the beings on that side track will be killed instead. The composition of beings on the main and side tracks can be varied, and the participant is asked to make a life or death choice by deciding to allow the trolley to continue or to throw the switch directing the trolley to the side track.

In the lifeboat dilemma it is proposed that a ship has sunk and there is a lifeboat with survivors, but, given the limited capacity of the lifeboat, some individuals have to be thrown overboard. The composition of the occupants of the lifeboat can be varied and the participant is asked to choose who is to drown.

Results supported the conclusion that using such fantasy material reveals basic aspects of human nature, unfettered by the laws, norms, and traditions of culture. The decision pattern was the same for all categories of participants, regardless of country of origin, language, sex, race, and religion. In addition, people were more likely to let something happen rather than acting to cause it to happen, even though the outcome, in either case, would be the same. The different kinds of people we have studied were more likely to cause something to happen if the alternatives were phrased in a Save wording rather than in a Kill wording. This wording effect has been found to be of major importance in studies of other kinds of dilemmas, such as making a choice between hypothetical health plans that differed in whether the outcomes were deterministic (killing all the people with a certain probability) or probabilistic (killing only a proportion of the people, with the same probability) (Tversky & Kahneman, 1981; Wang & Johnston, 1995).

In general, for all groups (students in Arizona, California, and Mississippi) and cultures (United States, China, Taiwan, and Mexico) the same dimensions were found to be important, with the same order of importance. The important factors determining the choices were those that would be expected to be effective, based on the actions of evolutionary mechanisms promoting increased reproductive success (RS) by enhancing direct and indirect fitness. Direct fitness is enhanced when people favor their own offspring over almost anyone else; indirect fitness is enhanced when they favor kin over nonkin, close kin over distant kin, friends over strangers, and pets over other animals, and disfavor members of a genocidal social group (Nazis). There are tendencies to save more rather than fewer individuals (or kill fewer rather than more)—but only if other things are equal—that is, none of the primary factors is involved in the dilemma. They favor people who are in jeopardy accidentally over those who are in a situation because they freely agreed to be (e.g., employees working for the industry whose operations have placed everyone in jeopardy), and strongly disfavor people who have violated a social contract (e.g., bank robbers or stock swindlers). There is a weaker tendency to favor people because they are members of an elite (e.g., productive scientists, physicians, or artists).

I have argued that one way to understand evolved aspects of human nature is to have people resolve fantasy dilemmas that involve situations in which the normal rules of society do not provide guidelines. Another way to examine basic underlying mechanisms is to consider decisions that are made when extraordinary circumstances prevail, such as deciding between unpalatable options in the conduct of warfare and the allocation of resources in battlefield situations. Cannibalism will be viewed from an evolutionary perspective. In times of famine, disaster, and isolation the normal rules of behavior do not apply. All of these avenues of approach provide only indirect information regarding the processes of natural selection that might be at work, and each of them has different shortcomings. However, if a consistent pattern runs through each of them, and this pattern transcends particular cultures, then it is compelling to argue that we are catching glimpses of basic human nature.

If the principles that influence behavior in these extraordinary situations are consistent with those involved in well-understood situations, we can have greater confidence that we are dealing with basic evolved mechanisms. Considerable success has been realized in understanding basic human mating strategies (Kenrick & Keefe, 1992; Thornhill, 1991), different patterns of sexual jealousy shown by men and women (Wilson & Daly, 1992), patterns of homicide (Daly & Wilson 1988, 1990), sex differences in the characteristics preferred for mates (Buss, 1994), and sex-specific aesthetic preferences of males and females that are related to reproductive value (Thornhill, 1998).

In our research we have identified what seem to be two basic underlying dimensions that provide the foundation for human morality. The most important one is a nepotism factor that includes kinship—and the immediate factor determining the outcome is the recognition of someone as kith or kin. This direct perceptual event that directly regulates the behavioral choices is called a proximate mechanism in evolutionary terms. I have argued (Petrinovich, 1999) that this proximate mechanism is based on, and develops from, the mother—infant bond, which appears full force at birth.

This nepotism factor is influenced by degree of relationship, with direct kin being the strongest component, community members next, then human strangers and foreigners, and lastly members of other species.

A second factor promotes community adhesion—a tendency to cooperate with others, which includes an expectation of reciprocation. This factor has two powerful components; the strongest is a negative one—to punish and exact revenge on those who violate explicit and implicit agreements between people—what is referred to as a social contract. People are able to detect cheaters, as well as those who would harm us and ours (e.g., Nazis and others who threaten the orderly furtherance of our RS). The positive aspect of this component leads us to cooperate with those who can reciprocate our good works. Another positive aspect is called mutualism—a tendency that is developed as a result of experience with others, which enables us to understand deception. People also develop a tendency to engage in a self-deception that we often use to modulate our behavior. This component of cooperation and mutualism provides much of the glue that holds communities together.

X. T. Wang (1996), using a different set of fantasy dilemmas, found that the group size that defined kith and kin was many times larger in China than in the United States, suggesting these dimensions can be nuanced by ecological variables. We now are investigating this effect further in the United States and China.

THOUGHTS ABOUT MORALITY

Patterns of behavior that appear during instances of survival cannibalism are consistent and similar to the pattern of decisions made when fantasy dilemmas are resolved, and both conform to expectations based on principles of evolutionary biology. It has been remarked (Seagrave, 1988) that cannibalism is a social affair; when marooned with somebody else you can commiserate, quarrel, and feud like newlyweds, and when things really get difficult you can always eat the other, or vice versa. Seagrave (1988, p. xiii) stated it as follows: "When the going gets tough, the tough get eaten." Marc Hauser (personal communication, 1999) suggested it would be better described as: "When the going gets tough, the tough chow down." Thomas (1835, p. 183) described a case of two seamen stranded in a lifeboat with no food or water: "Each knew the dreadful alternative to which nature would urge them. The cannibal was, already, in their looks, and fearful would have been the first attack, on either side, for they were both brave and stout men, and equal in strength and courage."

There is an obvious benefit to individuals who engage in cannibalism when it is necessary to survive. Although there is strong emotional revulsion by members of most societies to the idea of eating other people and to being eaten by them, survival cannibalism is seldom punished when it occurs. Even more surprising is that it does not meet with moral censure by the general public or its official guardians when the perpetrators return to organized society. This is particularly true if no one was killed for consumption, or if a fair lottery had been conducted (but who is to know?).

The abstract revulsion people have to cannibalistic acts has been used by authority figures to threaten reprisal for acts committed by and to drive terror into the very being of real or potential enemies. The strong emotional loading also makes it possible for the practice to be given ritualistic meanings, whereby deceased persons are honored by consuming some portion of their body, thereby incorporating their desirable qualities into oneself. Another common practice is to consume portions of defeated, but valiant enemies in order to acquire their admirable powers, usually by consuming the heart or brain, or even the muscles of fast runners. These primitive ritualistic meanings are but a short step from the incorporation of cannibalism into religious rituals, which often leads to the practice of ritual sacrifice of various animals and people to please and appease the Gods. In western societies such rituals are considered by some to be symbolically present in contemporary religious practices, such as the Catholic practice of taking Holy Communion. In the year AD 1215 Pope Innocent III decreed that when the phrase "this is my body" was spoken at Mass, the faithful were required to believe that the bread and wine were transubstantiated into the body and blood of Christ.

An apt metaphor to what I am suggesting here is to think of the flower vegetable of the daisy family—the artichoke. Anatomically the artichoke is well armored by its coarse outer leaves—hard and prickly except for the fleshy parts at their base. Even these outer layers have an attachment to the edible base of the flower. As more and more of the outer protective leaves are removed, the edible fleshy parts become more extensive, until a layer of tough, stringy innards is reached that we call the "choke"—which is inedible. It should be noted, however, that this choke is made up of the flowerets, which if allowed to bloom turn a beautiful deep violet-blue. Beneath this choke is the heart of the artichoke—the gourmet's culinary delight.

Metaphorically, we might conceive of human nature in similar terms. The protective layer that preserves and protects the whole is composed of the rules, laws, regulations, institutions, armies, and ideologies that we display to the world in order to protect ourselves from real and imagined threats of all kinds. Even these coarse protective elements are joined to the flower and heart of humanity to the extent that we must not thwart ultimate reproductive success—if we did we will have built a moral *ought* that violates the underlying biological reality—the *can*. If such a violation takes place the individuals in the society would not be able to reproduce at a level adequate for the community to continue as a viable, competitive entity. As Sober and Wilson (1998, p. 23) remarked: "It doesn't matter how many offspring you have; it only matters that you have more than anyone else." They expanded this idea to a convincing defense of a pluralistic brand of group selection, using the ideas of frequency and density-dependent selection, that does no violence to the basic tenets of individual selection.

As layers are peeled away there is more and more that is culturally palatable, able to provide the sustenance on which society depends—cooperation, mutualism, communication, language, and reciprocation. The situation improves until suddenly we encounter the "choke"—the harshness produced by the necessity to compete for resources with others, and to protect ourselves from those who might contest for whatever is necessary and available for us to survive and prosper. However, adjoining this choke of xenophobia is the fruit of human nature—the biological bases of the reproducing entity (our flowerets)—which is composed of the emotional bonds between kin, particularly the mother and neonate. Even this choke can be used to advantage if the ideological flowerets are allowed to bloom so that they are formed into the flower of social justice, rather than used to sustain hate and violence.

POLITICS AND CANNIBALS

There is a point of view within the social sciences, particularly prevalent among some cultural anthropologists, that questions the idea that cannibalism ever existed in human societies. This view is based on a basic misunderstanding of evolutionary theory, a political agenda that is often not apparent at first glance, and is supported by bad scholarship. One basic misunderstanding regarding evolution concerns the differences between proximate and ultimate levels of causation; complete evolutionary explanations must refer to both, with the ultimate level defined in terms of the reproductive success of individuals in the breeding population. Social scientists often ignore (or do not recognize) this ultimate level of causation, and concentrate exclusively on proximate behaviors deployed by individuals in various societies to further their ultimate goals. Questions regarding proximate mechanisms concern "what" takes place and "how" these events are controlled, ignoring the underlying concern of "why" they take place—what functional ends they serve. Failing to understand the distinction between these two levels produces major misunderstandings regarding how evolved processes act to influence human nature and the structure of society, as well as how it molds norms of acceptable behavior. The problems and misunderstandings become particularly serious when the specter of genetic determinism—which implies that there are genes that provide a blueprint determining what will take place—is added to cloud the picture.

Cook (1999) discussed several examples in which anthropologists committed what he called the Projection Error, mistakenly considering a behavior that is condemned in our culture but is condoned in another as having the same meaning. The error is that the focus is on the superficial similarities of the behavioral acts, rather than on the functional context within which they appear. He noted that Eskimos sometimes leave their old people to freeze to death in the snow. However, this is not the same as leaving my grandmother to freeze to death in a snow bank in Idaho. Even though the grandmother dies in both instances, I would be guilty of murder within the context of my society, but within the context of Eskimo society the Eskimo would not.

Acts must be viewed within the context of the cultural circumstances and environmental exigencies within which the Eskimo and I live. When considered within an evolutionary context, it can be argued that the Eskimo was acting to increase individual inclusive fitness by engaging in an accepted practice—accepted by the Eskimo, the grandmother, and members of the community—and furthering the ultimate goal by the proximate action of abandoning the grandmother. However, I was not doing anything that would enhance my inclusive fitness. In fact, I might well have decreased it: granny could have provided assistance to me and my offspring in the future, and if found out I could be arrested and deprived of my personal freedom, thus disrupting the functioning of a family within the community.

One underlying political issue is a tendency to view prehistoric and primitive peoples as "noble savages" who have been corrupted by the evil ways of modern society (read western, white, paternalistic). This has led to a denial that cannibalism ever existed [except possibly as survival cannibalism, which Arens (1979) regards as a regrettable act, rather than custom] as well as to a rejection of the archaeological evidence for it. Arens presented a revisionist view that has enjoyed considerable popular success, as well as widespread scholarly citation and rebuttal. He alleged that the view of the savage cannibal sprang from the heads of travelers who did not understand the cultures or languages of individuals from unfamiliar societies, was promoted by the greed of Europeans who wanted to conquer and exploit native peoples and to convert them to Christianity, and who projected their own cruel fantasies on the hated and despised "Other." I agree with Lestringant (1997), who characterized Arens as more of a sensation-hungry journalist than an exact historian, and with the Oxford anthropologist P. G. Rivière (1980), who characterized Arens' book as an example of bad scholarship. I will address these issues fully in Chapter 7.

Throughout, I will examine the various lines of evidence for cannibalism of several types, and use that evidence to challenge Arens' myth of the myth of man eating.

HUMAN STARVATION

Before launching into the narrative regarding cannibalism, it will be instructive to consider some of the physiological, behavioral, and psychological changes that occur when humans suffer severe starvation. These studies of starvation provide a background regarding the deterioration people experience when disaster strikes, which might make it easier to accept and understand why people engage in cannibalism. A valuable source of information is an extensive study of human starvation conducted in Minnesota (Keys, Brozek, Henschel, Mickelsen, & Taylor, 1950). The subjects for this laboratory study were young, healthy, and well educated conscientious objectors who had been drafted during World War II, had refused military duty, but volunteered to participate in this study of semi-starvation. In all, they were a select group of healthy, intelligent, well-adjusted, and motivated men, not a representative sample of the general public.

The baseline diet was nutritionally balanced and provided 3492 calories per day; during a semistarvation phase each person was allowed two meals a day, with an average daily intake of 1570 calories. Common dietary standards for a man weighing 70 kilograms involves the consumption of 2400–2500 calories for sedentary individuals, and 2700–3000, 3000–3400, and 3400–4500 calories for individuals engaged in light, moderate, and hard activity, respectively, reaching a high of 8600 calories for individuals in some occupations, such as New England brickmakers.

The two-volume report contains a detailed presentation of a variety of biochemical, physiological, and behavioral aspects, but they will not be presented here. Only those general aspects of starvation that are relevant to the incidents of disasters and famines to be discussed throughout the rest of this book will be examined.

Body weight dropped about 24% within 2 weeks and remained relatively constant throughout the 24-week semistarvation period. This weight loss was accompanied by a marked decrease in fat content of the body and skeletal musculature. Although the effects of weight loss in this study were severe, they were experienced under benign and constant environmental conditions, rather than the extreme environmental conditions and physical demands that are forced on individuals starving as a result of disaster or famine.

Studies of natural starvation victims indicate that the brain and spinal cord lose little weight, the soft tissues (such as liver and intestines) suffer to the greatest extent, with the heart and kidneys losing less weight in proportion to body weight loss. In the Minnesota experiment, basal oxygen consumption promptly and steadily declined to about 39% of normal.

Natural selection should favor physiological processes that allow individuals to cope with starvation, given that starvation certainly has been a major factor since the beginning of civilization. A large number of physiological adaptations are found during starvation that would serve to conserve body heat. It is common to find problems in water balance that causes the passage of a large volume of urine, an elevated fluid intake (although thirst is not mentioned as a complaint), accompanied by a marked salt hunger, which leads to the consumption of several times the normal amount of salt if it is available.

There is a decrease in muscular endurance and strength, a deterioration of coordination, and a slowing of voluntary movement, all of which were found in the laboratory study as well. Difficulties are experienced when performing any action that requires strength, such as pushing open a door or carrying heavy objects, even for a short distance. However, there are no striking changes in accurate movements of small muscle groups, such as those involved in typing.

Famine victims frequently experience episodes of fainting, particularly when they are required to stand upright suddenly. The sensory mechanisms of starving individuals are extraordinarily well maintained, with hearing becoming even more acute than normal, and there seem to be no changes in night vision acuity. Measured intellectual performance did not change for the Minnesota volunteers during starvation, although the willingness to engage in mental effort and level of achievement both suffered. There was a decrement in spontaneous activity that extended to intellectual pursuits, but there was no alteration in mental capacity. These findings suggest that only minimal neurological changes take place with starvation.

It is usually reported that during famines food becomes the central topic of conversation and writing, and this was true for the Minnesota volunteers. They tended to become irritated when food service was slow, and were very annoyed if food was not served hot. During meals they ate slowly and deliberately, devoting total attention to the food and its consumption. They markedly increased the use of spices and salt, and abandoned any semblance of manners—always licking their dishes to obtain every last bit of food. Cookbooks, menus, and information bulletins on food production became intensely interesting, even for those who previously had little interest in dietetics or agriculture.

A report made by a survivor of an Arctic expedition who had experienced severe chronic semistarvation is typical (Keys et al., 1950, p. 817):

"For my own part, I can think of nothing but food. At first my thoughts dwell with food recollections upon all sort of dishes, but gradually they concentrate themselves upon sandwiches—Danish sandwiches, with no top slice, very different from the dull, dry things one gets in England." Although this remark suggests there might be a greater sensitivity regarding food types, such was obviously not the case; foods that had been rejected earlier by the Minnesota volunteers were readily accepted when included in the menu during the starvation period, and there are many accounts of starving people eating anything, including lamp oil, hides, shoes, shoelaces—almost any material that contained protein. There was a large increase in gum chewing, smoking, and the consumption of tea and coffee, both in the laboratory study and in natural field conditions. The menu containing the most bulk was the most popular of the three used with the Minnesota volunteers, and this preference for greater quantity overrode the desire for variety.

During a rehabilitation period most subjects overate and became overweight, an effect probably due to a continued tendency to take a long time to eat meals (a pattern that developed during the starvation period), to eat large quantities of food at each meal, and to punctuate meals with many snacks throughout the day. This excessive consumption was not matched by a corresponding increase in physical activity or work. They reported a sensation of hunger, even after eating a large meal. This pattern is typical to that found for rescued survivors of shipwreck, Arctic, mountain, and airline disaster episodes.

The overall picture of the psychological changes the Minnesota men experienced included depression, irritability, nervousness, and general emotional instability. There was social withdrawal, narrowing of interests, and difficulty in concentration. Speech was slow, but there was no evidence of faults in memory or logic. Their personality changes were characterized as "psychoneurotic" in type, and although not grossly pathological, they became increasingly ineffective in daily life, with depression and apathy being the dominant feature of their behavior. After reviewing the literature, Keys et al. (1950, p. 906) concluded: "This description could easily serve as a synthesis of the results of 'natural' starvation as recorded in scores of reports." The disasters to be discussed in the remainder of this book support this conclusion; this pattern of behavior is seen time and again during natural starvation as a result of disasters and famine.

Keys et al. (1950) discussed several situations in which people starved, particularly cases occurring in prison camps. They noted that generally men appeared to be less resistant to semistarvation than women, and this seems to be the case in many of the situations that will be discussed here. They characterized the terminal stages of starvation in humans: Loss of appetite is an ominous sign, probably related to cessation of the secretion of digestive juices, which seems to signal the approach of a terminal stage; there was a tendency to constipation, although diarrhea was occasionally present; there was exhaustion and changes in reflex responses; finally a psychosis develops that is marked by hallucinations, and subsequent changes were, as a rule, irreversible. Again, many of these symptoms are evident in the accounts of starvation considered in this book.

THE COURSE TO BE TRAVELED

This chapter introduced questions regarding the morality of consumption, and discussed some of the conditions under which it is permissible to eat another human being. Although most consider it permissible to eat non-humans, under what circumstances is it permissible to eat humans? A classic case of cannibalism following a shipwreck was presented to set the stage for the events that are to follow. I stated the premise that there is evidence for cannibalism throughout the ages, in different types of societies, have identified different types of cannibalism, and discussed the general nature of the physiological and psychological changes that occur with starvation.

Chapter 2 is devoted to instances of cannibalism during the U.S. westward expansion that took place in the mid-1800s. Settlers and gold-hunters attempted to cross the western deserts and the Sierra Nevada Mountains; the starvation and cannibalism that occurred in the Donner Party are contrasted to the absence of cannibalism among the starving Mormon Willie Handcart Company, who experienced similar (though not as severe or prolonged) hardships. Reasons why there was cannibalism in the one and not in the other are suggested. The sequence of consumption that occurred with the Donner Party is what would be expected on the basis of evolutionary considerations. Special attention is devoted to clarify the evolutionary concepts of adaptation, natural selection, inclusive fitness, reciprocal altruism, and parental investment. These concepts are of central importance if we are to understand those evolutionary biological tendencies that influence human moral systems.

In Chapter 3, several instances of cannibalism following the sinking of sailing ships are discussed. There is a stable pattern of reactions by the public, the sailing community, and the legal establishment when cannibalism is discovered to have occurred. The patterns of choice of victims to be consumed are consistent with those revealed in the preceding instances of survival cannibalism, and these patterns conform to evolutionary expectations. This chapter will also contain a discussion of legal arguments regarding necessity, with the issues considered within the broader perspective of triage.

In Chapter 4, two modern instances involving airplane crashes are discussed—one in the Andes and one in the mountains of Idaho. These instances, as well as those that occurred during westward emigration, reveal the expected evolutionary patterns discussed throughout this book. There are very few instances because airplane crashes usually leave no survivors, the crashes occur at airports, or modern electronic gear on the plane allows survivors to be found quickly. The prevalence of cannibalism, construed as the eating of others of the same species, will be considered for species other than humans to consider general ecological influences and how cannibalism might promote the RS of members of those species. At the end of the chapter, an instance of cannibalism in the Arctic will be discussed, because it has been thoroughly documented and serves as a compelling summary of the material in Chapters 2–4.

In Chapter 5, cannibalism in prehistory is discussed, beginning with a consideration of archeological methods and evidence that suggests that under certain circumstances cannibalism has been widespread throughout human existence. There is abundant physical evidence that cannibalism was practiced by the Anasazi Indians in Southwestern Colorado (White, 1992; Turner & Turner, 1999). Some ruminations regarding basic human nature will be presented, and placed in the context of the universality of warfare between human societies. The case of the Aztecs will also be examined in this chapter. One of the major questions addressed is whether the Aztecs practiced cannibalism, and if so what type was it—ritual or dietary; if the latter, did it have a significant nutritional impact.

Early historical instances of cannibalism among the Caribs, and in Africa, South America, and the New Hebrides, are described in Chapter 6. The consequences of the pattern of cannibalism that has been described among the Fore of the New Guinea Highlands are profoundly disastrous, leading to the development of a fatal malady, kuru, which is related to a degenerative disease of the brain, Creutzfeldt—Jakob disease in humans and scrapie in sheep. The early spread of kuru among the Fore was the result of mortuary cannibalistic practices, and it has disappeared with the abolition of those practices. The same degenerative processes are present in the bovine spongiform encephalopathy identified in cattle in Britain— what is being called "mad cow disease."

The discussion in Chapter 7 focuses on currents of thinking within the social sciences, particularly by cultural anthropologists, that lead to widespread denials that human cannibalism ever existed beyond rare instances of survival cannibalism. This view is the result of a faulty perspective used by many social scientists and humanists, and produces major misunderstandings of the way evolved processes can act to influence the structure of society and its norms.

The political issue is raised because there has been a tendency to view prehistoric and primitive peoples as "noble savages," as discussed above. Arens' book, *The Myth of Man Eating* (1979), will be examined in detail, and the flaws in his arguments and scholarship will be discussed. The chapter will conclude with a brief discussion of problems field workers encounter when they study another species or culture.

In Chapter 8, frightening modern instances of cannibalism resulting from political innovations that produced widespread famine in Russia and in China are discussed, as well as the use of cannibalism as a tool of repression and political control in both countries. In addition, a few instances of wartime cannibalism during and after World Wars I and II are discussed, particularly those that took place during starvation in Gulags, concentration camps, and prisoner of war camps.

Finally, in Chapter 9, I will consider some classic depictions and discussions of cannibalism found in fiction, poetry, and film. Part of my thesis has been that the universal fascination with all aspects of cannibalism is strong and evocative. The various aspects of cannibalism attract strong interest and concern, even though it is often viewed as an aberrant breakdown of human rationality. The literature discussed will bear on a variety of cultures, religions, times, and nationalities.

The goal of this book is to develop and defend the thesis that human cannibalism has been widespread throughout the time humans have been in existence, and that this ubiquitous behavior can be understood more adequately when viewed through an evolutionary lens. This way of viewing events might provide helpful insights regarding the functioning of complex behavior mechanisms: Darwin was able to understand the expression of emotions using an evolutionary approach; Daly and Wilson (1998) discovered consistent patterns to homicide and sexual jealously using evolutionary considerations. When societal taboos against cannibalism break down in the face of dire necessity, the resulting patterns of consumption are those that would be expected based on evolutionary considerations.

2

Cannibalism during Western Migrations

Human liver is better than lean beef.

—Lewis Keseberg—Stewart (1960)

One of the best known and well-documented incidents involving survival cannibalism took place in the High Sierra Mountains of California, where a group of citizens, separated from society at large, facing incredible hardships and repeated disasters, resorted to cannibalism to avoid starvation. The Donner Party attempted to cross from Wyoming to California in 1846–1847, and was stranded in the mountains during one of the harshest winters on record (Stewart, 1960). There are also some well-documented incidents involving emigrating Mormons who faced hardships and starvation, but for whom no cannibalism occurred during their journey from Missouri to Salt Lake City (Stegner, 1964). The events that took place with the Donner Party were similar to those that took place in another disaster, which will be described in Chapter 4, involving an amateur rugby team from Uruguay whose plane crashed in the High Andes in the winter of 1972 (Read, 1974).

When a group of individuals is lost and starving, such as was the case with the Donner Party, the sequence of action individuals take to survive makes sense in terms of evolutionary expectations. Suicide seldom occurs; as hardships become more extreme and prolonged, animals are consumed in a reasonable order—first those brought for food, then work animals, and finally pets; when animals have all been consumed those parts usually considered inedible, such as hides, are boiled and consumed. When all of these food resources are exhausted, cannibalism begins. There is always an unwillingness to eat dead members of one's own family. As I will discuss after describing the events, this pattern is what would be expected in light of the proximate mechanisms that promote ultimate reproductive success (RS).

The pattern of behavior in the situations discussed in this chapter, as well as that occurring in shipwrecks (discussed in Chapter 3), is coherent. This coherence supports the idea that dimensions important in the studies of the structure of people's moral beliefs using hypothetical dilemmas (discussed in Chapter 1) are indeed important when real social dilemmas must be resolved. These cases all suggest that underlying evolutionary biases come strongly into play when those rules that regulate normal society are no longer applicable. I will argue that when people reach intolerable levels of starvation, combined with a low expectation of relief, cannibalism will always occur.

THE DONNER PARTY

The most authoritative and compelling account of the disasters faced by the Donner Party are contained in a book by the California writer, George R. Stewart, *Ordeal by Hunger*, first published in 1936, and reissued in an expanded edition in 1960 (the edition referred to here). Stewart (1962) later published a general history of the experiences of others who migrated west over the California Trail. There is also a volume containing fascinating letters, narratives, and memoirs written by survivors or based on interviews with them (Johnson, 1996), and a history of the Donner Party based on direct interviews with survivors (McGlashan, 1947; first published in 1880). Although there are minor differences of opinion regarding certain details, and some disagreement regarding the assignment of relative blame for the unfortunate events (see King, 1992, for a revisionist view), there is general agreement concerning the sweep of events as described here.

The Donner Party was composed mainly of a group of substantial midwestern farmers and businessmen who had packed up their possessions, formed a wagon train, and undertook the arduous journey west to enjoy the benefits of California abundance. They were mainly American-born inhabitants of the Mississippi Valley, and although they may have been pioneers they could not be called frontiersmen—they were country-folk and townspeople, not mountaineers. They were not accustomed to camping, most had never seen a mountain, and there was a great deal of sickness early in the trip.

There was considerable dissension among members of the company from the very beginning of the journey, and many petty differences of opinions and interests surfaced as the trip progressed. McGlashan (1947) considered these factors to be among the fundamental causes of the calamities that befell the party. Stewart (1962) and Brodhead (1997) agreed that the

Donner Party was too small (only about 10 wagons), with too few mature, sturdy adults to make it possible for them to overcome the adversities encountered at the journey's end. Also, the natural leader of the party (James Reed) was driven off for killing another male member of the party during a fight. Following Reed's banishment, George Donner, a prosperous farmer who was 62 years old and the father of 15 children, was elected captain of the train on the basis of his kindly, patrician manner. Stewart characterized the party, even in the early stages of the trip, as a shattered and beaten army, over which hung the threats of death from starvation, snow in the mountains, and Indians who shot at hunters from ambush and stole oxen and cattle.

After traveling across the prairies, the party left the camp of no return in Wyoming on July 19, 1846, crossed the Great Salt Lake Desert, September 3–8 (with considerable suffering due to an insufficient supply of water; they had badly underestimated the distance, and hence the number of days required to cross the Desert), and camped by the Truckee River to recover a bit longer than they should have. On October 15, after undergoing numerous severe hardships, they moved up the canyon of the river to Truckee Meadows, near what is now Reno, Nevada, and reached Truckee Lake (now called Donner Lake) by October 30. There was heavy snowfall in the mountains on October 28–29, and the party failed in its attempts to cross the pass with wagons between October 31 and November 3. On November 4 they returned to Donner Lake and established camp. Afraid of being trapped in the high mountains for the winter, they attempted and failed to cross the pass on foot on November 12 and again on November 21. By this time there had been a series of intense storms, and they now faced the prospect of spending a winter in the mountains with many feet of snow covering the ground, making it impossible to hunt or to forage for edible vegetation.

The original 87 members of the party had experienced immense difficulties prior to reaching the mountains and had lost most of their belongings, including many of their cattle and oxen, which either died due to a lack of water and food or had been stolen by Indians. The party was short of provisions, and almost all were in poor physical condition by the time they arrived at Donner Lake. Of the 87 who had camped at the Great Salt Lake, 5 died before reaching the mountain camps, 34 died later, either at the camp or while trying to cross the mountains, and 1 infant died after reaching the safety of the valley. Two Indian guides who were sent with supplies from Fort Sutter also died, with the final total being 42 dead and 47 survivors. All oxen, horses, mules, and dogs perished, and Stewart emphasized that communal sharing was not part of the group's way of looking at things; too many personal hatreds split the group into factions.

There were initially 81 people at the camps. Sixty people were at the

Donner Lake camp by about November 4: 19 men (18 years or older), 12 females, and 29 children (of whom 6 were breast-feeding babies). At the campsite occupied by the Donners, 5 miles back on the trail, there were 21 people: 6 men, 3 women, and 12 children. The occupants of the two camps built shelters and were able to communicate with one another. On November 12, the first clear day since their arrival, 13 of the hardiest men and 2 of the women set out to cross the pass, each with a small piece of beef, but the snow around the lake was soft and 10 feet deep, forcing them to return to the cabins by nightfall. On November 21, 16 men and 6 women made another attempt to cross the pass, taking 7 mules with them, but deep snow, coupled with exhaustion and a prevailing sense of despair, forced them to return the next morning.

"Forlorn Hope"   The first person, a 25-year-old single male, died at the Donner Lake camp on December 14, probably from malnutrition. Following this death a group of 5 women, 10 men (including the 2 aforementioned Indians and a single man—Charles Stanton—who had been sent in from California by Capt. Sutter with mules and supplies), and 2 boys attempted, on December 16, to cross the mountain pass using roughly constructed snowshoes—an attempt later dubbed "Forlorn Hope." One of the boys and a single German male, neither of whom had snowshoes, turned back after 1 day. For 6 days the group traveled about 5 miles a day, suffering immense hardship, cold, and hunger. On the sixth day Stanton was unable to continue, and remained at the campfire, smoking his pipe, and died. The last of the group's provisions had been used by that time, and after traveling about a mile the next day snow began to fall. Fearing they were lost, they stopped. After a day and a half without food, they moved into a valley on the ninth day. They halted, huddled together in the storm, and discussed what could be done. It is reported that at this time their thoughts included "maniacal cravings for food"—and they began to regard their comrades as offering new possibilities. As Stewart (1960, p. 101) wrote: "Man might eat beef—good! Man might eat horse, too . . . and mule. He might eat bear and dog, and even coyote and owl. He might also—and the relentless logic drove on—yes, man might also eat man."

One member of the group proposed (and another seconded the idea) that they should draw lots to see who should die to furnish food for the others. Stewart (1960) claimed that the proposal was dropped because the consent to proceed was not unanimous. Jacob Harlan, a member of another party that (successfully) preceded the Donner Party, presented a slightly different version of the lottery event in a memoir first printed in 1888 (Johnson, 1996). He reported that he was told the lottery was held, but that the loser was a popular member of the party, and they could not bring themselves to kill him. It was then proposed by the person who seconded the original lottery that two men should each take a six-shooter and fight until one or both were killed. They would, therefore, die in "hot blood, not slaughtered like a pig—It was a man's way." There was still no unanimity because, as Stewart wrote, "the scruples of civilization were dying hard." Finally, it was decided they should struggle on until someone died, and that person should be eaten. One of the single men (a Mexican male) died, but due to an increasing storm, accompanied by the loss of their fire, he was not eaten right away. Franklin Graves, a 57 year-old-male then died— and as he died, according to Harlan, he told his two daughters that it would be justifiable for them to eat his flesh to save themselves, and Harlan endorsed that position; they had eaten every other animal substance they could find.

After having spent 9 days in their attempt, 4 of those days without food, only 11 people were still alive, and they were close to madness. Stewart (1960, p. 104) wrote that "They dreamed maniacal dreams of hunger, and awoke trying to sink their teeth into hands or arms of their companions. At times they wailed and shrieked." After 5 days of starvation some of the survivors cut the flesh from the arms and legs of those who had died, roasted it by the fire, and ate it, "averting their faces from each other and weeping."

Once the taboo against cannibalism was broken it became easier to engage in, harvesting by members of the expedition became more efficient, and there seemed to be little moral revulsion to the practice. This initial resistance against engaging in cannibalism, followed by an unquestioning acceptance by most, is to be found in almost all of the instances of survival cannibalism to be described.

The day after the first consumption of human flesh, meat was stripped from the bodies and roasted. Some was eaten and the rest dried so it could be carried as they continued their attempt to escape the mountains. It was reported that no member of a family consumed the flesh of their kin, although they had to observe parts of kin being roasted and eaten by others. The party, now having human meat, rested 3 days, after which 10 were still alive (all of the dead were men), with the survivors being 2 Indians, 5 women, and 3 white men. In the course of another week they had crossed the mountains and were moving through a valley. However, they had no more human flesh and were reduced to eating the rawhide thongs from their snowshoes. After 3 more days without food they once again considered drawing lots to determine who should be killed and eaten. Instead, it was suggested that the 2 Indians should be eaten. However, one of the men of the party believed that the Indians deserved a chance because they had crossed the mountains with Stanton and the mules, saving the lives of the company. The Indians responded appropriately by promptly taking their leave from camp. Another of the white men died and was eaten, as was a deer that was shot as it chanced by. By this time 3 weeks had passed, and the group now consisted of 5 women and 2 white men.

One of the men argued that one of the women (who could not keep up) should be killed and eaten, but this was opposed on the grounds that she was a wife and mother, whereby the same gentleman proposed that because two of the other women were not mothers, and the husband of each already had died, one of them should be killed and eaten. At this point the group happened to cross the tracks of the 2 Indians who had left camp, and the aforementioned gentleman found them collapsed and near death, whereupon he killed them, and they were consumed. This is one of the few instances (except for shipwrecks) in which people were killed in order to be consumed, and as often is the case, they were members of another race.

Finally, one man went ahead and reached a ranch in the valley (ironically, with the aid of some Digger Indians whose village he had stumbled into), and help was sent to bring out the surviving members of the Forlorn Hope party. Of the 10 men and 5 women who began the trek, 8 men had died, with only 2 white men and all 5 women surviving the 33-day ordeal. They arrived at Johnson's Ranch in Bear Valley (a total journey of 70 miles) on January 18.

Stewart (1960) commented regarding the degeneration the party had undergone. They started as civilized men and women who delayed to enable a comrade who fell behind to catch up. Later, they decided it was not proper to draw lots to see who should be killed and eaten, nor would they eat a man already dead. Then, as starvation approached, they plotted to kill men of another race, and it was suggested they kill women of their own race with whom they had traveled for many months. By this time comrades were left behind when they could not keep up, they had tried to kill each other in at least one open fight, and on finding the 2 Indians who had slipped away in fear for their lives, they killed and ate them. When the story became known following rescue, the survivors were not criticized by either authorities or the general public for having eaten human flesh; it was excused on the grounds that cannibalism was necessary to survive. This judgment was strengthened by the survivors' denial that any of the party was killed to be consumed (except the 2 Indians, who seemed to matter little).

Camp Cannibals   Meanwhile, back at the Donner Lake camp, the situation was just as desperate for those who had remained. Almost all animals had been killed or stolen by Indians, or had been allowed to wander off and could not be found, having died and become covered by deep snow. Thus, by December, most of the cattle, horses, and oxen had run off and died in the snow and the available beef had been eaten, as had most of the dogs. Before Christmas the main food consisted of animal hides that were cut into strips, the hair singed off, scraped, put into a kettle, and boiled for hours. Boiling continued until the mass became soft and pulpy, and this was cooled until it stiffened into a glue-like jelly, which was consumed. There was no salt available and only a little pepper. By this time 4 of the 21 people in the cabin occupied by the Donner family had died, the first being Jacob, the 65-year-old brother of George Donner, as well as 3 other men.

During the first week of the New Year the last remaining dog, the children's pet, was killed and eaten, and hides were all that remained. Another snowshoe party of 3 women and 1 man attempted to cross the pass on January 4, but they failed, 1 woman returning after 1 night and the others after 4 days. They were able to get over the pass, but lost their way and ended up where they started. By the end of January, even hides were becoming scarce, and people began squabbling over them.

A relief party of 7 men started from the California side on February 4, managed to cross the pass, and (after experiencing numerous and prolonged hardships) reached the Donner Lake camp on February 18, almost 4 months after the party became trapped in the mountains. The return trip was begun, on February 22, by a group consisting of 23: 3 men, 4 women, and 16 children (2 of the Reed children had to turn back the first day because they were too small to follow in the footsteps of the preceding people), with a group of 17—2 men, 3 women, and 12 children—left at the lake. Eighteen of the party survived the journey, reaching Sutter's Fort on March 4, bringing a total of 26 of the Donner Party reaching safety to date, with 28 dead; 2 of those who had reached safety earlier returned in an attempt to rescue the 31 who still were starving in the mountains.

A second relief party (headed by James Reed, the man who had been banished early in the journey, but whose family was still with the Donner Party) reached the lake on March 1. Twenty-eight people were still alive at the two mountain camps. There was evidence that the situation for those who had remained at the camps was so severe that by February 26 some of the survivors had begun to eat the dead. The relief party left the lake on March 3 with 17 survivors: 1 man, 3 women, 2 boys of age 14, and 11 children ranging in age from 11 down to infancy. The party encountered a fierce winter storm on the return trip and had to leave 13 people behind in a temporary camp, which became known as "Starved Camp." A third relief party was able to reach those stranded emigrants in mid-March; 3 had died and the rest had survived by eating the dead. Part of this rescue party continued to the lake where they found 10 people still alive in the two lake camps. They returned, leaving at the lake camps only 5 survivors who were unable to travel.

A final expedition reached the lake on April 17, and only Lewis Keseberg was still alive. He had a pot of soup made of human flesh, and was reported to have said that the flesh of Mrs. Tamsen Donner, who had probably died of hypothermia (Johnson, 1996), was the best he had ever tasted (Thornton, 1996). No traces of her or the other woman who had been in the camp were found. Later, Keseberg professed a preference for human brains and liver to almost anything else. He was taken to Johnson's Ranch on April 25. Eventually, according to Stewart (1960), he went to Sacramento where he bought a hotel, and with questionable taste, opened a restaurant. He was reported to have boasted in his barroom that human liver was the best meat he ever ate. He finally lost his business and his money, and dropped out of sight, dying in Sacramento in 1895. By the time the ordeal of the Donner Party ended, 48 of the original 81 members of the company had survived.

Stewart (1960, p. 232) concluded that many of the survivors had engaged in cannibalism, and he believed they should not be held culpable. One large family of survivors (the nine Breens) were Roman Catholics, and Stewart's opinion was that in the view of a priest they would have committed no sin, and would have no penance to perform because "in overcoming natural scruples in order to preserve his life a Catholic is thought as much to practice virtue as to commit a sin." This view is similar to that expressed by the Jesuits who dealt with the Andean survivors (discussed in Chapter 4). Stewart argued that cannibalism, although regarded as a taboo practice, should be "regarded as one of the unclean things, like certain practices of sex, not to be discussed or even thought of." Even though it is unthinkable, there seems to be a lot of thought about it by starving people, and even more by commentators reflecting on the disasters for years thereafter.

AN EVOLUTIONARY ANALYSIS

To place these events in an evolutionary perspective a few basic principles must be understood to appreciate the richness of what is now called Neo-Darwinism. I will briefly discuss but a few aspects of the basic theory of evolution to illuminate critical aspects of one of the topics of major concern in this book—survival cannibalism. Those aspects include natural selection, adaptation, inclusive fitness, and reciprocal altruism. A fuller appreciation of the richness of evolutionary theory can be gained by consulting books by Williams (1966), Ghiselin (1969), Mayr (1970, 1982), Sober (1984), and Bell (1997), or a couple of less technical overviews by Dennett (1995) and Dawkins (1996).

Natural Selection

Darwin's great idea [which Dennett (1995) called "Darwin's Dangerous Idea"] is natural selection, with adaptationist reasoning being the "heart and soul" of evolutionary biology—it is not optional. Ideas regarding the ways in which natural selection works might require modification and supplementation from time to time, and flaws will appear and have to be corrected, but if natural selection is displaced from its central position in biology, it would result in the downfall of Darwinism and the collapse of our understanding of much of modern biology and medicine. The attitude of modern biologists toward Darwinian theory has been caught well by Mayr (1991, pp. 162–163), who wrote: "The basic theory of evolution has been confirmed so completely that modern biologists consider evolution simply a fact . . . as much of a fact as the observation that the earth revolves around the sun rather than the reverse."

There are three important points regarding evolutionary change. First, the process driving evolution works on physical manifestations of the organism (the phenotype), and in that sense it is not primarily a genetic event, although any characteristics that are to be selected must be heritable. Mutation is important to supply the gene pool with a source of genetic variation that contributes to random change, but the direction of evolutionary change is due to natural selection. As Cronin (1991) remarked, it is selection that does the "thinking."

Many people, from the very beginning of Darwin's work, have considered it too improbable to imagine that complex organisms with their complicated organs could have evolved through natural selection working on chance occurrences. The eye has been taken as the exemplar of a structure that is so complicated it could not have arisen through a process of chance. Many critics continue to object that too many complex, interdependent manifestations have to appear in the right order and with the right timing to construct a functional eye; and such complexity leads them to conclude it is necessary to invoke a plan with a designer—an objection that reveals a basic misunderstanding of evolution as well as an impoverished sense of imagination.

Among the many who have discussed such reasoning, Dawkins (1996) devoted a chapter to debunking this objection, noting that eyes have evolved independently around 40–60 times in different species, which suggests there may be functional regularities that develop to cope with the environments encountered by animals of many species, and that these regularities predispose organisms to develop some form of light detection mechanisms. These independent evolutions have resulted in eyes of quite different types; all, however, effectively sense the presence of light and transmit veridical light-related information through the eye. It is not difficult to imagine that the ability to sense light and to resolve what that light represents would confer an advantage to an organism that must eat, avoid being eaten, reproduce, and make a good living under a variety of circumstances.

Dawkins (1996) asked rhetorically why it is so hard for even sophisticated scientists to grasp the simple point that Darwinianism is *not* a theory that relies on random chance. Although random mutation occurs, there is the important caveat that cumulative natural selection is *nonrandom.* Dawkins used the metaphor that the task of evolution is to climb a mighty mountain (which he designated "Mount Improbable") starting from surrounding lowlands. Anti-Darwinian critics look at the height of the sheer cliffs of the mountain to be climbed to arrive at such a thing as the complex eye, and decide it is just too improbable that those sheer, lofty heights could be conquered by a sudden coming together of chance events—a mighty leap to the top. As Dawkins (1996, p. 77) wrote: "You don't need to be a mathematician or physicist to calculate that an eye or a haemoglobin molecule would take from here to infinity to self-assemble by sheer higgledy-piggledy luck."

There is, however, another way to ascend Mount Improbable than by one mighty leap, and that is to break the ascent into small, manageable parts; as he puts it (p. 77): "smearing out the luck needed, going round the back . . . and crawling up the gentle slopes, inch by million-year inch. Only God would essay the mad task of leaping up the precipice in a single bound." He continues with the observation: "And if we postulate him as our cosmic designer we are left in exactly the same position as when we started." This designer would have to be intelligent and complicated beyond all imagining in order to be able to construct the dazzling array of living things—and Dawkins considers such complication to be just another word for improbable, which still demands explanation. He suggested that Darwin's great achievement was to discover the nature of the gentle gradients winding up the other side of the mountain. Bell (1997, p. 13) concurred, noting that "Evolution can leap only very small gaps."

A second important point is that physical and behavioral characteristics are not normally the product of a single gene; therefore, any single mutation usually will not produce a character change—such change requires major or minor reconstruction of the entire genotype. Bell's (1997, p. 10) admonition is apposite: "Selection will cause progress, but it is a constrained and restricted sort of progress, with advance in one direction being associated with regress in others. Perfection is unattainable."

And third, the selective value of a gene is not absolute, but is largely determined by peculiarities of the external environment and the developmental system within which the gene operates. Different populations of individuals are likely to have evolved by different routes and arrived at different destinations. The particular route taken by a population is contingent on the fortuitous occurrence of those variations on which selection can act, and the enormous range of variation possible means that different individual variants are likely to arise at different times in different populations. A large number of genes contribute to the shaping of any phenotypic trait, making it unlikely that a polygenetically based trait will be modified easily by natural selection. Selection can build only on the foundation laid by previous generations.

Once again, Dawkins (1996, p. 83) has put it nicely: "Any animal that has succeeded in reaching an age to become a parent must already be pretty good. If you start with something pretty good and change it at random, the chances are that you'll make it worse. And, as a matter of fact, the great majority of mutations do make things worse." Dawkins (1996, p. 99) continued: "however many ways there may be of being alive, it is certain that there are vastly more ways of being dead." These statements emphasize the point that most mutations have been deadly rather than helpful. Successful genes are ones that are good at cooperating with those other successful genes that constitute the gene pool of the species.

Bell (1997, p. 15) characterized evolution through selection as resembling a blind and fumbling process, yet it leads a population toward a state that is unlikely to be improved by any feasible modification, even though a superior design might be possible. He concluded: "If progress can be made only by the demolition and wholesale reconstruction of the present design, then progress will simply not be made; the abrupt appearance of a novel creature superior to its ancestors is so unlikely it can be neglected. Selection provides no blueprints, and no alternative engineer is available." All adaptive characteristics are the result of natural selection, but all characteristics are not adaptive. It matters less that an organism does well in the competition for survival and reproduction than that it does better than others in the game. An appreciation of the concept of adaptation is crucial if we are to understand evolution, but it must be invoked with caution to enjoy the benefits of the heuristic value that increases understanding of organic systems.

A final point is that the rate of a gene's self-replication is the only attribute that can be selected directly, and everything else rides on that fact. Other attributes certainly can be selected, but their selection is indirect in the sense that they occur through connection with altered rates of self-replication.

Heritability and Inclusive Fitness The discussion to this point has been primarily about genes and their effects on an organism's structure and function. No matter how advantageous or deleterious any change is to an organism, that change must be heritable or it will disappear with the demise of the particular individual hosting that change. Individuals do not evolve—they develop, reproduce, and die. The characteristics of organisms in the population, however, may change through time to the extent that those characteristics are heritable. Selection of a gene is heritable when that gene is passed to offspring, and fitness may be increased if those offspring, in turn, are able to pass that gene to their offspring—the RS of that lineage is enhanced. Natural selection requires variation if it is to work its way. For evolution to take place those variants selected must be able to be inherited by future generations, and evolution through selection is the necessary consequence of heritable variations in fitness.

Because an individual is the bearer of genes, it is important to think of genetic lineages—both in terms of components making up an individual (such as cells) and as communities of individuals (such as families). We can speak of the direct fitness of an individual, which is the direct physical transmission of genes through the individual's sex cells. If individuals who possess a heritable trait leave more offspring than those who do not possess it, there will soon be a larger number of individuals with that trait than without it. This is the direct component of fitness, which can be defined as the reproduction achieved by an individual, independent of aid provided by relatives. Aspects of this personal fitness affect the robustness and the likelihood an individual will reach a developmental stage at which the reproductive episode can proceed efficiently and effectively.

This direct component has an important indirect component added to it—reproduction achieved by kin. The reproductive line can proceed efficiently if an individual assists descended kin, and if those kin also assist that individual. I can transmit my genes into succeeding generations by creating offspring who contain some of my genetic component (and in sexually reproducing organisms, so my partner's genes will also be transmitted), and also by helping genetically similar individuals create their own offspring. Cooperation within kin groups can be considered to be a universal, and when the direct and indirect components of fitness are added together we have the components that determine inclusive fitness.

It can be understood, then, how a trait that reduces the reproductive capacity of an individual might be selected, as long as the trait enhances the reproduction of enough related individuals in the population. This enhancement of RS is called kin selection, and the effectiveness of such selection is what is known as the coefficient of relatedness (r) of different individuals. Parents and offspring share one-half of their genes ($r = 0.5$), as do full siblings (for identical twins $r = 1.0$), and the amount of sharing decreases as relatives become more remote: For an uncle and a nephew the sharing is one-quarter ($r = 0.25$); with a first cousin it is one-eighth ($r = 0.125$). Obviously, people do not go around calculating coefficients of relatedness before they decide to assist someone. It was likely that in the environments of evolutionary adaptation (EEAs), the members of a small group that was stable across time would be kin, and the tendency to help such social companions would increase an individual's fitness. Just being raised in the same household with someone could be a fairly good clue that those familiars are likely to be genetically related—leading to the selection of traits to cooperate with and help them, even though not inbreeding with them—which is undesirable for several genetic reasons. What is important is that kin are *affected* differentially, but it is not important for them to be differentially affected *because* they are kin.

Any trait that enhances social cooperation could be favored by selection. Selection should favor genes that result in traits leading to cooperation as well as to altruism among kin. In one sense, altruism by kin is not altruism at all, but serves the selfish genetic interests of those involved. Cooperative behavior among kin is selected because cooperative individuals attain a greater relative fitness. Sober (1984) suggested that kin selection merely means that selectively significant interactions are nonrandom with respect to kinship.

Reciprocal Altruism

Although it is understandable that altruistic helping among kin could be selected, it is more difficult to understand how altruism develops among nonrelated individuals. If the evolutionary game is replication of one's genetic lineage, wouldn't the best bet be to compete with everyone to their disadvantage? If social interactions involved only single encounters between individuals who will never meet again, then cooperative behavior could not evolve. If there are stable groups, however, and they contain both genetically related and unrelated members, then kin selection could lead related members to engage in altruistic behavior. Cooperative traits will be selected within a population at large because cooperative individuals have a greater relative fitness. If one helps unrelated members of the community, then the helper could profit, providing the help is reciprocated at another time by recipients. Helpers would gain the reputation of being trustworthy individuals who can be counted on, and they might profit from reciprocated aid given to them in times of need.

An example of how these ideas can be used is provided by considering the case of parental care given to neonates. There is no problem in understanding how a gene would be selected to favor such care; the care allows one's progeny to prosper, and that progeny represents the replication of half of a parent's genes. Generally, two related individuals differ from two unrelated ones in the probability that they carry replica genes inherited through their genetic lineage. Thus, a gene might be selected to provide care to neonates, even though that neonate does not carry replicates of the caretaker's genes, and even though it might be disadvantageous to the bearer's direct fitness—as long as it allows the bearer to confer a sufficiently large advantage to relatives who share replica genes with the care-taker.

There can be, then, a tendency to perform an action detrimental to one-self if, for example, the action benefits siblings ($r = 0.5$) at least twice as much as the loss to oneself, or produces at least two surviving young. It is worth helping a half-sibling($r = 0.25$) in order to gain at least four times the cost to one's direct reproduction, and a first-cousin ($r = 0.125$) to gain at least eight times the cost. Thus, in a pure genetic world, no one should be prepared to sacrifice their life for any single individual (probably not even an identical twin—even though it is a one-to-one tradeoff)—but everyone might be expected to save more than two siblings, more than four half-siblings, or more than eight first-cousins, particularly if there were limited chances to breed. For all of this to work, the ability to recognize close relatives must be favored through the process of natural selection, and the proximate factor probably takes the form of favoring those with whom one has been raised.

Selection can act in several ways to increase my relative fitness. I could mate a lot with many different mates in order to increase my direct fit-ness—as rich and powerful men do in some societies. They are able to do this because they can contribute sufficient resources to ensure that the re-sulting offspring will be viable and fecund, and these men also devise and control the social customs that make such mating strategies permissible.

I could breed less and help my mate raise fewer young. It does no good to fitness to propagate if none of the propagules survives. There are mech-anisms, such as infertility during lactation, that help the female control her rate of reproduction, permitting the allotment of more maternal care to the vulnerable infant. Both parents also could profit by not having more chil-dren, but by making sure their existing young live to reproductive age and are able to reproduce. Such strategies are successful because grandchildren have a coefficient of relatedness of 0.25 with each parent. I could, instead of reproducing more (or even at all), help my siblings ($r = 0.5$) to reproduce; after all, $r = 0.25$ with the young of my siblings (my nieces and nephews). Or I could (as birds of several species do) help my parents produce more sib-lings—who will have an r of 0.5 with me. Or I could seek to work within a large extended family and help a lot of young nephews and nieces or a gag-gle of cousins to reproduce, given that they all carry a portion of my genes.

To estimate what the contribution of a given act is to my fitness, the di-rect fitness has to be calculated, then the indirect fitness component added, as well as the results considered over my entire lifetime (to determine my lifetime RS). It is also necessary to know the reproductive value and relat-edness of all the players, and add in the benefits due to the actions of re-ciprocal altruists. Again, no one calculates these things consciously, but the game of natural selection works according to these rules, and individuals are driven to develop proximate tendencies that serve the ultimate evolutionary ends of reproduction and genetic propagation.

This concept of reciprocal altruism is important, because it supplies an evolutionarily based social glue that solidifies cooperative tendencies between those within the community, even though they are not kin. As will be discussed below, the downside of this community cohesion is a fear and distrust of outsiders, which would have been valuable to enhance survival and reproduction in the EEA, but that results in what may well be maladaptive acts today, leading to intergroup rivalries, distrust, hate, and genocide.

Another factor is an evolved tendency to favor members of our own species over those of others. The reasons to expect that such strongly evolved tendencies will greatly influence behavior patterns constitute the thrust of the argument of *Darwinian Dominion* (Petrinovich, 1999). In that book, the centrality of the concept of a biological species is discussed in light of evolutionary biology and the bearing of the species concept on issues regarding human morality is developed at length; I will therefore not repeat those arguments here. The conclusion reached was that it is evolutionarily sound for people to favor individuals of the human species, because those individuals make up the potential breeding population, all of whom share heritable genetic material. There are essential differences that disqualify animals of other species from full moral agency, and the humanness of people endows human moral patients (those lacking full moral standing, such as infants, mental defectives, and the senile) with a higher standing than that accorded to animal moral patients.

The establishment of a social contract is another consideration that must be recognized. A smoothly functioning society is held together by a tendency to honor social contracts voluntarily entered into by human moral agents. It is also important to honor morally imperative social contracts that agents have toward human moral patients, even though the latter cannot voluntarily enter into such agreements because they cannot understand the ideas of causation, rules, and obligations. In the same way, it is important to honor those social contracts we strike with individuals of other species if we are to have a just, humane society. Wanton cruelty is not permissible whenever we have shouldered the responsibility of assuring the welfare of animals as pets, companions, or partners in the struggle for day-to-day existence. However, as we shall see, the strength of these contracts is weaker when the necessity to survive rears its ugly head.

BACK TO THE DONNER PARTY

Now what does this evolutionary musing have to do with the events experienced by the unfortunate Donner Party? Everything! Many disastrous instances of cannibalism can be understood when viewed as the direct expression of evolved aspects of human nature. It is interesting to compare the events that occurred in the Donner Party with those that occurred in the next situation to be discussed, the Willie Handcart Company. These people, too, suffered greatly under somewhat similar circumstances, but cannibalism did not occur. This nonoccurrence may help to identify those culturally accepted social norms that must be overridden for evolved behavioral tendencies to surface and permit cannibalism.

Various episodes of starvation cannibalism are discussed throughout this book to make it clear that it is not advantageous to be a member of another species, of a different race, or even to be a stranger when people are driven by starvation. The best thing is to be a member of a family group, and not to be too young or too old. The sequence of events indicates that the "new rules" that survivors develop to survive make sense in terms of evolutionary expectations. People do not voluntarily commit suicide, an act that would completely eliminate one's reproductive value, and also make it impossible to assist kin or other members of the community who could contribute to one's indirect fitness.

Even though it could be expected that you might kill yourself to provide food for a number of kin, this does not happen. Often dying individuals urge surviving kin and friends to eat them when they die, but the surviving kin sometimes find it difficult or impossible to do so. This reluctance to eat dead kin and close friends reflects a strong respect for the person who was. This respect could be based on an interest to ensure, in normal circumstances, that a person's own goods, wishes, and bequeaths will be respected on death. Another deterrent is that although it might make immediate genetic sense to kill oneself to feed a number of kin, the act of suicide certainly cuts off any future reproductive value the individual might have.

The above argument is based on three major considerations. The first is that of inclusive fitness, in the sense that people tend not to kill direct kin (Daly & Wilson, 1988). The second is the power of the social contract that supports altruistic tendencies and serves to bind the community into a cohesive unit. Such a contract is strong between members of a family and neighbors within the community (Petrinovich, 1999). These social bonds support the tendency people have to honor the memory and wishes of the dead. The third is a tendency to disfavor those who are not members of the community. This xenophobia would have been adaptive in an EEA that was inhabited by small groups of foragers and hunters. Strangers from another group could quite likely be a source of danger to the members of the community and their goods. This tendency to disfavor those not like us, therefore, is based on what was once a highly adaptive trait. Its existence leads people to find it acceptable to kill and eat those of other races when the necessity arises.

As expected, animals of other species are most vulnerable, and are high on the menu list. The order in which animals are consumed conforms to expectations. First, those brought along to provide meat or products, such as milk and cheese, are consumed. Next, work animals (oxen and horses used to ride or pull wagons) and then working animals usually not eaten, such as dogs used for hunting and as watch dogs, are consumed. People next boil and consume sources of protein, such as animal hides, that usually are not eaten and are not particularly palatable. This starts to occur at about the same time pets, usually dogs, spared as long as possible in respect of the terms of the social contract struck by human owners when they took on the responsibility of having companion animals, are finally killed and consumed.

Throughout these initial stages, people still refuse to eat the flesh of dead humans. Almost all do consume human flesh after necessity leads the practice to begin, however. There is always an unwillingness to eat dead members of one's own family. The pattern of events is what would be expected in terms of the proximate mechanisms that developed to increase ultimate RS; eat foodstuffs, then animals who normally are not food, then animals to which you have a social bond, then usually inedible protein, then those of another race, strangers of your own kind, then friends, and last of all kin.

It is clear that members of a different race do not have a protected status. Early in the journey of the Donner Party it will be remembered that James Reed was banished from the party for killing another white man in a "fair" fight. Although the emigrant train was isolated and removed from the machinery of U.S. justice, one of the party's own people had killed another, and that was not permissible. The interesting fact is that this killing occurred near the place where a member of another party had earlier shot and killed an Indian who had startled him, even though the Indian had raised his hand in a sign of friendship. The Indian was left to die, but another member of the party rode up, and seeing he was dying, shot him through the head to "put him out of his pain." There was a call for retributive justice, but the killer was allowed to disappear and was not seen again. Members of this party also poisoned the meat of wounded oxen so that Indians would die if they consumed the meat.

The only incident discussed to this point in which people were killed to be eaten involved the two Indian guides of the "Forlorn Hope" escape party. Although the Indians had brought mules and supplies to the Donner Party and had served as guides, they were the only ones killed for consumption, as far as is known. To this point there is an orderly pattern of consumption of animals of other species, followed by humans of another race.

A strong case regarding the power of kinship is provided by the ordeals

James Reed endured to rescue his family. Although Reed was banished from the party, his wife and four children remained with it, and those sympathetic to Reed's situation promised to care for them. Reed, after undergoing considerable hardship, reached Sutter's Fort, convinced Captain Sutter to provide him with mules, horses, and provisions, and immediately set out for the mountains. Severe storms forced him to turn back about a dozen miles from the pass, and he returned to Sutter's Fort. Reed then made his way to what is now San Francisco, where he gathered funds, supplies, and volunteers, and returned to Sutter's Fort, once again heading into the mountains with a relief party. He met the returning relief party, which contained his wife and two of his children, but continued on to Donner Lake to rescue his other two children who had been forced to turn back. He successfully reached the Lake camp and returned with his children and 15 other survivors.

Another event that attests to the compelling power of kinship also indirectly involves James Reed. William Eddy had left with one of the relief columns, returning to find that his son had died. Lewis Keseberg had resorted to cannibalism, but there was no proof that he had killed anyone for food, although there were several reports that he threatened to do so (Farnham, 1856). In any event, Eddy believed that Keseberg had killed his son, and after the rescue armed himself and set out to kill Keseberg. It is reported that Reed persuaded him to give up this idea (Stewart, 1960). This is the only instance of anyone attempting revenge for the death of any of the victims.

**Demographic
Analyses**

Grayson (1990, 1993) analyzed the demographic pattern of the Donner Party deaths, and in 1997 analyzed the timing of the deaths. He found that there were more males in the Donner Party as compared to the "white" population in Illinois at that time, with the overrepresentation greatest in the 60–69 year age class (due to the age of the heads of the two Donner families—62 and 65). There also was a heavy representation of single males, which was the case for most western emigration parties. A disproportionate number of males typified California-bound parties: Stewart (1962) estimated that of the 45,000 migrants in 1850, only 1% were women and 2% children; among 52,000 migrants in 1852, 13% were women and 17% children. As mentioned earlier, Stewart (1962) and Brodhead (1997) agreed that there were too few mature and sturdy adults in the party to conquer the extreme adversities encountered.

Death rates were highest both for the youngest (ages 1–4; 62.5% mortality) and oldest (ages 50–69; 83.3% mortality) members of the party (compared to 45% over all ages), figures rather similar to those found for human societies in general. Mortality rates for males were higher than for females in all age classes (56.6% for males; 29.4% for females); males succumbed at a rate that was approximately twice that of females (and they died sooner). Grayson (1993) noted that the initial round of deaths removed those people who were doomed by their age and sex. Such sex-related mortality differences are found for most human societies.

Under the stresses the Donner Party encountered it has been proposed that women were favored by, for example, their smaller size, greater proportion of subcutaneous fat, and lower basal metabolic rate (see Grayson, 1993). These factors would afford them greater protection from cold stress, particularly during the periods of inactivity that prevailed under conditions of extreme starvation. It is likely that tasks requiring short-term physical exertion were done primarily by men, which would have increased their later vulnerability to stress. The lowered mortality of females was due directly to this greater ability to endure cold stress and famine (Grayson, 1990). The most extreme stress was encountered by the 15 members of the Forlorn Hope party; 8 of the 10 males died, but none of the 5 females.

An interesting analysis of sex discrimination in disasters supported Grayson's conclusions. Among a number of findings, Rivers (1982) reported that important differences in the death rate of victims based on sex can be the result of differences in social roles that affect the victim's exposure to punishing environmental conditions. Rivers suggested that men suffer from basic flaws in nutritional design; adult men are on average larger than adult women, and body size is a major determinant of nutritional needs. In conditions of cold stress, women have an advantage due to their relatively thick deposits of subcutaneous fat, which results in a lower critical temperature (the temperature below which the metabolic rate starts to rise as the external temperature falls) than men. Under conditions of cold stress women have a 10% smaller increase in metabolic rate than men. This means that women have a lower energy need, and thereby suffer a smaller physiological deficit caused by conditions of starvation.

Under normal living conditions, longevity is positively related to the size of an individual's social network, particularly the size of the immediate kin group (Grayson, 1993). A major factor that mediated death for the Donner Party was family size: For those between 5 and 40 years of age the average kin group size for surviving males was 8.4 compared to 5.7 for nonsurvivors; for females it was 10.1 for survivors and 4.0 for the one nonsurvivor. For those 25 individuals between 20 and 39 years of age, the average kin group size for survivors was 6.8, but only 2.3 for nonsurvivors. There were no single women in the party, but there were 15 single men between the ages of 20 and 40. Of these 15 men, only 3 survived. A remarkable fact is that all members of the two larger families survived: all 9 of the Breen family and all 6 of the Reed family. Seven of the 10 members of the Graves family survived, but of the combined 16 members of the two Donner families only 8 survived. The lower number of Donner survivors was due to the fact that the wife of George, Tamsen Donner, refused two opportunities to come out, staying to care for her injured husband, and keeping two of her children (who perished) with her.

Grayson (1990, p. 241) concluded: "When read as biology, the story becomes one of natural selection in action." The fact that fewer men survived would be of little consequence in terms of the overall reproductive value of members of the party. The limiting factor in a breeding population typically is the number of females; this factor would be particularly important in the frontier communities they were entering, because there was a scarcity of women. Stewart (1960) remarked that almost before the frostbite was out of their toes the girls were receiving advances and accepting suitors. Those men who survived would have been among the sturdiest, having been severely tested, so natural selection would have preserved those whose reproductive value was probably the highest (and who had good luck on their side, as well). Many of the male and female survivors assumed important roles in the communities they entered, and not only did they survive, but most of them prospered and went forth to reproduce.

WILLIE HANDCART COMPANY

The Mormon Church, having been driven steadily westward from Ohio since 1832, fled from its base in Nauvoo, Illinois, reaching what would be the site of its City of Zion, Salt Lake City, Utah in 1847. Several parties were sent back and forth between Missouri and Salt Lake City to pick up supplies and recruits, and to rescue faltering companies. The first pioneer company not only performed these functions, but also was instructed to note the site of good campgrounds, wood, water, and grass; distances were measured, mileposts established, bridges built, sites established where rivers could be forded, and rafts and ferry boats were constructed for the use of later parties. Stegner (1964) remarked that they left men with the ferries to "make an honest dollar ferrying the Gentiles."

Stegner noted that these parties were not composed of groups of young and restless adventurers, as were many of the early pioneering parties, nor were they isolated families or groups of families, as was the Donner Party. They literally were villages on the march, and the members possessed a sobriety, solidarity, puritan masochism, and discipline that not only was unheard of on the western trails, but was infrequently found in the settled United States. Stegner (1964, p. 184) characterized them as follows: "Only their faith, the authority of the priesthood, and the peculiarly coherent social system that their faith encouraged made them different from the adventurous, independent, and violent men who made the trip under other auspices." And they had a determined, effective, and authoritarian leader, Brigham Young.

The pioneer caravan to Salt Lake City, led by Young, was substantial; 3 women, 2 children, 144 men and boys, 72 wagons, 93 horses, 52 mules, 67 oxen, 19 cows, 17 dogs, and some chickens (Stegner, 1964). Only one of the 149 people in this party who started from Missouri failed to get to Salt Lake City, and this failure was attributed to the fact that he, a fiddler for dances, turned back on the first day, claiming illness. It was also suggested that his failure was a result of being "weak in faith."

Later Mormon parties were not as fortunate, running into early snow-storms as they journeyed toward Salt Lake City, and did not have the benefit of the stern dominance of Brigham Young, whose presence eliminated any threat of dissension. One such company was reduced to eating the brains from the frozen heads of a donkey and a mule they found, their rawhide saddlebags, and then a worn-out mule they killed. They did not kill the children's pet dog, but traded it to Indians for a piece of dried buffalo meat—there is no indication of what the Indians did with the dog. The members of this party were not reduced to cannibalism because yet another company caught up with them on the relatively well-traveled road, and together the two companies made it to winter quarters.

Between 1856 and 1860 the Mormon Church enlisted new members to travel from Iowa City to Salt Lake City, a distance of 1300 miles, pushing handcarts. There were 10 such handcart companies, a total of about 650 handcarts and 3,000 emigrants. These carts had hardwood wagon beds, hickory shafts and side pieces, and axles with wheels as far apart as normal wagon wheels. Each cart carried 400 to 500 pounds of food, bedding, clothing, and cooking utensils, and required two able-bodied people to pull it. Five people were assigned to each cart, and each company included one ox-drawn commissary and baggage wagon for about every 20 handcarts. These wagons carried large public tents, each of which would accommodate 20 people, and a captain had charge of 5 tent groups. This organization was remarkable in comparison to what prevailed for most wagon trains, and particularly for the ill-fated Donner Party.

Ten years after the Donner Party disaster one such company, the Willie Handcart Company, left Iowa City late, encountered early snow, and lost 16% of their group, as contrasted with the Donner Party, which eventually lost 46% of its original party. The members of this party had originally embarked from Liverpool, crossed the Atlantic Ocean to Boston or New York, and traveled by train to Iowa City, where they were provided with handcarts. This company was large: almost 500 people, 100 handcarts (unfortunately, quickly thrown together of green lumber), 5 wagons, 24 oxen, 4 mules, and 25 tents. The first sign of trouble occurred when the green wood of the carts started to disintegrate, requiring constant repairs. Further misfortune was caused when they were overrun by stampeding buffalo, which cost them 30 head of cattle. They had expected to replenish their supplies at Fort Laramie in eastern Wyoming, but nothing was available, the weather turned bitterly cold, and people began to die from exposure to cold and malnutrition due to inadequate food supplies. The company continued, but had to camp embedded in snow over a foot deep with their food stores almost exhausted. When Young heard that the Willie Company and one other, the Martin Company, were still on the trail and in serious trouble he organized rescue parties. An advance party informed the Willie Company they would receive supplies, and when those supplies arrived they continued west, from time to time encountering wagon loads of food sent to them from the west.

By the time they reached Salt Lake City some 70 people had died. During the ordeal some of the emigrants lost toes, others fingers, and others whole hands and feet. Stegner (1964) reported that a young girl, sleeping in a tent shared by her family and a pair of boys, awoke screaming with pain in the night to find one of the boys eating her fingers. Dragged away, he began to eat his own fingers, and in the morning he was dead. This is the closest the company came to cannibalism.

Grayson (1996) examined the patterns of mortality for the Willie Company in the same manner as for the Donner Party. He noted that the Willie Company differed from the Donner Party in at least four ways that may have impacted mortality profiles. First, the Willie ordeal was shorter—5 weeks as compared to 6 months, and they had direct assistance from rescuers. Second, they walked and pushed or pulled carts loaded with children and goods. Third, the women as a group performed far more energy-intensive labor than did the Donner Party women. And fourth, the Donner Party contained no women traveling alone or traveling without fathers, whereas the Willie Company included 26 families led by mothers, with 27 more women traveling on their own. There were 33 single men.

He was able to identify 437 individuals, and found that a relatively large number of the women were between 20 and 39 years of age, a percentage that was significantly greater (64.0%) than the percentage in Utah at that time (51.6%). As for the Donner Party, the highest mortality rates occurred among the oldest and youngest age groups. For the Willie Company, the male mortality rate was 2.93 times higher than for females, but for the Donner Party, male mortality had been 1.93 times greater. This increased ratio of male to female mortality for the Willie Company occurred despite the increased heavy labor required from the Willie women.

An odd occurrence is that both for males and females, mortality in families led by single mothers was significantly lower than for families led by mother–father pairs. Grayson suggested this was due to the fact that fatigued children often had to be carried, and that fathers bore this load most often, which led to higher levels of mortality among fathers. He also remarked that members of larger families had to pull heavier loads, whereas members of the Donner Party never pulled or walked, and this difference could have eliminated the advantage in survival for larger families in the Willie Company. A striking fact is that for individuals 40 years or older, the odds of a man dying were 10.4 times higher than for a woman.

Grayson concluded that the patterns of mortality for the two companies were similar, and where they differed it was due to differences in the magnitude of the ordeals faced by the two groups, by the way resources were allocated, and how energy was spent by different members of the group. He believed that the patterns of mortality due to exposure to severe cold and starvation are explained adequately by the interplay between human biology and environmental challenge.

There appear to be several factors that account for the absence of cannibalism in the Willie Company. The ordeal was not as long or as severe, there was always hope that help would reach them in time (a hope that was confirmed periodically), they were well organized and supervised on the trail, and they had a strong faith in the theological righteousness of their cause. Stegner (1964) considered the justification for Mormon polygamy to be less in terms of personal liking or pleasure than a belief that the greater glory in heaven resides in the practical eugenics of a stock breeder—an apt Darwinian view.

Whether cannibalism would have commenced had supplies failed to come through, accompanied by a longer time and increased level of starvation, cannot be determined, but it is clear from the one incident cited that they were close to the limit. It should be remembered that for the Forlorn Hope group the first step toward cannibalism was described as maniacal cravings for food—a craving that included their comrades as possibilities. The maniacal episode of the finger eating could well have been the first step toward cannibalism had help not arrived.

Mormon Cowboys Stegner (1964) described another ordeal by starvation that took place in 1857, when 21 Mormon cowboys tried to overwinter with a herd of about 275 cattle in the mountains. They started with inadequate supplies and their cattle, because they were in poor condition, became bait for packs of wolves. To have food, the winterers were forced to kill the last 40 cattle before the wolves did. After a couple of months they had only unsalted beef to eat. Stegner remarked that 21 men eating nothing but meat can chew their way through 40 skinny carcasses in a very short time. When the meat supply was exhausted, they began boiling hides to produce a gluey broth, which made all of them sick. They then attempted to survive on little more than coffee, and it was still only early January. They enjoyed the luxury of adequate shelter and firewood in a solid cabin. This was a considerable improvement over the conditions that prevailed for the Donner Party, whose shelters consisted of hides (many of which were removed and eaten during the ordeal), and their cabins were, at best, dilapidated and drafty.

One might expect the cowboys to have held a lottery to see who should be killed and eaten, but as Stegner (1964, p. 263) phrased it: "the Mormons, whatever their other capabilities never showed any talent for cannibalism." Instead, they held a meeting and prayed for the Lord to direct them, and "He directed them back to the hides." They scraped the hair off, cut up the hides, and boiled them until they were soft enough to be chewed, but with enough consistency to be swallowed with ease. Again, in Stewart's phrasing: the Lord then passed on His favorite recipe for boiled hide: Scorch and scrape the hide to get the hair off (scalding gives it a bad taste); parboil for one hour in plenty of water and throw the water and glue away. Then wash and scrape again, rinsing in cold water. Then boil to a jelly and allow to cool. Serve with a sprinkling of sugar.

This they ate for 6 weeks until a mail coach made it to the cabin, and they were able to whip up a skimpy breakfast from the coach driver's supplies. At this juncture a lone Shoshone Indian appeared, and the coach driver, knowing the Shoshone language, was able to speak to him. The Indian led 10 of the men to the Indian camp and promised that his comrades would get buffalo meat if the cowboys would protect them from their enemies, the Crows. They did, and the cowboys returned with mules laden with buffalo meat, which lasted until early March, by which time all the meat and hides had been consumed, as well as moccasins, rawhide tires from hand carts that had been abandoned in the vicinity, rawhide wrappings from wagon tongues, and a chunk of buffalo hide that had been used for months as a door mat.

Once again, a mail coach happened by just as the cowboys had put a pack saddle on to simmer, and they were able to substitute the coachman's buffalo meat to make buffalo broth instead. Occasional mountain men came by, and by trading calico goods that had been left in the cabin the cowboys were able to obtain enough meat. This enabled them to survive until the weather warmed, making it possible for them to hunt, and for express wagons to reach them. Once again, their strong faith, combined with disciplined spirits, kept them going, and they avoided engaging in "unthinkable" cannibalism.

As will be seen in the next two chapters, once the thin veneer of civilized society is removed people will struggle mightily to protect kith and kin, as well as to sustain their own life. There is a strong tendency to save close kin, even at great risk to one's own being, and that is an evolutionarily sound strategy in most cases. One surprising thing about cannibalism is the regularity with which it occurs among normal people from conventional society. The Donner Party was not a harmonious group, but it was composed of solid, upright folks. The pattern of behaviors that occurred as the situation continued to deteriorate is very similar to what we will encounter in the Andean plane crash (described in Chapter 4) and in the many instances of seafaring cannibalism. I agree with Grayson's conclusions regarding the demographics of starvation, and generalize them to conclude that when starvation cannibalism occurs we encounter the raw biological forces of natural selection.

3

Shipwreck Disasters

Mrs. Patterson, the wife of the captain of The Francis Mary remarked after having eaten the brains of an apprentice seaman, that it was the most delicious thing she had ever tasted.

—A. W. B. Simpson (1984)

As mentioned in Chapter 1, when discussing the case of the *Francis Mary*, sailing vessels often suffered disaster and, lacking radios, the crew was unable to signal their distress. The resulting hardships either on a disabled ship or in exposed lifeboats led to deaths, to throwing people overboard to increase the availability of provisions or to lighten the boat, and to a number of instances of cannibalism. These cases provide historical instances similar to those involved in the lifeboat fantasy dilemmas we have used in empirical studies of moral intuitions, and the patterns of choice are similar in both the real and fantasy situations. The number of cases available in the literature suggest that those who have maintained that cannibalism is a rare event when disasters occurred did not bother to look very carefully.

Simpson (1984) discussed a number of cases, and a few will be considered here. In general, the legal defense of cannibalism is one of necessity based on an appeal to the "instinct for survival"—the principle of self-preservation that prompts people to save their own life in preference to that of another—although that defense has to be reconciled with a respect for the sanctity of human life. The argument of necessity has often been buttressed with an acknowledgment of the level of stress that had driven survivors to the brink of insanity, making them not accountable for their actions.

The common defense is that it is better for some to have survived by sacrificing one or more lives. Often the argument is a distinctly utilitarian one, for example, that those survivors with a chance to live, and who had dependents, were considered to be justified in killing a dying boy who had no dependents. The contrary position, which seldom prevailed in ship-wreck cases, is that the sanctity of human life must always be respected.

Animals are not accorded much respect, with those that are impersonal cargo going first. For example, there was one incident in which a "variety of cat species" was being shipped to New York. The ship met with bad weather and the sailors insisted it was occasioned by the evil presence of the cats, all of which they tossed overboard. The owner wanted to be com-pensated for the loss of the cats—a request that was resisted on the grounds that the destruction was necessary for the safety of the ship. In the end, the parties compromised on a financial settlement—little comfort for the cats.

The next to be sacrificed are those edible animals that are pets the crew had brought along, usually birds, cats, or dogs. In the case of the small sloop, *Betsy*, which sank off the coast of Dutch Guyana in 1756, the captain, mate, and two crewmen survived by killing the captain's pet dog, drink-ing the blood, and eating pieces of the dog with some onions they had aboard (Thomas, 1835).

This event is similar to one that took place in 1979 (Leslie, 1988). A young couple living in a cabin on the western coast of Alaska were forced to kayak out of the wilderness because they were running out of food and winter was threatening. They loaded their kayak with their pet dog, camping equipment, and what supplies they had. A storm forced them ashore, the kayak was destroyed, and most of their supplies were lost. They were able to kill a wolf, which they ate, and on the eighth day after leaving the cabin decided they must walk out of the wilderness. After they had been hiking for several days, the man lost hope and suggested they use the three re-maining bullets to kill the dog and the two of them, but the woman refused. After a few more days he decided they must kill and eat the dog, but should not waste a bullet. He called the dog, who climbed into his lap, "tail wag-ging." The woman held the dog's head, and the dog was stabbed in the chest. The dog was skinned and gutted, the heart and liver were removed, and meat from the hindquarters was cut off. Although the man expressed remorse at "killing a friend" they consumed the dog and used the fur to keep their feet warm until, on the nineteenth day, they were rescued by a helicopter. Again the evolutionary imperative appears: Do not commit sui-cide, kill and eat a wild animal, and finally kill and eat a beloved pet dog.

In several shipwrecks, after available animals are eaten, any turtle, bird, or fish that happens by would be pounced on, and in at least one instance the barnacles were scraped from the hull of the ship and eaten. Next, any edible protein such as leather and cloth, and finally such exotics as tooth-paste and lamp oil are consumed.

Simpson (1984) described a number of instances in which shipwrecked individuals consumed the dead in order to survive. Although it usually took a few days for cannibalism to begin, it is common, and no criticism is leveled at those who engaged in it to survive.

There are at least two cases reported in which a slave was killed and eaten before much time had passed, and these murders raised little, if any concern. In one case it was claimed that lots had been drawn, and the slave had lost. In the other case a slave was killed and eaten without any discussion of the formality of casting lots. In yet another, a slaver ship foundered after picking up a cargo of slaves in West Africa. An American, an Irishman, four Englishmen, and two Portuguese escaped in the ship's boat, abandoning the slaves and 15 crew members to drown. The survivors ate each other, starting with the Portuguese, and at the time of rescue only the American and Irishman still survived.

In yet another instance (discussed further below), the crew of the *William Brown* occupied an overloaded lifeboat and threw passengers overboard to keep the boat from sinking. They chose to throw male passengers over, including only women who interfered or insisted they go over with their husband or brother. The captain and crew were not prosecuted on the grounds that they were essential to the working of the boat and had to be preserved to allow any to be saved. In the case of the *Francis Spaight* (also described below), the crew decided that lots should be drawn among the boys of the crew because they had no families, and their death would not be as great a loss as would that of family men to their friends, wives, and children. In general, the order of survival is for the captain and officers to be favored over crew, next passengers, with women and children favored over male passengers, men with family favored over boys, foreigners being in jeopardy, and slaves being thrown over just after animals, which go first.

Rivers (1982) doubted that the principle "women and children first" was the operative rule in many disasters, citing instances that suggest such was not the case. When the steamship *Atlantic* sank on a trip from Liverpool to New York in 1879, 294 of the 295 women and children died, but only 187 of the 636 men. When the *General Slocum*, carrying 740 children and 640 adults, foundered in 1904, half of the 1021 passengers who died were children. Only one of the 23 crew was lost, and Rivers remarked that that crewman drowned because his pockets were overfilled with passengers' money. He also cited the sinking of the *Titanic* in 1912: 30% of women and children on the ship did not get a place in a lifeboat; only 60% of those who did get a place were women and children; and over half the men to get places were crew. Deaths were particularly high among women and children in steerage class.

There has never been any question regarding the practice of seafaring killing for consumption when lots are drawn. As Simpson (1984, p. 140) succinctly phrased it, "What sailors did when they ran out of food was to draw lots and eat someone." Because the eaten did not survive to testify to the fairness of the draw, we can question the fairness of the game or whether it was played at all; the survivors always swore it was, and who was left to complain. Maritime survival cannibalism was a common and accepted practice among seamen, and the public and the law concurred, provided any killing was preceded by the drawing of lots. One reason cannibalism was resorted to fairly quickly was that seamen of the sailing era were usually on such skimpy and substandard rations that they quickly developed signs of malnutrition when food and water were no longer available (Bisset, 1958). Samuel Johnson remarked that being on a ship was similar to being in jail, with the added chance of being drowned, and commonly in worse company than would be expected in a jail (Boswell, 1791).

FAMOUS SHIPWRECKS

The Nottingham Galley   An early case of shipwreck cannibalism was that of the *Nottingham Galley*, which departed for Boston from London late in the year 1710 with a cargo of butter and cheese and a crew of 14 men. A gale was encountered east of the Piscataqua River off the coast of Maine, and the ship struck a rock on December 11. The captain ordered the crew to go over the side, as he also did, and all managed to reach the rock. By morning the ship had disappeared and the only food that could be found was some cheese that washed up among the rockweed, as well as planks, timbers, sails, and canvas. They could see the mainland, which was about 12 miles away (Leslie, 1988). According to the captain's account the ship's cook died on the first day (Constable, 1812, v. 2) and the corpse was "put in a convenient place for the sea to carry him away." It was not suggested they eat the corpse at that time, but after being on the rock only 2 days they were entertaining thoughts of cannibalism—a relatively shorter interval than usual.

A boat was constructed, but it smashed in the surf and the craft was destroyed. It was extremely cold, the men suffered from hunger and frostbite, and they had not been able to start a fire. They survived on rockweed, two or three mussels a day per man, and water obtained from rain or snow melted in cavities in the rock. A raft was then constructed and two people sailed off, never to be seen alive again. At the end of December the ship's corpulent carpenter died. Through there is some discrepancy regarding who suggested it (Simpson, 1984; Leslie, 1988), it was suggested that he be eaten. Simpson (1984, p. 115) presented the justification as follows: "It was no Sin, since God was pleased to take him out of the World, and that we had not laid violent Hands upon him." The captain had the head, hands, and feet thrown in the sea, then skinned, dressed, and quartered the corpse. Three of the crew refused to eat the meat at first, but by the next morning all partook of it with rockweed to serve as bread. The meat was rationed by the captain until the 10 survivors were rescued on January 4. No one was criticized for cannibalism, and the captain later became the British consul in Flanders.

The Peggy
An American ship, the *Peggy,* sailed from the Azores on October 24, 1765 with a cargo that was mainly wine and brandy, bound for New York with a captain and a crew of eight men, one of whom was a Negro slave. On October 29 the ship was disabled by a severe storm that lasted for weeks. The ship carried barely enough provisions to last through a normal voyage to New York, and both food and water were severely rationed until the crew broached the cargo of wine and brandy, becoming riotously drunk for much of the remaining time.

On Christmas day, a ship was sighted and drew alongside, but after some discussion, refused to help and sailed away. The crew killed and ate their two pet pigeons, the ship's cat, barnacles scraped from the ship's side, tobacco, lamp oil, candles, and all the leather they could find, including that in the ship's pumps. All were still drunkenly alive on January 13, at which time the crew insisted they cast lots to see who should die to keep the others alive. The captain acquiesced, but would not command that the lottery be held. The men left the captain's cabin, returning almost immediately to announce they had drawn lots and the Negro had lost, whereupon he was shot through the head. Thomas (1835) commented that the lot had been consulted only for the sake of form and that the black was proscribed the moment the sailors first formed their resolution. One of the crew ate the liver raw, some of the rest of the body was cooked, and the remainder (cut up and referred to as "steaks") was pickled, with the head and fingers thrown overboard. It was claimed that the captain did not eat any of the meat.

According to one account (Dorling, 1927, p. 17), the crewman who ate the liver died in "a state of raving madness," but the superstitious sailors feared they, too, would become mad if they ate him, so they threw his body overboard. The body of the Negro lasted until January 26, and on January 29 they once again petitioned the captain to conduct a lottery. He agreed to do so, fearing that if he failed to supervise it and ensure that fairness prevailed, he would be the automatic loser. The loser, who was a very popular person, was said to have accepted his fate and asked to be put to death quickly, as had been the Negro, and by the hand of the same person. The crew delayed the killing until morning in order to commiserate with the loser, but after a few hours he "went deaf" and became "a raving madman." Meanwhile, the crew had prepared a fire on which to cook the victim. At that time a ship was sighted, all were taken aboard, and they reached Dartmouth on March 2. Two died during the passage, with only the captain and three crew surviving—the one remaining "a raving lunatic." Thomas (1835, p. 179) claimed that the latter sailor "was restored to perfect health, after having been so near the gates of death." The event is probably the inspiration for the shipwreck scene in Lord Byron's *Don Juan*. In the case of the *Peggy* we find another "fair lottery" being held, the loser being a Negro slave, then another lottery was held, with the loser accepting his fate, but going mad and being rescued before the killing could take place. Again, there was neither criticism nor surprise at the sequence of events.

The Dolphin, Tyger, and Zong   The ship *Dolphin* was dismasted on a voyage from the Canaries to New York in 1759; the eight persons aboard were adrift for 165 days, and without food for 116 of those days (Huntress, 1979). Their stores had been exhausted for more than 3 months and they had eaten their dog, their cat, all their shoes, and everything else that was edible. Starving, they cast lots with the recipient of the shortest lot to die, and the holder of the next shortest to be the executioner. A Spanish passenger was the loser, and he was shot through the head, which was thrown overboard. When the gentleman had been consumed the survivors started casting lots a second time, but the alarmed captain remembered he had a pair of breeches that were lined with leather (Simpson, 1984). The leather was removed and the captain allowed each man a piece about an inch and a half square as a daily allowance, and they were able to survive for about 20 days on that with a garnish of the grass growing on the deck. When rescued the survivors consisted of the captain and seven others (Constable, 1812, v. 2).

In yet another tale (about which there have been questions regarding how much is fictional) a ship, the *Tyger*, was wrecked in 1766. A French captain, his wife, son, and Negro slave reached land but suffered greatly from hunger. The captain remembered that in such cases mariners often cast lots to determine who should die to keep the rest alive. However, he dispensed with the formality of casting lots and killed, smoked, and ate the slave, rather than put himself or his family at risk. So, on two of the above occasions a lottery was held and the outsider, a Negro slave and a foreign passenger, just happened to be the losers, while in the third the lottery was dispensed with and the slave was "it."

Simpson (1984) reported on one other case that highlights the fact that it did not pay to be a slave aboard an English boat—the slaver *Zong* of Liverpool. Although English commentators had extolled the civilized virtues of English officers and sailors, particularly their devotion to protecting passengers, the captain of the *Zong* had 132 African slaves thrown alive into the sea in 1781, allegedly out of necessity. There was no prosecution for murder, but there was a suit to collect the insurance policy on the cargo—the slaves had been insured for £30 each.

The Medusa A famous disaster occurred in June 1816, when the French frigate *Medusa* sailed from France bound for Senegal. This disaster is remembered because it inspired Géricault's painting *Radeau de la "Meduse,"* which is now in the Louvre. The captain of the ship apparently was a less than competent commander and navigator, lost the course, and became entrapped among shoals and reefs that extend from the African coast. He crashed into the rocks and the ship became stuck in the sand in water only 16 feet deep (Paine, 1921). Given that the coast was but 40 miles away and the ship was in danger of breaking up, it was decided to abandon ship. The process could have been routine given five seaworthy lifeboats and the availability of provisions, water, skilled seamen, carpenters, and mechanics. In addition a large raft was quickly thrown together that would accommodate many more people. However, there was no semblance of order and panic ensued. The five boats left lightly loaded with the captain, senior officers, and some soldiers. It was expected that the boats would tow the raft, but they sailed off (quickly reaching the coast), leaving about 150 people aboard the raft, which, being overloaded, was partially awash. It was not unusual for the captain and officers to abandon other survivors, as we shall see in the instance of the *St. James* (described below), and also with the loss of the British man-of-war the *Centaur*. In the latter case the captain considered that he should remain with the ship and perish with the ship's company, but "love of life prevailed" (Thomas, 1835), and he and the mate descended into the only lifeboat and sailed off with several seamen who had launched the boat, reaching land after a few days.

In the *Medusa* disaster, few provisions were available: enough biscuits for one meal when soaked in wine, of which, unfortunately, there was a considerable quantity. By the morning of the second day 20 people had died or been swept overboard. The sea worsened, the soldiers and sailors drank to excess and mutinied, and the officers had to attack and subdue them (Adams, 1877). About 60 people were dead and 67 alive in various states of well-being. On the fourth day (the third, according to Simpson, 1984) the mutineers began cutting pieces from the dead and drying them for consumption. Some flying fish became entangled in the raft and were eaten, mixed with human flesh. Another mutiny occurred the next night and by morning of the fifth day only 30 were left alive (Lee & Lee, 1971). Two soldiers were thrown overboard for stealing wine, a punishment that was claimed to have been agreed on earlier. About half the people were wounded or extremely ill (including the one woman left), so it was decided that because they could survive for only a few days the weakest should be thrown overboard to conserve rations. A doctor selected those to be jettisoned (Simpson, 1984). The unlucky 13 (chosen by lot according to Paine) were thrown over by 3 soldiers and a sailor. Only 15 men were on the raft when they were rescued on the seventeenth day, with 6 of these dying after being taken ashore.

Paine (1921, p. 71) considered the acts of murder to be justifiable, likening them to wartime triage decisions, whereby "the hopelessly wounded have been put out of the way in preference to leaving them in the wake of a retreat or burdening a column with them." The French government investigated the event and agreed the murders were justifiable, and no one questioned the necessity of cannibalizing the dead.

The Essex Yet another famous disaster is that of the Nantucket whaler *Essex*, which was sunk by a sperm whale on November 20, 1820, and immortalized as a chapter in Melville's *Moby Dick*. She was whaling in the Pacific Ocean about half-way between the Hawaiian and Galapagos Islands, and while the whaleboats were hunting away from the vessel the whale rammed the ship. The mate of the ship was of the opinion that the attack by the whale was intentional—in retribution for the killing of three whales in the shoal of prey.

Before the ship sank the crews of the whaleboats brought out casks of bread, fresh water, boat nails, a musket, two pistols, a bit of powder, and light sails and spars to outfit the boats in order to make them seaworthy enough to reach land. On November 22, they set off in three whaleboats, but had not been able to recover charts or navigation instruments from the ship. In all, the abandonment and preparations had been extremely orderly and competent, in contrast to the state of affairs for the *Medusa*.

For the first few weeks they ate the bread, rinsed their mouths with sea water, and drank their own urine (a practice common for shipwrecked sailors), with occasional flying fish dropping into a boat and being eaten raw. At this point, considerable effort was expended to keep the boats together in a spirit of common cause. On December 20, exactly one month after the *Essex* sank, they landed on Henderson Island, which was uninhabitable (Leslie, 1988). The 20 men in the party rapidly exhausted the island's few resources and realized they would probably starve. Three elected to stay behind rather than venturing across the ocean in an open boat, and ultimately were taken off safely. The others left on December 27, with the first of the sailors dying and buried at sea on January 10. The mate's boat became separated from the others on January 12.

Lee and Lee (1971) cited the captain's report that a black man, in one of the boats accompanying his, died on January 25, and was eaten. On January 23, a black man in the captain's boat died, and his body was shared for food between the crews of both boats. On January 27 a black man died in the other boat, and on January 28 yet another black man died in the captain's boat, both of whom were eaten. When they were out of food a lottery was held, and a cabin boy lost and was shot and eaten. When rescued on February 23, only the captain and a young crewman were alive in the captain's boat, having survived on the body of the boy who was killed and that of one other seaman who they claimed had died.

In the mate's boat that had become separated from the others, one man died on February 8, and as they were preparing the body for burial, after having reflected on the matter all night, they decided to keep it for food, thereby avoiding the necessity of having to draw lots. The mate reported that they separated the limbs from the body, cut all the flesh from the bones, took out the heart, and then committed the rest to the sea. They ate what they needed immediately, and dried the remainder in the sun. This body lasted for 6 to 7 days, and the mate remarked that they still had some bread available. By February 15 all the flesh was consumed, and they then finished the last morsel of bread—two cakes; they were rescued on February 18.

No one was prosecuted or criticized for murder or cannibalism because it was sworn that there had been a fair lottery to determine who should be killed, and the others had died natural deaths. Once again, however, it seems that the blacks had the bad luck to die first, and a young cabin boy had bad luck in the lottery. The contrast between this story and the preceding one is remarkable, attesting to the value of having a strong authority present to prevent panic and maintain order to enhance the likelihood of survival. Another interesting point in all of these stories is that quite often the hands, feet, and head are thrown in the sea after a person has been killed. It is as though they remind those about to eat that it is a human entity they are munching, and it is easier to enjoy the meals if those reminders are removed.

LOTTERIES AND NECESSITY

In several of the preceding disasters in which living persons were killed the issue of whether and under what circumstances a lottery should be held was raised, as well as the problem of deciding whether a lottery was fair, and even whether it had been held at all. The word of survivors regarding fairness usually is accepted, even though there have been some remarkable runs of bad luck among those low on the pecking order. The crews of English and American ships were likely to be racially and ethnically mixed, and Malchow (1996) remarked on how often non-Anglo-Saxons, Irish, Spanish, half-breeds, Negro or mulatto slaves or freedmen, and ship's boys were the big losers when lotteries were held. The preceding cases of the *Essex*, *Peggy*, and *Tyger* were typical of those in which lotteries (fair or otherwise) were held and a person was killed and eaten. In these cases, the killing was held to be justifiable because it was sworn by survivors that a lottery had been held. A second issue concerns the legal argument regarding the appropriateness of using the defense of necessity against a charge of homicide, whether there had been a lottery or not.

Simpson (1984) claimed that the earliest recorded instance of lottery-driven cannibalism took place between 1629 and 1640 (the only direct account of it having been published in 1641). Seven Englishmen set out from the Dutch island now known as St. Kitts in the Caribbean on a voyage expected to last but one night. A storm blew them to sea and they were afloat for 17 days. During that time it was decided to cast lots to determine who should die to feed the rest. The lot fell on the one who had suggested the process, and lots were also cast to select an executioner. It was claimed that the victim consented to be killed, after which his blood was drunk and his body was divided and eaten. When they were eventually cast up on the island of St. Martin they were accused of homicide, but pardoned by a judge who considered their crime to be "washed away" by "inevitable necessity."

At times not all individuals are included in the pool of vulnerability. An example is provided by the wreck of the *Francis Spaight* in 1844 (Simpson, 1984). The ship sunk and the 15 survivors had neither food nor water. After about 15 days the captain decided one should suffer for the rest, and that lots should be drawn among the four ship's boys; as they had no families, their loss to society would not be so great because no one depended on them—which of course spared the officers and all the crew. One of the boys objected to limiting the lottery to the boys, but acquiesced when it appeared that if he did not join in the men would proceed in a more summary way. When the lots were cast the boy who had objected lost, and Simpson suggested that the procedure had been contrived to select him. The boy was killed and the captain ordered the cook to bleed the boy because it was the function of the ship's cook to prepare meals for the crew, but the cook refused. However, he finally agreed and did the deed. This responsibility of the cook was described by Simpson (1984, p. 260) to be "in accordance with the proper tradition of the sea." Later the same day another of the boys was killed and bled after he "went mad." The survivors lasted 20 days, at which time 11 of the original 18 were rescued. No attempt was made to conceal what had occurred, and there were no legal proceedings against the captain or crew.

Three further incidents will be discussed that bear directly on the issues of lottery and necessity: The first involves the American ship the *William Brown;* passengers were thrown overboard by the crew to drown without benefit of lottery, as had also occurred in the *Medusa* disaster. The second was the *Euxine* incident in which it seemed obvious the lottery was not honest, but no proceedings were filed. The third was the case of the *Mignonette* , in which a dying sailor was killed and eaten without the formality of a lottery, and charges were pressed and sustained.

The William Brown

The wreck of the *William Brown* is discussed fully by both Simpson (1984) and Leslie (1988) because of its centrality to the question of the responsibilities of captain and crew toward passengers in terms of a necessity defense. The ship was sailing from Liverpool to Philadelphia with a crew of 17 men, 65 male and female passengers (mainly Irish with a few Scottish emigrants), and a general cargo. On the evening of April 19, 1841, she struck an iceberg 300 miles southeast of Newfoundland. The ship began to sink and two boats were lowered in about half an hour. As was usual in those times, there was not enough space in the lifeboats to accommodate all the crew and passengers. The two boats were roughly the same size—about 20 feet long; one was rigged as a sailing cutter and the second was a shallow longboat propelled by oars. The captain, second mate, seven sailors, and one enterprising woman passenger commandeered the cutter, with the longboat left for the rest of the crew and all of the passengers. The longboat was able to hold 9 crew and 33 passengers; 30 or 31 passengers were left to drown as the ship sank. No order was maintained regarding which passengers were to be left and which were to be taken in the longboat. The captain would not permit any of the people from the overloaded longboat (which contained 42 people) to transfer to his boat (which contained only 10), even though the former's gunwales were only 4 or 5 inches above the water and it was leaking. The captain's boat remained in the vicinity through the night, but in the morning he gave the first mate, who was in charge of the longboat, a chart, watch, compass, and quadrant (even though the mate was a poor navigator). The mate was heard to tell the captain that given the severe overloading of his boat, it would be necessary to draw lots to determine who was to be thrown over, unless the captain took some of them with him. The captain commiserated but did not issue any command, and sailed off shortly thereafter.

When darkness arrived the crew, after unanimously agreeing among themselves, began to throw passengers overboard. Their justification was that the crew was required to sail the boat, and if they did not lighten the boat everyone would be lost. The sailors decided to jettison men rather than women. Although the mate had given the order it was stated that he did not participate. One of the crew, Holmes, had to forcibly throw a man overboard who was resisting seriously, and for this he was the only one to be tried in the case: *U.S. v Holmes*. Almost all of the men were thrown overboard, plus one sister who did not want to live if they killed her brother; his second sister was thrown overboard as well, although she begged not to be. I guess they strove for fairness, believed that families should stay together, or something. Although the sailors claimed that all those jettisoned were nearly dead, this probably was not the case, as later testimony would indicate.

At six in the morning, just after 2 male passengers who had been hiding were found and thrown overboard, an American ship appeared and took the survivors off. It seems, with hindsight, that it was not necessary to kill anyone, given that rescue took place so quickly, but that could not have been known at the time. Altogether, 14 male passengers and 2 women were thrown overboard to certain death by drowning.

The rescue ship landed in Le Havre with the survivors, and the mate and his eight sailors were arrested and imprisoned. The captain's boat, incidentally, was rescued after 6 days; the occupants suffered from frostbite, and one died in the hospital. The captain was not charged because he was not considered to have committed any legal offense. Holmes was tried and found guilty of manslaughter, but the jury recommended mercy. He was sentenced to 6 months at hard labor and fined the lordly sum of $20. Because he already had been in jail for over 6 months he was released, and the fine was remanded, but an appeal to the U.S. president for a full pardon was denied.

The defense had argued successfully that the killings were justified by necessity, and it was concluded that Holmes reasonably anticipated that the eventual survivors would have died had the others not been killed. The argument that it was imperative for the sailors to survive to operate the boat, in preference to passengers, was successful. It was concluded by the judge that it would have been better to draw lots among the passengers, but that was not a prudent course of action, given the dire nature of the immediate circumstances. Simpson remarked that this is a leading legal case because it explicitly accepts the existence of a defense based on the necessity of homicide, and is the only case that explicitly states the desirability of selecting victims by lot (which was not done here), but only if circumstances permit (it was concluded they did not).

The case of the *William Brown* was used by Bedau (1997) as an exercise in casuistry, which he described as a method of practical reasoning that relies on intuitionism to arrive at some set of moral norms more or less beyond dispute. He considers this method of practical ethics to be superior to theoretical ethics; it is a bottom-up strategy that triangulates the boundaries of the ethical region determined by the relevant ethical principles. He identified the principles of selection on which the crew acted in deciding whom to throw overboard to be not to part man and wife and not to throw women overboard. The passengers were not consulted nor were lots cast, and none of the crew was put overboard. Bedau dubbed the operative selection principle to be "Save Families Plus Crew" (even though some of the crew—for example, the cook—were no more adept at handling a small boat than were some of the single male passengers). He remarked that it was not likely many would come to the defense of a single male passenger, and that members of the crew, being fit, might resist strongly, and such a struggle would be in no one's interest.

The Euxine   The loss of the *Euxine* could well have been the basis for a leading case involving the argument of necessity and the practice of conducting a lottery to determine who was to be killed and eaten. However, there was a series of questions regarding the proper judicial jurisdiction, and because of political interests of members of the government they wished the matter to be set aside. These issues, combined with a mishandling of documents, and just plain incompetence on the part of authorities, resulted in the case not being brought to trial, and the memory of the events were allowed to fade away, until Simpson (1984) searched into the matter.

The *Euxine* left the port of South Shields in the United Kingdom on June 12, 1874, carrying a cargo of coal. During a severe storm on August 1 the cargo shifted and had to be leveled under difficult sea conditions, a process that took 3 days. On August 5, smoke was seen coming from the coal, which had ignited spontaneously, a common source of disaster in that era. On August 8, the crew of 30 abandoned ship in three boats. On August 9, the ship caught fire and the convoy of boats set out for the island of St. Helena in the South Atlantic Ocean. The captain, a skilled navigator, located the island with no difficulty.

The boat of concern here was in command of the second mate, and contained seven members of the crew. It became separated from the other two boats and was not seen by them again. Although the mate's boat had navigational instruments and a chart, as well as provisions and water, his lack of skill in navigation led them to lose the course, and after 12 days they still could not find land and the mate did not have the ability to establish the longitude. It was decided to sail for Brazil before the trade winds, a trip of more than 2,000 miles. On August 27, the boat capsized three times, and there were only five survivors. All navigational materials, masts, food, and water were lost. When they were rescued by a ship on August 31, 22 days had elapsed between leaving the other boats and rescue.

The survivors had no reticence in telling the following story to the British consul; on August 30, they managed to set a small sail, and by August 31 it was suggested lots be drawn to decide who to kill and eat. The survivors claimed that all agreed, even though one "dark-skinned Italian boy," 20 years old, spoke only enough English to say "yes" and "no." The lots were to be drawn three times, with the losers of the first two draws pitted against one another for the third. What bad luck for the Italian boy! He lost both of the first two draws, refused to draw a third time, so someone else drew for him, and lo and behold he lost once again. He acquiesced and was tied up and killed by cutting his throat. All drank the blood, the heart and liver were cut out and eaten, the head and feet cut off and thrown overboard, and the rest of the body stored. A few hours later they were rescued. The question of whether the lottery was held or was a sham was raised by both authorities and journalists, particularly given inconsistencies in the various tellings, some of which required the Italian loser to comprehend English far better that he was able.

The attorney general in Singapore examined the record and concluded (Simpson, 1984, p. 182) "that there was no necessity for any Judicial Enquiry and that the men who committed the deed are free to engage themselves on any vessel requiring their services." Later, he wrote that the case, "as dreadful as it is, might be palliated with the plea of necessity." A Captain Harrington wrote a letter in a Singapore paper calling for action in the interests of disabusing sailors of their belief that they are justified under certain emergencies to sacrifice one of their number. He recommended prayer, not cannibalism, in such emergencies.

The attorney general decided the matter should be put in evidence, particularly to determine the fairness of the drawing of lots. However, there was no agreement about where the trial should be held—in England or Singapore. Finally, after much political maneuvering and stalling, the men were released without proceedings being brought against them, the certificate of the second mate was renewed, and he obtained his first mate's certificate and his master's certificate 2 years later. Rather than being a leading case it just vanished, although it left the sailor's tradition of killing and eating people after a lottery intact in the folklore of the sea.

In yet another case, three Scandinavian sailors were rescued on January 7, 1893, from the foretop of a ship disabled on December 22. The legless and headless remains of another sailor, a Dutchman, were found hanging on board. The survivors testified that he was stabbed and had been consumed after the head and hands were cut off and thrown in the sea because they had been so dreadful to look at. All swore that a lottery had been agreed on and that the Dutchman lost on two consecutive draws and complied with the luck of the draw. Again, it seems that foreigners often tend to suffer bad runs of luck in the game of lottery. Although the Norwegian public prosecutor stated that a homicide had been committed, he requested that no charges be brought. It was noted that the shortening by some hours of one individual's death struggle is insignificant in relation to the good obtained—the rescue of all the others. Under similar questionable circumstances a Norwegian ship foundered in a hurricane, with the last three men (two Scandinavians and one Austrian), not liking the flesh of those who had died, deciding to hold a lottery to determine who should be killed for fresh meat. Simpson remarked that, predictably, Hoffman, the Austrian, lost the lottery, and although no details of the lottery could be recalled by the two survivors, no charges were ever brought. The argument of necessity based on utilitarian grounds prevailed in these cases, even though the circumstances of the lotteries were highly suspect.

The Mignonette

The most important legal case involving cannibalism involved the yacht *Mignonette*. It is important because it was the only trial in which a captain was convicted of killing a dying sailor without holding a lottery, with the captain and his two companions surviving for 4 or 5 days by eating the victim until rescued. Simpson (1984) devoted much of his book to a discussion and analysis of the events and their legal significance, and I will rely primarily on his account.

On May 19, 1884, Captain Dudley, three crew members, but no passengers or cargo, left from Falmouth to sail the yacht to Sidney, Australia. They crossed the equator on June 17, but on July 5 the yacht was stove in by heavy seas, sinking within 5 minutes. There was a 14-foot dinghy lashed to the deck that was lowered, but being of fragile construction it was damaged during the process. Through a crewman's mistake the water cask was lost in the sea, and of six tins of provisions only two 1-pound tins of turnips survived the transfer to the dinghy. The Captain tore loose the sextant and chronometer from the yacht and secured them in the dinghy. The hole in the boat was plugged, a sea anchor constructed, a shark fended off by hitting it in the head with an oar, and a course set for the nearest land they could possibly reach—the coast of South America, more than 2,000 miles away. There was general order, Captain Dudley was in command, and he had made the best of a bad situation.

The turnips lasted until July 7, and on about July 9, the fourth day in the dinghy, they captured a turtle on which they lived until about July 16—there being about 3 pounds of meat available for each survivor. All had begun to drink their own urine, but followed the conventional wisdom and did not drink any seawater for fear of going mad. On about July 20, the fifteenth day adrift, the youngest of the crew, 17 years old, began drinking large quantities of seawater, which made him violently ill. He began suffering from diarrhea, which dehydrated him even more, and became delirious and comatose. Simpson noted that none of Dudley's written accounts of the story mentioned any proposal for a lottery to sacrifice one for the sake of the others, although there were verbal accounts that he had wanted to do so, but one or more of his companions had objected.

On about July 24, the young seaman was lying on the bottom of the boat; Captain Dudley believed the boy was dying. He noted that he, the Cap-. tain, had a wife and three children, one of the others a wife and five children, and that human flesh had been eaten before. It was decided to kill the boy before he died in order to secure his blood to drink. Simpson (1984, p. 65) characterized the series of events to have involved three stages; agreement that *someone* must be killed, selection of the young crewman by the Captain, and ratification by the senior of the other crewmen. Simpson wrote: "The law treated accelerating death as murder; popular culture did not necessarily accept this rigorous line."

Captain Dudley had once been a cook steward and knew butchery; he decided the boy was comatose and dispatched him by thrusting a penknife into his throat. After the blood was drunk the heart and liver were cut out and eaten. The Captain then dismembered the body using the dinghy's brass oar locks as a block in order to avoid damage to the thin planking. They all consumed the meat, which lasted for the next 4 to 5 days, and about half of it remained when they were rescued on July 19, the twenty-fourth day in the open boat. There was no attempt to conceal the remains, and Captain Dudley said, without embarrassment, that one man had been killed and eaten.

The Captain made no effort to conceal what had happened, and during the trial, when asked who killed the boy he said "I did," and demonstrated to the court using the actual knife. The public generally accepted that he had acted properly, and there was great surprise when the three survivors were placed in custody. They were released on bail, usually not permitted in capital cases, and the only public discussion concerned why lots had not been cast. In Falmouth, public opinion was strongly in favor of the three survivors, and once the facts were known they all became heroes. One editorial writer was quoted as having justified the killing by invoking Darwin's "survival of the fittest." In general, sailors were not sympathetic to criminal prosecution in cases of shipwreck.

The men were tried because some in the judiciary believed it was essential to have a trial and conviction to emphasize that one person must not take the life of another person when his own life is in danger, even if such an act is necessary to save himself. However, the sentiment was that the men, if convicted, should receive "an hour's or other light imprisonment, and thus assert the sacredness of human life." The case was also brought to trial to further the political aspirations of a judge (who committed severe breaches of judicial conduct), and who Simpson characterized as being an opinionated, domineering man, able to persuade juries to reach the decision he thought correct. Both the Captain and the senior seaman were convicted (the other serving as a witness against them), but received a pardon from Queen Victoria on condition they be sentenced to 6 months in prison, not at hard labor. According to Simpson, these were the first and only individuals who ever faced a murder trial under circumstances involving killing for survival after a shipwreck. On release, Captain Dudley and his convicted companion both requested that their lost certificates as master and mate be restored, and the requests were granted. Dudley emigrated to Australia and established a business making tents, tarpaulins, and sails, and died of the bubonic plague on February 20, 1900, at the age of 46.

Survival cannibalism has been common in many extreme situations, both on land and sea, and it meets with no disapproval as long as killing was not involved. If killing occurs it is permissible, as long as lots were drawn. The type of individuals in the vulnerable pool is sometimes allowed to vary, and this variance seems to reflect both a utilitarian bias, a respect for social bonds, and the exercise of arbitrary authority. Even when killing has been done arbitrarily there was only the one case of prosecution, and the conviction in that case was politically motivated and resulted in light sentences.

TRIAGE

An interesting perspective within which to view the events that take place in the course of shipwrecks is that of triage, from the French word for sorting or choosing. Given limited time and resources, medical personnel in the field of combat must determine which of the many combat casualties are to be treated and which are to be left to die untreated. The usual procedure is to give preferential treatment to those whose likelihood of recovery is judged to be greater, given the less severe nature and type of wound. These decisions are considered morally permissible because the medical personnel do not actively kill anyone, but merely allow dying to take place. Intuitively, it is less socially dangerous to fail to save someone than to actively kill, and we consistently have found this to be the case in our studies of moral intuitions.

Devine (1978) suggested that it is better to allow a natural lottery to run off rather than to make a decision to set up a lottery. He proposed a hypothetical situation in which there is a machine containing two children, John and Mary. If a button is pushed, John will emerge unharmed, but Mary will be killed. If the button is not pushed Mary will emerge unharmed, but John will be killed. Rather than flipping a coin to decide what to do, Devine believes the right thing is to do nothing, letting John die, rather than killing Mary, assuming that how they got into their respective places is not known or relevant. In his view, the coin has already been flipped through the ac-

tion of the natural lottery that brought about their relative positions. Just
such reasoning seems to prevail in most cases of shipwreck. There is no
censure when someone is allowed to die and is then eaten by the survivors;
the natural lottery has decided who is to die, and the living can eat the
dead. The problem arises when no one is drawn by nature to die, and a lottery must be held to determine who is to die. Once again, if the lottery is
agreed to by all voluntarily and is fair, then no blame is assigned to those
who kill and eat the loser.

Triage is also of concern in cases in which scarce resources must be apportioned among a group of individuals. I have discussed this issue in another context when considering the allocation of resources to provide
health care for the citizens of the State of Oregon (Petrinovich, 1996). In this
instance a set of priorities was established for treatments to be provided by
the state health plan, and it was decided not to support treatments that
would be futile (e.g., to treat a cancer that had spread throughout the body,
with further medical treatment resulting in only an estimated 5% chance
of a 5-year survival time). I concluded that in the United States, such a medical priority system should be established so that limited and finite medical resources could be apportioned to enhance maximally the quality and
length of life for a maximum number of people. Although this is a lofty ideal, it is attainable if there is a willingness to face economic, political, social,
and moral implications of the decision and to assume the duties and responsibilities the system would impose on society.

In instances of shipwreck there seems initially to be an equitable distribution of food and water among all survivors. However, when it becomes
apparent that if nothing is done all will die, with the alternative being that
some will survive if others are sacrificed, we face a triage situation. One
such instance occurred in the sinking of the *Medusa* discussed above. It was
clear the raft would sink because too many people were aboard. The crew
made the decision to lighten the ship by throwing male passengers overboard. They justified this decision by reasoning that it was necessary for
the crew to remain intact if there was to be any chance of keeping the craft
afloat and sailing (which probably was true) and that the passengers
thrown overboard were near death anyway (which probably was not true).

The Portuguese vessel the *St. James* sank off the coast of Africa in 1586
(Thomas, 1835). When it became apparent that the ship could not be saved,
an admiral, the captain, the first pilot, and several seaman commandeered
a lifeboat and sailed off with the promise of seeking a landing where they
could construct a vessel large enough to convey all of the crew and passengers to land. They decided instead to sail toward the continent of Africa,
not returning to rescue the others. The remainder of the original comple-
ment of 500 men and 30 women had but one boat to accommodate them.
It was decided that people must be thrown overboard to lighten the over-

loaded lifeboat. A captain was elected, and his method of triage was to point at each of the weakest in the boat. In one instance a man was selected, but his younger brother demanded a delay, pleading that his brother was a skilled professional, his father and mother were very old, and his sisters were not yet settled in life. Although the younger brother could not be of service, his older brother could. The younger brother was therefore thrown overboard instead. The captain who sailed off was apprehended and put in prison, but as soon released and assumed command of yet another ship.

A logic seems to prevail in shipwrecks similar to that used by military combat doctors, only the killing often is active rather than passive, which leads many to find the killing morally objectionable. There often is a suggestion (sometimes not followed) that a lottery be held. However, the urgency of the situation and the necessity to take immediate action often make the lottery procedure difficult to implement. Also, the crew, who usually are the physically fittest of all the survivors by far, would be placed in jeopardy, and they do not relish being placed in such a position. In the case of the *Mignonette,* the captain followed a similar logic when he killed the weakest member of the lifeboat survivors, but in this instance it was judged impermissible because no lottery had been held prior to the killing. The punishment exacted was relatively mild given the fact that the act was judged to be murder. I conclude that cannibalism is common in disasters when survival is threatened—on both land and sea, and even in the air, as we shall see in the next chapter.

4

Airplane and Arctic Cannibals

"It's just like beef jerky." Remark by a survivor of a plane crash regarding human flesh that had been dried in the sun.

—Gzowski (1980)

Does the pattern of events that occurred for the Donner Party and among sailors generally prevail? There is another well-documented account of human cannibalism brought about by starvation that reveals a similar pattern. This disaster has been described in a book by Lopez (1973), one by Cunningham (1973), and another by Read (1974), which was made into a movie in 1992. Although there are a few discrepancies in the different versions regarding the sequence of events, I have pieced together a coherent narrative that preserves the essentials as told by all three writers. After the events of the Andean incident have been discussed I will consider briefly a small plane crash that occurred in the mountains of Idaho. The sequence of events in that instance testifies to the generality of those events that took place in the Donner and Andean incidents. I also will describe an episode in which a U.S. Army expedition that had been sent to the Arctic to map and make weather observations was stranded for 3 years before being rescued. At the end of this time there was cannibalism. The case is discussed here because it can be used to pull together some of the threads running through these last three chapters regarding the nature of events that lead to and prevent cannibalism under severe conditions. Finally, I will discuss the prevalence of cannibalism in other species, and consider the conditions that predispose species to be cannibalistic.

ANDEAN SURVIVORS

The story begins on October 12, 1972, when a plane of the Uruguayan Air Force took off on a chartered flight with members of an affluent Catholic boys school rugby team, The Old Christian Club Rugby Team. They left from Montevideo, Uruguay, to go to Santiago, Chile, for a rugby match. The team members, ranging in age between 19 and 25 (Lopez, 1973), were accompanied by 3 relatives and 17 friends, with a flight crew of 5 (Lopez, 1973). Bad weather forced the plane to land in Mendoza, Argentina, on the western side of the Andes. Twenty-four hours later the plane left on what is usually a 1-hour flight to Santiago, but disappeared in the High Andes. Immediately on losing contact with the plane, authorities sent out air search parties (to the wrong areas) for 8 days, but nothing was heard from or about the plane for 10 weeks. The plane had crashed on October 13, on the Argentine side of the border in an 11,500-foot valley surrounded by 14,000-foot peaks, apparently because the co-pilot, who was flying the plane, had mistakenly assumed he was over the mountains and began his descent to the valley on the other side, striking the mountain (Lopez, 1973). The eventual survivors spent 10 weeks in heavy snowstorms with night temperatures falling considerably below 0°F. Thirty-two people survived the crash, 4 died shortly thereafter, and 16 lived to be rescued. After 10 weeks, a Chilean peasant saw two of the survivors who had struggled across the mountains in search of help.

Of the crew, the pilot, co-pilot, navigator, and steward died in the crash, with only a mechanic surviving. Members of the crew who knew how to operate the radio were all dead, leaving the survivors with no hope of establishing radio contact with the outside world. At such a high altitude, and given the depth of the snowpack, there were no trees, plants, or animals available. There was plenty of drinkable water because a method was devised to collect water from snow by melting it in the sun and collecting the runoff in a trough made from a metal seat backrest. For provisions they had wine, some liquor, odds and ends of food such as chocolate bars, caramels, several pounds of cheese, salted crackers, dates, a great deal of toothpaste, and about 130 cartons of cigarettes (which had been put on board for sale on the black market, and over which there would be continual controversy among the 13 smokers). Throughout the ordeal they had a radio that could receive news broadcasts. These constant broadcasts alternately gave them hope they would be rescued when they heard the search was continuing, and dashed those hopes when the searches were called off from time to time.

The first few days were spent burying the dead, treating the injured, establishing a living area, and searching the skies for rescuers. This is a pattern of behavior that commonly occurred in those shipwrecks in which the captain was able to maintain his authority. After two planes had passed over the area without seeing either them or the fuselage of the plane (which had a white top) a large cross was trampled into the snow. One person calculated the amount of food that was available and rationed the portions at each meal. In all, the group organized efficiently to perform essential tasks, displayed strong religious faith, and sustained the hope that they would soon be rescued. Even the lapsed Catholics among them became devout.

Four days after the crash some began planning to cross the surrounding mountain peaks, but others told them that if they did not freeze to death in the snow they would starve to death. Among the survivors there was continual talk of elegant meals they had eaten, accompanied by elaborate descriptions of favorite restaurants. One person who wanted to attempt the escape was quoted as saying that to survive, he would cut meat from one of the pilots, "After all, they got us into this mess." No one took the suggestion seriously at this point.

An escape party of four people started out on the fifth day and failed, having to turn back by the end of the day (Read, 1974). On the eighth day one of the survivors died, and on the tenth day, the others gave up all hope of being able to scavenge for plant food in the deep snow. Given that dead bodies were well preserved by the intense cold, there was talk of eating the bodies of those who had died in the crash—one person remarking that it might be the only way to survive.

Gradually the realization dawned that the dead would have to be eaten if any were to survive, and this became the topic of private conversations between several survivors. These discussions included more and more people until all 27 discussed whether they should eat the bodies of the dead to live. Some argued it was the moral thing to do because God had wanted them to live; if He had not they would have been killed in the crash and He would not have given them the means to live by providing the dead bodies of their friends. Besides, it was argued, the souls of the dead had already left the bodies and were in heaven with God. It would be wrong to reject this gift of life because of squeamishness against preparing and consuming the flesh. Another justification was devised to the effect that if the survivors were among the dead, they would want whoever was still alive to use them for food, with one quoted to the effect that "if I do die, and you don't eat me, then I'll come back from wherever I am and give you a good kick in the ass." At this point, an agreement was struck that if any more of the surviving members died, their bodies were to be used as food.

A group of foragers decided to remove flesh from an unidentified corpse, the buttocks of which protruded from the snow. According to Lopez (1973) the meat was cut into thin strips and rolled into pellets that could be swallowed raw with little difficulty. Initially, the pellets were rolled in melted chocolate, until all the chocolate was exhausted. Finally, thin strips of meat were placed on the roof of the plane to dry in the sun. One of the foragers prayed, and forced himself to swallow the meat. Later that evening small groups of boys followed this example. Some had difficulty eating human flesh for the first time, one deciding it was acceptable because it was like Holy Communion. Another was quoted by Read (1974, pp. 90–91) as having said: "Think of it as the body and blood of Christ, because this is food that God has given us because He wants us to live." This concept was accepted by all except two of the survivors. Reaching an agreement that they would live off the dead, the stronger boys organized a party to cover corpses with snow to preserve them, and the weaker undertook the task of melting snow in the sun to gather water. Coca-Cola crates were burned to cook the meat, which made it easier to overcome the revulsion of eating it raw, and it was remarked that it seemed similar to beef, which induced the only two holdouts to consume the meat.

The repugnance of eating close friends was partly overcome by having one group cut the meat from the bodies (an unpopular job, but with the major advantage that, working unobserved, they could appropriate some extra meat). Another group, neither knowing the identity of the source nor having to see the bodies, divided it for consumption.

The corpses first had to be dug out of the snow and thawed in the sun. Those cutting off the meat found it was easier if the eyes of the corpses were first closed so that they would not have to cut into a friend while under his "glassy gaze." In maritime disasters it will be remembered that survivors who resorted to cannibalism tended to cut off the head and throw it overboard, often with the hands. These actions, too, probably were done to depersonalize (dehumanize?) the process. They also agreed not to eat the three dead women (none of whom was eaten), and some were either reluctant or refused to eat relatives until the very end. A medical student in the party convinced the others they should eat the livers for their reserves of vitamins. Having taken this step enabled them to eat the heart, kidneys, intestines, and later the brains. The health of all improved noticeably when this expanded menu became available.

Eight more people died in an avalanche that struck the plane. It was decided to allow three (Read said there were four) of the boys to have extra rations so that they could be strengthened and sent out as expeditionaries to seek rescue, using the plane's compass to guide them. To equip the expeditionaries Read claimed that stockings were fashioned from human skin. The expeditionaries set out to reach civilization, with one returning after 3 days, although he had reached the summit. He returned because the group realized there was such a great distance still to be traveled that there was not enough food for three. After 10 days of hiking over a series of ridges the remaining two expeditionaries followed a stream downward, reached a valley, and encountered the Chilean peasant who summoned aid. They were taken to the peasant's house 70 days after the plane crash.

The peasant provided them with cheese, which they ate ravenously. When the peasant left them in order to tend his cows they took what remained of the human flesh they still had with them and buried it under a stone. Read claimed that some of their earlier revulsion toward eating human flesh had returned once it was no longer necessary to do so. As soon as the news of the two survivors was radioed out by the police who were sent in to check the story, they were accosted by what Lopez referred as "a jackal-pack" of writers, cameramen, and reporters who had rushed to the peasant's cabin.

The police ordered two military helicopters sent to the cabin to rescue the fourteen survivors on the mountain, and they took off for the crash site with the two expeditionaries to guide them. When they arrived at the site they were not able to land because the helicopter would sink through the ice-crusted snow and be unable to take off again. It was decided to hover a few inches off the ground, land three mountain climbers and a medical attendant, and take the six most disabled aboard, leaving eight survivors behind with the climbers and the attendant. Then all eight of this initial group were taken to the base camp where the two expeditionaries had been found, and they were subsequently flown to a city hospital.

While awaiting news of the two expeditionaries, and hopefully rescue, the survivors were beginning to run low in their ready supply of corpses, and began to search for those that had been dispersed in the snow during the crash. They also began consuming more of the bodies, partly due to the supply shortage and partly because they needed variety from their bland diet of meat with neither salt nor spice. They all savored bone marrow from the start, then blood clots, and finally began eating the small intestines, brains, liver, heart, kidneys, and lungs—parts that had been initially rejected. They heard the radio news that the two expeditionaries had been found and that a rescue expedition was under way. After some discussion, they decided not to hide the remains of the bodies they had eaten. Their reasoning was that there was no need to hide what they had done, even if it had been possible to dig a pit in the frozen snow, because they had done nothing wrong.

The remaining eight survivors were rescued the next day and were ferried to the base camp and then to a hospital in Santiago. Eventually all sixteen survivors were brought together in Santiago. It was found that although all had lost 30 to 80 pounds apiece, they were in reasonable health. When asked what they had last eaten they told the doctor who examined them, "human flesh." Lopez (1973, p. 119) wrote that the doctor remarked that "Once they had decided to break that ancient taboo, they did it with great maturity and wisdom." The doctor summoned a young priest who was taken to the private wing of the hospital where the survivors were being kept, and all attested to the fact that it was their devotion to God that had sustained them throughout the ordeal. When one survivor asked to confess the priest responded, "You have confessed in this conversation," and told them they could take Communion without confessing, or if they wished to confess, it should be to unburden themselves for other sins.

It is the teaching of the Roman Catholic Church that eating human flesh is permissible *in extremis,* and this dogma ensured the peace of mind of these devout Catholics. A Jesuit priest endorsed their decision to eat the dead because of the sober and religious spirit in which they made the decision, but he rejected any relationship between cannibalism and communion. The Auxiliary Bishop of Montevideo agreed that the cannibalism was blameless, and that one should not blame himself for something he would not "blame in someone else and which no one blames in him." The Archbishop concurred (Read, 1974, p. 308): "Morally I see no objection, since it was a question of survival. It is always necessary to eat whatever is at hand, in spite of the repugnance it may evoke." Read noted that another theologian provided an ethical justification on the grounds that they fed themselves with the only food available to avoid a sure death. It is legitimate to resort to lifeless human bodies in order to survive.

No one in the church hierarchy concurred with the view that eating human flesh was equivalent to Holy Communion. The Auxiliary Bishop was quoted by Read (1974, p. 308): "the use of the term communion is not correct. . . . At most it is possible to say that it is correct to use this term as a source of inspiration. But it is not communion."

Another interesting church view concerned the one instance in which a survivor could never bring himself to eat human flesh, but secretly disposed of his portion. This individual died from starvation. The Auxiliary Bishop was asked about this, and it was his view that the refusal to eat flesh in no way could be understood as suicide because he did not *act* to kill himself; he merely let death happen. This is the doctrine of double effect that Catholic theology uses to justify performing an abortion to save a mother's life; the intent is to save the mother's life, and the killing of the fetus is considered to be a foreseen and intended side-effect.

On release from the hospital the boys were transferred to a hotel, where they displayed a ravenous appetite at the hotel restaurant, some of them eating until they became sick, returning yet again for more food, and continuing at night, ordering from room service. This appetite persisted, with some becoming overweight in only a few weeks. The Chilean townspeople feted the survivors as heroes who had triumphed over the Andes, and considered them to be the living embodiment of an apparent miracle, although at this time the cannibalism had not been revealed to the public.

The reaction of the relatives of those who had been eaten was an initial expression of shock. However, they soon accepted the conclusion that if all 45 had survived the crash no one would still be alive. Some said they saw their dead sons in the survivors; all wished to forget the events and preferred to think that by the time the bodies were eaten the souls were in heaven. One bereaved father was quoted by Lopez (1973) to have remarked that his son's body had a more beautiful destiny than mere decomposition, likening the eating of the flesh to the transfusion of blood, which does not evoke a feeling of horror.

Koch (1993) reported in *The Boston Globe* that the survivors now live in a prosperous suburb of Montevideo, and most are successful professionals; one is a physician who ran unsuccessfully for the presidency of Uruguay. They all were described as charged with a spiritual element acquired during the ordeal. It appears that, as with the Donner Party, cannibalism was accepted as a reasonable solution to the problem of starvation, as long as there was assurance that people were not killed to be eaten (an exception being granted in the case of the Donner Party when it involved members of another race). Based on these two cases it seems that the prohibition against killing is strong, active suicide is not an acceptable alternative, and cannibalism is permissible whenever it is necessary to survive. A similar pattern was evident in seafaring cannibalism. Members of neither the Donner nor Andean group knowingly ate their own relatives, and in the Andean case it was decided they would eat the dead women last. One of the Andean survivors, on finding his cousin's body among the wreckage, asked the others to have that body used last.

Another interesting point is that when the possibility of eating human flesh was first raised, it was proposed to start by consuming those who were not members of the community—the pilots. This suggestion is what one would expect in terms of both evolutionary and social contract considerations. Those who are members of the community include kin and also nonkin who could reciprocate favors should they survive. This biologically established social contract is strengthened by the rules society uses to maintain order. It is also to be expected that there should be a willingness to eat the dead crew members who caused the problems in the first place. They were hired to take risks, and when disaster occurred they bore the responsibility, much as we have found in our studies of moral dilemmas.

Although at the outset a strong effort was required to eat human flesh, once consumption started an appetite developed, leading Read (1974, p. 214) to observe that "the instinct to survive was a harsh tyrant which demanded not just that they eat their companions but that they get used to doing so." By the end of the 10 weeks the lungs and intestines were eaten because a need developed for a stronger taste, given the absence of salt, pepper, or spices.

AWAY BEYOND THE HILLS IN IDAHO

There is a journalistic account of yet another instance of survival cannibalism involving the crash of a small plane in the mountains of central Idaho

(Gzowski, 1980). The plane contained a pilot, a father and daughter, and the husband of the father's older daughter. The summits of the range of mountains reach over 10,000 feet, and have been referred to as the Alps of America. Because of a sudden intense storm system over the mountains, a course had been plotted that should have avoided most of the reported weather, skirted the highest peaks, and followed a route through a series of mountain passes.

Unfortunately, the pilot flew into a canyon that did not provide a pass through the mountains, but ended in a high cul-de-sac that the pilot was unable to avoid or fly over. A tree trunk sheared a wing, the plane bounced against a rock, and careened over rock and snow, finally driving into a snow bank. The skull of the pilot was pierced by the handle of the throttle, the shoulder of the son-in-law was broken, he suffered deep cuts to his neck muscles by broken glass, and his jaw was smashed. The daughter had broken bones in her wrist and hand, deep cuts on one hand, and her feet were injured. When the two young people regained consciousness a few hours after the crash they realized that the father was dead, but his leather jacket had been draped over his daughter's chest, an act he must have performed just before dying. The son-in-law was quoted to as saying, "He's dead, but he wanted you to live."

The pilot's injuries were severe, with brain tissue laid bare, and he could not speak coherently, although he seemed to comprehend what was said to him. The pilot left the plane, then returned and found a can of oil, with which he started a fire. The two young people decided it was better to return to the plane to escape the wind and to concentrate on securing the cabin against the elements. The pilot rambled about, came back to the plane, and tried to take the coat off the daughter, desisting when the son-in-law began screaming at him.

The only thing available for sustenance was a can of Pepsi, which they shared—the first nourishment they had had for more than 24 hours; they had skipped meals in order to get to Boise before dark. They then thought, mistakenly, that they saw cars on what could be a road below them, and the pilot headed downhill that way, disappearing from sight, not to be seen alive again. Subsequently, his body was found less than one-half mile downhill from the plane.

The crash occurred on Saturday, and by Monday the two survivors prayed, and began going through the luggage for warm clothes and what scraps of food they could find—half a box of candy-covered chocolates, a granola bar, a package of shelled sunflower seeds, and some toothpaste. They also found the plane's first-aid kit, which contained aspirin, a few bandages, and surgical soap. They cleaned and bandaged what they could of their wounds, siphoned gas from the fuel tank, and built a fire on the floor of the plane's cabin.

After 40 hours they became more desperate, talked of God, covered the dead father's face, prayed, and sang a hymn. Their thoughts turned to food fantasies; mounds of fresh strawberries with whipped cream, steaks and chops, dishes of potatoes and green vegetables. They recalled fine meals and the skills of cooks they knew. After 5 days they removed a seat and found a bottle of Pepsi under it. They agreed to ration the soda, but drank it all within a half-hour. They found a package containing seven cigarettes and some matches, which the son-in-law, the only smoker, chain-smoked, "to conserve matches."

The storm had weakened, and by the end of the week they began talking about the father's sacrifice of his coat to save his daughter, and how much he had wanted her to live. They discussed the story of the Andean plane crash and decided that the South American students had done the logical thing by eating the bodies of the dead to stay alive. It was decided that the only way to stay alive would be to eat the father's body, and that he was watching over them, just as was God. They concluded that he was saying (Gzowski, 1980, p. 90): "I hope they eat that old body down there, because it's no use to me. I've left it." It will be recalled that the logic of this episode is almost identical to the reasoning followed by the Andean students. The son-in-law, who had experience hunting, killing, and dressing deer, believed he could do the butchering. But he couldn't bring himself to make the first cut. They prayed to know the right thing to do, and with the idea of communion in his mind, he performed the cutting, pounded the meat flat, and dried it in the sun.

The next day the son-in-law felt better and began keeping a notebook, which was recovered. He expressed hope that they could gain enough strength to walk out. In the journal he made a rather bizarre entry, stating that when they were able to walk out they would have everyone over to his place for a barbecue! He later wrote that he wanted to barbecue a piece of boneless ham about a foot long that had been injected with a strong orange sauce, cook it until just about done, glaze it, and add crushed pineapple. By the middle of the second week they were gaining strength.

Concerted search efforts had been started on the Sunday after the crash, at first checking emergency landing strips in the area, asking for information from the small radio stations and telephone systems in the back country, and then searching a 128-mile grid that had been broken into rectangles, each of which was searched from the air. After exhausting all possibilities, and even consulting a clairvoyant (which had also been done by the parents of the Andean survivors), after a week or so the search wound down.

By this time the survivors had gained strength, walked the 200 feet to the ridge above them, and were able to start a signal fire with twigs, igniting it with gasoline from the plane. At the end of the second week they packed what gear they thought they would need, cut a supply of meat that they dried, sang a hymn, had a service for the father, and set off to the ridge and down toward a valley. They continued moving ahead for a couple of days, by which time they had moved below the snow line. On the nineteenth day after the crash they walked into a mine site that was occupied by a family, and their ordeal in the mountains was over.

The two survivors never denied they had been able to live by eating parts of the father. They emphasized their reliance on prayer and divine guidance, and likened the consumption of human flesh to the Roman Catholic rituals involving the taking of bread and wine as the transubstantiation of the body and blood of Christ. They were not subjected to blame by relatives, clergy, or the law, and expressed no feelings of guilt. It was widely agreed that they did the proper thing to survive, and that the father would have wanted his kin to preserve themselves after his death. The parish priest told them they had been morally right to save their lives through cannibalism, and the widow of the father affirmed that what they did was right, and that the father would have wanted them to do it and would have been proud of them.

The two airline incidents described here involved widely different circumstances, a quite different cast of characters, and contrasting challenges. One strong similarity was a religious belief that allowed them to justify their cannibalism in terms of the Holy Communion. In both cases, religious authorities agreed that the cannibalism was necessary to sustain life, but were not willing to endorse the Communion argument.

In the Andean crash, there was resistance to eating kin, but they were able to do so because of the manner in which the anonymity of the source of meat was guaranteed. In the Idaho crash, it was necessary to consume the dead father because he was the only source of food. Once again, in both instances, there was no blame because no one was killed to be eaten. This was the same pattern found in all of the events involving seafaring cannibalism, although people seemed willing to look the other way when killing was suspected, or when the fairness of lotteries that were claimed to have been held led to rather suspicious outcomes—particularly when the losers were slaves, foreigners, or boys. Although "unthinkable,"eating flesh is standard practice for the starving.

ABANDONED IN THE ARCTIC

The experience of a group of explorers that was stranded in the Arctic for 3 years provides a useful narrative to characterize the events that occur in disaster situations such as those discussed in these last three chapters. In the summer of 1881, a U.S. Army party, the Lady Franklin Bay Expedition commanded by Lt. Adolphus Greely, was organized and sent to the Arctic. The party was to be visited by a supply ship in the summer of 1882, and repatriated by ship in 1883. The purpose of the mission was to map the Arctic more completely, gather meteorological data to enable more accurate and timely weather prediction, and to go farther north toward the pole than anyone had before (a record then held by the British). The party suffered numerous setbacks after the first year, and were stranded for 3 years, the last 2 years under extremely severe conditions, resulting in the death of all but 6 of the party of 25. Their story is chronicled in a book, *Abandoned*, by A. L. Todd (1961), who had access to an extensive amount of material: books, letters, the diaries kept by several members of the party, transcripts of remarks made at the time, and the cooperation of the Greely family and the Historical Division of the U.S. Army Signal Corps. It is unusual to have such detailed first-hand accounts made throughout the course of a disaster.

Instead of being composed of explorers or people who could deal with the Arctic seas, the party consisted of regular soldiers of the U.S. Army infantry, freelance civilian specialists temporarily in uniform as army sergeants, civilian specialists (a physician and a photographer), three infantry officers with experience on the western frontier of the United States (Greely, Kislingbury, and Lockwood), and two Eskimo sledge drivers hired in Greenland. The party was put ashore in the Arctic with no problems, and Greely immediately had a sturdy building constructed (which he named Fort Conger after the Senator who sponsored the bill funding the project), began meteorological projects, made trails, collected coal from nearby deposits, and sledged the coal back to Fort Conger and to depots up the north coast to be used during exploration trips in the spring. Hunters were bringing in musk oxen, which provided enough meat to provide each man with a pound a day. More than a hundred eider ducks were shot; altogether they had three tons of meat and an equal amount of offal for the sled dogs. Greely also began Psalm reading on Sundays, a day declared as one of rest, with no games permitted.

When spring arrived the 24 hours of darkness began to give way to the sun, and preparations began for the season's sledging before it became so hot that the heavy winter ice would melt, making travel difficult. The major project was for one of the officers, Lt. Lockwood, to take a sledge party to break the Farthest-North record that had been set by the Royal Navy—which they did. In all it was a very auspicious beginning and a profitable first year.

The ship that was to resupply the party cleared St. John's, Newfoundland on July 8, 1882, with supplies, meat, and additional men to replace any who were ill or whose performance had not proven to be satisfactory. However, when they reached the southern tip of Greenland on July 13 the ship was unable to proceed due to obstruction by the ice flow. When the ice broke to the north on August 7, the ship became helplessly caught some 200 miles short of Fort Conger. On August 29, the captain had part of the stores landed at a point that had been agreed on a year earlier, and sailed south on September 5 with three-quarters of the supplies that were to have been provided for the party still aboard.

Initially, Greely had equipped the party with abundant supplies to enable them to survive, so no panic ensued when it was realized that there would be no ship to resupply them, and the dull winter routine commenced once again. Minor incidents of insubordination began to occur, but discipline was restored when Lt. Greely immediately reduced offenders to the rank of private and threatened court-martial on return if the offense was repeated.

Lt. Kislingbury, with whom Greely had clashed from the outset, resigned his position and was relieved of formal duty, with his new orders designating him as "temporarily at the station awaiting transportation." The doctor, although a good physician whose services were indispensable, was causing problems. He believed he should be in charge of the expedition, quarreled with Greely, and refused to follow orders. He was placed under arrest for disobedience of orders, and Greely announced his intention to have the doctor tried by general court-martial upon return. The doctor did, as a good physician should, continue his medical duties.

The agreement back in 1881 was that if a ship could not reach Fort Conger in the summer of 1883, the party would, using the boats they had with them, make its way to a rendezvous point to the south. Fort Conger was abandoned and the party began the trip to the rendezvous point on August 9. Meanwhile, two ships had cleared St. John's harbor on June 29 to bring the party home, and the main ship, the *Proteus*, carried supplies to leave for Greely should they not locate him before being forced to leave the ice zone. The *Proteus* attempted to sail north but became entrapped in ice, was crushed by it on July 23, and sunk. The army personnel aboard attempted to save the supplies intended for Greely, while the ship's crew occupied themselves with saving their personal effects and preparing their ship's boats for the emergency.

The events that occurred on the sinking of the *Proteus* illustrate an essential difference between maritime tradition and military procedure in those days. As noted in Chapter 3, when a civilian ship sinks the crew is no longer subject to the orders of the officers or the shipowners because their contract, as well as their wages, go down with the vessel. However, military personnel must maintain disciplined respect for the orders of military superiors no matter what the circumstances. The soldiers in this incident attempted to retrieve every box of supplies that had been thrown overboard. Todd (1961) noted that almost as if acting on orders, the sailors left the ship by one side, tossing their gear down to their friends on the ice below. The soldiers' party left the ship by the other side, and had an officer as a leader with authority; he had his men continue the mission by saving everything they could to supply Greely.

There were three boats for the 21 members of the *Proteus* crew and two for the 16 army personnel. A major contrast between the two groups was that the Newfoundland sailors had grown up around boats, whereas the soldiers were all landlubbers who scarcely could fit an oar in an oarlock. Four of the sailors were persuaded to transfer to the army boats and help the soldiers, which made it possible for the army party to land a few rations on shore, although most of the rations were carried away on the ice flow. The entire party then moved south to meet the second ship, with the members of the crew refusing to share their adequate stores with the underprovided soldiers. The party was rescued on September 2, but with the remaining ship too frail to work the ice, it was too late to attempt to contact Greely. The rescue party then steamed back to St. John's.

The Greely party journeyed for 2 months, the second month drifting on an ice flow. Before being stranded on the ice flow, they survived by using supplies that had been cached by Greely in 1881, as well as those in another cache that had been established earlier by the English. The members of the party suffered considerable hardship. When matters became difficult the doctor and Lt. Kislingbury proposed a mutiny, but it failed to materialize. On August 30, there was food for 50 days; with rationing it could be stretched to 60. Rations were cut to half the normal Arctic ration, causing severe suffering because two to three times the normal diet is required at such low temperatures. When they reached land on September 30 they began preparing three stone and ice huts for shelter, which they completed October 8. Messages were found at the site of recently cached food informing them that the *Proteus* had sunk and that the second ship had returned to St. John's. The available food had to be stretched until April 1, which was 173 days off, meaning that rations had to be cut to a fourth of normal. The decision was made to abandon the huts and the dogs, move closer to the remaining cache sites, and build yet another shelter.

By the time they arrived at the place at which the cache from the *Proteus* was located there was only 6 hours of daylight left each day. They had been reduced to eating raw seal intestines (which they usually fed to the dogs), and were less than pleased when the cache was found to contain only 100 rations of meat, instead of the expected 500, along with 10 pounds of tobacco, two boxes of lemons, and three boxes of raisins. They established a campsite from which they could see Greenland, built a winter shelter, and gathered supplies that had been scattered along the coast. The shelter was made of stone, with the roof consisting of an overturned whaleboat. Rations were cut to one-fifth of the Arctic ration—4 ounces of meat, 6 ounces of hard bread, and 4 ounces of all other foodstuffs. The meat and other foodstuffs were combined with alcohol, seal blubber, and burned tarred rope to constitute a stew. As happened with the Andean plane crash survivors, foragers were sent out, in this case to gather distant caches of food, and as with the Andean survivors these foragers were allowed a few extra ounces above the normal rations for several days to build up their strength.

The men were constantly hungry and started eating moldy food that would have been rejected earlier. As usual in such instances, there was much talk of food that members of the group liked, of menus, restaurants, and meals they had consumed. By October 27, they realized that someone had begun stealing food from the commissary, and Greely vowed he would find and punish the culprit. The thefts continued, however. One of the foragers collapsed during a trip, and while trying to quench his thirst by eating snow froze his fingers, nose, and feet. Another of the foragers returned to camp and a rescue party was sent to bring the frostbitten individual back. He recovered, although he lost most of his fingers and his feet. The theft of food continued and the group demanded that the thief confess, with no results. Greely noticed that the doctor was stealing food from the frostbitten patient's ration as he fed the man (who had no usable hands), but decided he could do nothing about it because the doctor's services were becoming ever more essential.

The first death occurred on January 18, when an engineer died of starvation. His early death was attributed to the fact that he had been a heavy drinker, and this intemperate life was a contributing factor. Members of the party began drawing up wills, and a sense of hopelessness prevailed. By February 17, the last of the beef and seal meat had been used, leaving only bacon and pemmican. One soldier suggested they should eat everything and die at once, but Greely refused to permit it. The first talk of cannibalism was recorded on March 7, and again on March 11 when someone expressed fear of the other occupants of a group sleeping bag. By this time the party consisted of 24 starved men, of whom 2 could not walk and another 6 would not be able to carry anything if the party should attempt to walk out.

It was agreed by all who the food thief was, and there was a call to put him to death. Greely resisted, putting the soldier under close arrest and forbidding him to leave his sleeping bag without permission or to leave the hut unaccompanied. It was found that the almost inedible tiny shrimp at the water's edge could be caught in quantity, although they had little nutritional value, being two-thirds shell. They were added to whatever the stew du jour was, combined with seaweed.

One of the Eskimos died on April 4, followed 2 days later by a soldier, and 2 days after that by Lt. Lockwood. On April 10, the doctor surprised everyone by volunteering to chop the ice to be thawed for cooking. Incidentally, the pond at which ice was obtained was in the direction of the ridge where the dead had been placed—half-buried and half-exposed. When the bodies were removed by the eventual rescue party, it was noted that some of them had pieces of flesh carved off, with what was described as the skill of a surgeon.

At this point good fortune provided a medium-size white bear, which was shot, and every part of the animal was consumed; the blood was used to thicken stews and inedible parts were used as shrimp bait. Another soldier died that day, and a week later Greely decided the ration should be reduced from 1 pound per man to 10 ounces in order to make the food last until May 15, by which time it was hoped a rescue ship might reach them.

The second Eskimo drowned when his kayak sunk, leaving 18 still alive. The food thief struck again and was caught, and Greely had become too ill to leave his bunk. The doctor became insubordinate, which caused Greely to declare (Todd, 1961, p. 222): "If you were not the surgeon on this expedition, I would shoot you." Clearly things were near the point of dissolution; but after this flare-up everyone merely sank back into lassitude, and soon resumed discussing the meals they would have on rescue.

On May 12, Greely decided to have the remaining rations divided up, which would have to last until noon on May 15, making it necessary to survive after that on shrimp, seaweed, and anything that could be killed. The doctor, meanwhile, began to spend an increasing amount of time at the lake. Another soldier died on May 19, one on May 23, and yet another on May 24.

On May 25, sealskin thongs were cut up and introduced into the shrimp stew, and pieces of other thongs were burned to a cinder and eaten, followed by boots with their soles and oil-tanned sleeping bag covers. This is a pattern that occurred for the Donner Party, shipwrecked seamen, and Mormon cowboys: Acceptable foodstuffs become an ever-expanding category. The astronomer died May 27, leaving 14 still alive. Kislingbury died June 1 and another soldier died on June 2. Greely had ordered that with one more theft the thief should be shot at once: He did and he was. Three soldiers were assigned to do the deed; they decided to confront the thief rather than using stealth, drew lots to determine who the shooter should be, and swore among themselves never to identify who shot. The executed man's possessions were found to contain stolen sealskin, tea, knives, a valuable silver chronograph, as well as a pound of bear meat.

Another soldier and the doctor died that day—it was suspected that the doctor had died by self-administered poison. There were now nine alive, and they were surviving on lichens and the occasional birds that were migrating to their breeding grounds. On June 12 another soldier died and one person (one of the strongest in the party) suggested that the stronger of them should abandon the others and each should work and cook for himself alone—a suggestion that was rejected. The sealskin covers of all spare sleeping bags had been consumed by this time, ptarmigan droppings were tried, as were caterpillars, worms, and saxifrage blossoms. On June 18 another man died, leaving 7 survivors.

The survivors were rescued on June 22 and taken aboard ship; the amputee died on July 8, 3 days after surgeons had amputated his ankles to save him from blood poisoning, bringing the number of survivors to 6 of the original 25. The reaction of government officials and the press to the news of the rescue was all positive at first, hailing Greely and his party for their courage and perseverance. The initial reaction of President Arthur was a bit sour: Quotes indicated that he had never favored these explorations because the geographic and scientific information secured could not compensate for the loss of human life. The *Chicago Tribune* chimed in, maintaining that Arctic exploration was an immense waste of money and life, the *Philadelphia Inquirer* agreed that with rescue of the the Greely party there should be a cessation of "the monstrous and murderous folly of so-called Arctic exploration," and the *New York Times* joined the call for an end to such folly. Still, the reaction of the public was positive overall, and the front pages of the newspapers were full of accounts of suffering and heroism by members of the expedition.

Trouble began to brew when the *New York Times* raised questions regarding the summary execution of the thief, along with rumors that cannibalism had taken place. The military authorities had not shown any inclination to consider these matters, nor did they offer criticism of the execution, justifying it as necessary to maintain discipline. The *Times* articles, seldom accurate regarding the events, were given a sensationalistic spin, with claims that there was widespread killing of unwilling, screaming victims. The line was that this was the most dreadful and repulsive occurrence in the long annals of Arctic exploration. Todd characterized public sentiment, however, as still generally favorable, considering it appropriate to eat the dead in order to avoid dying of starvation—sentiments similar to those that prevailed in all of the other disasters discussed.

At this juncture the family of Lt. Kislingbury had his body exhumed to examine the state of the remains. It was found that large pieces of tissue had been cut from the thighs and trunk of the dead officer (by his close friend the doctor?). Greely repeated an earlier statement that if there was any cannibalism it was done in secrecy and entirely without his knowledge. He remarked that all of the survivors had assured him separately that they were innocent and knew nothing of it and noted that he could not tell whether they told the truth or not (given the fact that he was incapacitated during the time most of the cannibalism would have occurred); he doubted that an investigation would reveal who the cannibals were. The military tended strongly to support Greely for maintaining discipline and the survivors were praised. One correspondent wrote a message to Greely that was similar to that reported in the Andes incident (Todd, 1961, p. 295): "If I had died of their number I would have been glad to have them eat me."

The autopsy of Lt. Kislingbury revealed that fecal matter removed from his intestine contained moss, bits of sealskin, and bits of human muscle and tendon, which led to the conclusion that he had fed on (or as the *Times* put it, was forced to feed on) the flesh of his comrades, just as he later had become food for the survivors. Subsequent examination of the 12 bodies that were recovered revealed that six of them had parts missing.

The matter became increasingly ugly when a source, an unnamed junior naval officer, was quoted as having heard horrible and detailed accounts of grisly acts of cannibalism from an unnamed survivor while aboard the rescue ship. Another newspaper repeated the story, attributing it to a Third Officer Kelly on the rescue ship as well as to one of its cooks (there was no man named Kelly among the officers or crew of any ship of the rescue mission). This same unnamed junior officer was said to have provided yet another story to the effect that the doctor had been killed and eaten by those outside the "Greely clique"; because this group was not in favor its members had been denied their fair ration of food and therefore were hungrier than the rest. Later reports stated that one of the survivors was munching on a raw duck, with blood dribbling down his beard, when the rescuers reached the camp—a story that was published by the *New York Times* and copied by other papers.

Shades of present day journalism: Reporters presenting fantasy as fact, sources that did not exist, and anonymous, well-placed, knowledgeable sources (today lawyers or politicians familiar with testimony offered during privileged and secret legal proceedings). *Plus ça change, plus la meme chose.* Another interesting aspect of the newspaper coverage is that at the time this sensationalism was taking place, charges had been made that both presidential nominees, Grover Cleveland and James G. Blaine, had sired illegitimate children. The *Times* made a plea that there be no further agitation of these presidential scandals. A rather different twist from what we see now: Then printing lurid stories regarding cannibalistic misconduct of members of the military was more important than an inquiry into alleged sexual peccadilloes of presidential candidates; now, alleged presidential sexual peccadilloes command center stage over weighty matters of government.

Todd (1961, p. 297) was of the opinion that the early stories of cannibalism were inspired by an ice pilot who had been discharged for habitual intoxication and had been hired by the *New York Times* to act as its correspondent with the rescue fleet. When in his cups, the pilot revealed a flair not only for strong drink but for the dramatic as well. He claimed to have been the first man to greet the first survivors at the camp, and that he had called out: "Greely, are ye there?" and from within joyful voices called out: "It's Norman! It's Norman!" This claim was made in spite of the fact that the members of the party could not have heard his voice for 3 years, and his only contact would have been as a mate on the ship that landed the rescuers.

No charges were brought against Greely or the other survivors, and in 1887 Greely was appointed Chief Signal Officer of the Corps, with the rank of brigadier general—an unusual honor given there was no previous record of anyone reaching general-officer rank after starting out as a volunteer private, as had Greely. It will be remembered that such official approval had also been accorded to the cannibalistic captain of the *Nottingham Galley,* who was awarded the post of British consul. The data obtained by the expedition were summarized and published by Greely in two volumes, which provided the most important source books of Arctic data available to the scientific world for some time. The experiences of the party led to the realization that improved instruments were needed to record weather information under conditions as extreme as those found in the Arctic, where temperature could be below −40°F. It seems that the expedition was a success, both in terms of providing scientific data and establishing a new exploration record for the United States.

The events that have been described in these past three chapters indicate that not only does cannibalism occur with regularity, but there is a strong similarity in the sequence of events that occurs as starvation under extreme circumstances proceeds. The breadth of things eaten becomes more and more inclusive until everything, no matter how unpalatable it would seem, has been consumed. Ways are found to make stews of almost any substance that can be put into a boiling pot. When all foodstuffs, animals, hides, shoes, and saddles have been consumed, cannibalism becomes the order of the day. The order in which people are eaten is standard: The dead go first, with dead kin last; then live slaves, foreigners, the young, strangers like us, and down the ladder to kith and kin; active suicide is almost never in evidence.

A major modulating variable that comes into play is the presence of strong leaders and a code that the leader can enforce. In seafaring cannibalism a strong captain can prevail and maintain discipline, and the order of killing and eating is a reasonable one, given the circumstances. With the Mormon and Army parties there was an established and respected chain of command; the former prevented cannibalism at all (although conditions were not as extreme as for the Donner or Army parties), and the commander of the Army party prevented public cannibalism among his command. There is every reason to suspect that the people who did resort to cannibalism in the Arctic incident were a civilian (the doctor) and an outlaw officer (Kislingbury). The food thief was subsequently revealed to have been of questionable character; he had been convicted of forgery while in the Army and had been dishonorably discharged, had killed a Chinese in a barroom brawl, and had enlisted using an assumed name. It appears that with strong leadership and a clear ethical code, the conventions of society will hold longer among group members who accept that code. Lacking this, the entire group abandons its customary ways sooner, disorder tends to take place, and killing and cannibalism begin sooner. When they do begin, however, the same orderly pattern that would be expected in terms of evolutionary considerations appears.

ANIMAL CANNIBALS

Extensive evidence for survival cannibalism among humans has been discussed and analyzed to this point. There is a large literature that indicates animals of other species eat their fellows as well. I will examine a bit of this literature in order to round out the picture of what we know about cannibalism, and to determine whether the pattern seen for humans is unique in the animal kingdom.

Properly, the term cannibalism should apply only to humans, given that the noun was derived from the Arawak word *caniba*, bestowed as an insult to their fierce Caribbean neighbors (see the discussion in Chapter 1). The biologists Elgar and Crespi, in their edited volume entitled *Cannibalism: Ecology and Evolution among Diverse Taxa* (1992a), defined cannibalism more broadly as the killing and consumption of an individual of the same species. They excluded scavenging of the dead from consideration, although among humans the eating of the dead is included. Interestingly enough, they specifically excluded human cannibalism from consideration in the belief that there was little cross-cultural or historical evidence for cannibalism in human populations, a conclusion that the material in this book contradicts strongly. As we have seen, the evidence for human survival cannibalism is strong, and it appears to exhibit many of the characteristics found for animals of nonhuman species.

Elgar and Crespi (1992b) made the somewhat obvious remark that cannibalism is a particularly antisocial form of behavior that would make the evolution of gregarious behavior impossible if it was commonplace between adults or juveniles. There are, however, circumstances in which the benefits of cannibalism might override the costs of the activity; if so its evolutionary development would be possible.

There are reports of intraspecific predation in approximately 1300 species (Polis, Myers, & Hess, 1984), and evidence of intraspecific predation for 75 species of mammals, distributed among 7 orders. Eighty percent of the papers dealing with mammalian cannibalism that specified the identity of both predator and prey referred to infanticide (including cannibalism). This led Polis et al. to suggest that infanticide often functions as part of a reproductive strategy. Cannibalism is found commonly among nutritionally stressed bats, as well as among 21 species of rodents. There is strong evidence that it is widespread among cats (Felidae) and dogs (Canidae), with the victims usually being juveniles.

Cannibalism has been observed in 15 primate species, and causal attributes that have been identified include conspecific density factors, nutritional stress, reproductive strategy, environmental stress, and population regulation. In many species, cannibalism occurs after infanticide has occurred, as well as during mating and courtship. Sometimes the elderly are eaten, as well as eggs, and cannibalism occasionally occurs in the course of competitive interactions. In general, males are the cannibals and juveniles are the victims. Cannibalism tends to occur when population density increases to high levels, making it difficult for individuals to satisfy their nutritional requirements. It has also been suggested that it functions as a reproductive strategy among primates. In nonhuman animal species mothers are able to recover some of their reproductive investment by eating their young when there is a strong likelihood the young will not survive. This consumption increases the probability the mother will gain enough strength to produce viable young later should environmental conditions improve.

Cannibalism often is found among humans; first the dead are eaten, and then living others are killed and eaten, as described in these past three chapters. Instances of human infanticide (both active and passive) are widespread under circumstances similar to those found for other animals: in ancient Greece, China, Japan, India, Brazil, nineteenth-century London and Florence, France, and among Eskimos (Scrimshaw, 1984). Cannibalism of human infants is seldom reported, except under conditions of extreme starvation, such as that described for the Donner Party in Chapter 2, in some instances of ritual cannibalism that will be described in Chapter 5, and in the severe conditions that occurred in Russia and China in this century (Chapter 8). Scrimshaw (1984) concluded that parentally manipulated infanticide improved the parents' reproductive success by improving the quality of those children allowed to survive: more resources could be directed toward the hardiest and most viable young, usually the first child to have survived the critical first year of life.

Dong and Polis (1992) suggested that there are three major factors that affect cannibalism for many species: prey vulnerability, density, and quantity and quality of food items. Prey vulnerability is defined relative to a predator's characteristics, with the size ratio of predator to prey, relative age, developmental stage, and hunger also being major factors influencing vulnerability. Usually the prey is smaller and younger than the predator, e.g., eggs, embryos, neonates, and nestlings in the case of birds. Cannibalism increases as the degree of hunger increases. As animals become more hungry, foraging activity increases, attack threshold decreases, and the range of acceptable prey increases, admitting previously ignored items (including conspecifics) into the diet. These factors are important in human cannibalism as well: As people experience severe starvation they begin eating all kinds of usually inedible substances (e.g., hides and saddles), then they eat dead humans, and finally they kill humans for consumption.

There are three indices of density that influence the prevalence of cannibalism: prey density (potential victims), predator density (potential cannibals), and gross density (prey plus predator density, plus density of other individuals and objects). Another factor, quantity and quality of food, is the most important environmental factor, directly affecting levels of hunger and malnutrition in interaction with density of food and competitors. Dong and Polis identified three feedback loops between cannibalism density and food availability: As conspecifics are eaten the population of intraspecific competitors declines and per capita food level increases; if density increases and food is the limiting factor, then per capita food and growth decrease, producing smaller and weaker individuals that are more vulnerable to cannibalism; as cannibals become satiated there is a decrease in both feeding rate and the stresses that predispose individuals toward cannibalism.

Among the costs associated with cannibalism is the fact that if a prey is attacked it might injure or kill the predator, particularly if the prey, because it is large, will provide enough energy benefit to the predator to make it worthwhile to take the risks. To enhance inclusive fitness one should not kill genetically related individuals. It appears that conspecifics are usually not considered as prey, particularly for humans. Killing and consuming conspecifics may result in threats of revenge and retaliation, may cause your reputation in the community to suffer, may sorely annoy the eaten one's relatives, and may increase the possibility of ingesting transmittable pathogens and parasites, a danger that has been found to have strongly deleterious effects among humans, as will be discussed in Chapter 6, when the transmission of kuru is considered.

Courtship and mating cannibalism have been studied in spiders and other invertebrates (Elgar, 1992), and it has been found to be widespread (particularly among scorpions and spiders). Females attempt to consume mates before, during, or after copulation. Because females of many spider species consume males even before copulation, a male should somehow signal that he is a mate, and not prey to be eaten at once or an intruding female. Some males emit visual cues signaling their status, particularly movements that distract the female, and others have developed elaborate behavior tactics and strategies to thwart the female. Obviously, it does the male no reproductive good to be eaten before copulation because he provides only food and no sperm for the female. If there is any possibility that a female will remain unmated, thus failing to reproduce, she should not be too adept at consuming all males before copulation. Females should attempt to cannibalize males to either increase their fecundity or to mate with larger males. However, the effectiveness of such a strategy will depend on the density of males: If the density is low then she runs the risk of remaining unmated. Experimental tests of premating sexual cannibalism indicated that the most important factors influencing a female's decision to cannibalize a male were the rate at which she encountered males and her expected food intake from other prey items. This state produces a strong reproductive conflict between the interests of the male and the female.

Males of some species have developed the strategy of providing a nuptial gift to the female that functions to distract her, enabling him to copulate while she is occupied with the gift. If he is able to fertilize her, then the gift, and even his own body will provide her with additional nutritional benefit, and this would help to provide sustenance for his young-to-be. Another strategy is to wait for the female to capture a prey item before starting to court her, and then to copulate while she is otherwise occupied with feeding. Yet another strategy used by males of some species is to gather in a mating thread, and use the thread's tension to spring away very rapidly from the female after copulation, thereby reducing the chance of her capturing him.

Elgar noted that if a female's reproductive success is limited by her ability to induce males to sacrifice their lives for her consumption, then selection would favor male coyness during courtship, which should, in turn, lead the female to advertise her fitness through elaborate courtship behaviors. These considerations increase the likelihood that postmating sexual cannibalism could evolve if the number of additional offspring produced as a result of sexual cannibalism is greater than the number the male would expect to produce if he was not cannibalized, but instead attempted to mate with other females.

In general, large male spiders are less likely to be cannibalized than small ones because their longer legs increase their ability to physically manipulate the female. For spider species in which males are relatively small compared to females, the males have relatively longer legs than would be expected for their body size, making it possible for them to maneuver the female into a position that is more responsive to copulation, while remaining at a safe distance from her. The best bet for a male probably would be to copulate and to escape to live to copulate another day, but there are few data available to evaluate the outcome of this struggle between the spider sexes.

There has been considerable interest in infanticide among nonhuman primates (see Hausfater & Hrdy, 1984). It has been found that cannibalism generally occurs following infanticide. Nonhuman primate males, after having taken a female from another male, often kill the female's infant, an act that causes the lactating female to come into estrus sooner, making it possible for the new male to fertilize her, thereby enhancing his RS. Such infanticide usually occurs in populations in which male–male competition for mates is extremely high (Hiraiwa-Hasegawa, 1992).

Cannibalism has been observed in the common marmoset (*Callithrix jacchus*). It was found that nonviable newborns were likely to be cannibalized, and that the mothers did not interfere unless the infant vocalized, which would be a sign of viability. Lacking this sign the infant was regarded as a piece of food by family members. Cannibalism was experimentally induced by feeding squirrel monkey (*Saimuri sciureus*) mothers a low protein diet during late pregnancy. There was a high rate of abortion and the mothers devoured their aborted fetuses. Hiraiwa-Hasegawa concluded that all victims of cannibalism recorded among nonhuman primates were infants, with cases of cannibalism reported for 11 species.

Chimpanzees are probably the most carnivorous nonhuman primates, and all age and developmental classes of both sexes (except infants) frequently cannibalize juveniles. Hiraiwa-Hasegawa concluded that cannibalism of the victim infants following infanticide is likely to be the norm, as long as the attackers possess the body of the victim. It appears that male chimpanzees might prey on conspecific infants whenever they can find a suitable victim, usually an infant unrelated to the killer. Cannibalism following infanticide has been reported for many other carnivorous animals, among them lions, puma, brown bears, polar bears, coatis, golden jackals, and ground squirrels.

Cannibalism is found not only among invertebrates and mammals, but is common in fish and birds. For example, the males of some fish species guard eggs, with females competing for mating opportunities with the males. Then the female raids the male nest, eats the eggs he is guarding, and then mates with him, leaving him to guard her fertilized eggs.

Adult–adult cannibalism is rare among wild birds, although many species of gulls (*Larus*) frequently cannibalize both the eggs and young of conspecifics (which are not usually close relatives), particularly after they have lost their own young (Stanback & Koenig, 1992). In two species, the barn swallow (*Hirundo rustica*) and the acorn woodpecker (*Melanerpes formicivorus*), cannibalism of conspecific nestlings has been observed. In the former case it was by a male who killed and ate the nestlings of a widowed female, with whom he then mated; in the latter a replacement female killed and cannibalized young nestlings, thereby gaining additional breeding opportunities.

Another common type of egg destruction and cannibalism occurs for species in which females use a joint nest to lay their eggs. In such cases the first female to lay eggs invariably has one or more of her eggs removed from the nest by later-laying females. Males also may engage in egg destruction and cannibalism of nondescendent kin in situations in which they are denied breeding opportunity (Stanback & Koenig, 1992). Cannibalism of nestlings has been documented in many avian families, but often it is not certain whether it was by parents, siblings, or both. It was concluded that many kinds of cannibalism occur in birds, but that it is rare (particularly adult–adult, sexually selected, and sibling cannibalism) in birds relative to other vertebrates.

An experimental study of cannibalism by tiger salamanders (*Ambystoma tigrinum*) was reported by Pfennig, Ho, and Hoffman (1998). They fed adults larvae of diseased and healthy prey, some of which were of the same species (conspecifics) and some of which were of a different species (heterospecifics). Cannibals that ate diseased conspecifics were less likely to survive, and grew significantly less than those that ate diseased heterospecific larvae. In a study of free feeding preferences the cannibals preferred healthy heterospecific over healthy conspecific prey. These results were interpreted to mean that individuals may be more likely to acquire pathogens from conspecifics than from heterospecifics because of a greater genetic similarity among conspecifics. Such a genetic similarity might make the conspecific cannibal less resistant to host immune pathogens because predator and prey have more similar immune systems and are thus afflicted by similar varieties of pathogens. Indeed, as shall be seen in the discussion of cannibalism among the New Guinea Fore in Chapter 6, the transmission of the disease kuru probably was due to the consumption of brains of conspecifics—in this case humans.

From this brief review of the existence of cannibalism in several animal species it can be concluded that cannibalism occurs with regularity, given appropriate environmental conditions combined with certain patterns of courtship and copulation. It appears that some of the factors influencing cannibalism in these different animal species are influential in human cannibalism as well. Major influences that uniquely moderate human cannibalism are the tendency of kin to protect and avenge harm done to their own, and to reject (and eject) cannibals, except in certain cases of ritual cannibalism to be described in Chapter 6.

5

Osteoarchaeological Evidence

"It is the patterned bone destruction and associated signatures of percussion and postpercussion processing that constitute the best evidence warranting the inference that bone tissue was being manipulated to obtain nutrition."

—Tim White (1992)

The preceding chapters discussed survival cannibalism that has taken place throughout recent recorded history, and developed an evolutionary interpretation and analysis of those events. There is no doubt that people of many kinds have resorted to cannibalism in order to survive, and that it was not a rare activity engaged in only by deranged, psychotic individuals driven to the edge of madness or beyond. Not only is cannibalism common in severe and chronic circumstances, but the sequence of events is predictable and is considered to make sense in evolutionary terms.

In this chapter, the question is whether cannibalism was something that began to appear only as human societies became more complex or whether it is an expression of basic human nature. The most compelling evidence for prehistoric cannibalism has been provided by archaeologists who have examined bone deposits from several sites occupied by prehistoric peoples. These deposits provide the best and most compelling direct evidence that survival cannibalism occurred early in human history, as well as evidence for ritual cannibalism. Archaeology is the best tool to use to investigate the existence and extent of prehistoric cannibalism; it can either validate the written information provided by anthropologists and historians or demonstrate its unreliability (White, 1992). I agree with the comment by Arens (1979) that archaeologists and paleontologists often are misled when they rely on the contributions of social anthropologists, whose research methods are often not rigorous. This observation, however, does not apply to recent evidence that has benefited from adequate methods of excavation and dating, evaluating the total context surrounding artifacts and using sound biological theories to develop ideas about the structure of prehistoric human communities.

I begin with a discussion of ritual human cannibalism among the Aztecs in Mesoamerica. A major issue is whether cannibalism among the Aztecs developed in response to nutritional needs or was purely a ritual activity. Although this discussion is not based on archaeological evidence, it establishes the fact that ritual cannibalism, which is the primary concern of Chapters 6 and 7, existed in the New World.

The widespread prevalence of cannibalism suggests it may represent a basic evolved tendency. It would be surprising if humans, being part of the primate mammalian line, did not exhibit tendencies to engage in cannibalism when faced with conditions similar to those associated with its occurrence in other animal species (most commonly other primates), particularly when under nutritional and environmental stress.

Following the discussion of the Aztec and archaeological evidence, some ideas regarding basic human nature as it might have existed before recorded civilization will be examined. Specifically, I will entertain the argument that human groups have always engaged in inter- and intraspecies competition, and conducted organized warfare against other humans. I have suggested (Petrinovich, 1999) that early human societies were founded on two strongly evolved components: The function of one is to establish and maintain the emotional bonding and cooperation that promotes a well-functioning society; the other is competition, with an attendant fear and distrust of strangers that enhance the likelihood kith and kin will survive and propagate, making it possible to protect goods and property from marauders. The influence of variable aspects of the environment will be discussed, because evolved basic human nature must be flexible enough to cope with a range of ecological differences if individuals in a group are to be successful at tasks that enable their long-term survival and reproduction.

In the past, anthropologists and biologists accepted the conclusion that only humans killed conspecifics, with animals of other species (particularly mammals) having evolved special mechanisms that prevented individual killing and organized warfare (e.g., Goodall, 1963; Roper, 1969). As field biologists began to conduct long-term studies with groups of known individuals, intraspecific killing was found for many animal species. In fact, in their edited volume surveying cannibalism among animal species, Elgar and Crespi (1992b) expressed doubt that aggressive cannibalism existed for humans, concentrating their attention on the widespread evidence of cannibalism for animals of species other than humans.

RITUAL CANNIBALISM AMONG THE AZTECS

The cases discussed in Chapters 2, 3, and 4 represent clear instances of survival cannibalism. The archaeological material discussed in this chapter could represent instances both of survival cannibalism and of ritual cannibalism that involved motivations such as revenge on an enemy or the symbolic acquisition of the desirable powers of an enemy.

Turner and Turner (1999) concluded that it is foolish to doubt that the practice of cannibalism existed among the Aztecs, and I concur. There has been an intellectual debate regarding the meaning of the well-documented occurrence of human sacrifice and cannibalism among the Aztecs. Harner (1977) was the first to suggest that the extensive human sacrifices that took place each year were done in the interest of cannibalizing the flesh, with the practice being disguised as sacrifice. He believed cannibalism was necessary to supplement the Aztec diet in times of drought and famine, necessitated by a depletion of wild animals, birds, and fish, combined with a lack of domesticated animals. This suggestion was defended by Harris (1979), who, in response to an article by Sahlins (1978), proposed that it was uniquely difficult for the Aztec ruling class (who supplemented their diets by consuming human flesh) to prohibit the other classes of society from consuming humans or to refrain from using human flesh as a reward for loyalty and bravery on the battlefield.

Harris (1985) published an extensive treatment of the issue, unfortunately before Ortiz de Montellano's 1990 book, to be discussed later. In a chapter entitled "People Eating," Harris made the useful distinction between two modes of cannibal production: peaceful acquisition and consumption of bodies as an aspect of mourning rituals and the acquisition of bodies through violent means as an aspect of warfare. Aztec cannibalism was of the latter type only, and although it probably did little to enhance the nutrition of the peasantry, it did benefit the elite. Harris considered the real dilemma to be why a society that constantly perfects the art of mass-producing dead human bodies on the battlefield finds humans good to kill but bad to eat.

Aztec Society and Sacrifices Before entering the fray regarding the possible nutritional significance of the Aztec sacrificial practices, those aspects of the Aztec state on which there are general agreement will be described. The Aztec civilization was of high population density and was located in an ecological zone that was subject to frost and low-rainfall from time to time. The Aztecs lacked domestic herbivores such as cows, horses, and pigs. Most of the time their agricultural systems and food plants allowed the population to remain healthy and well nourished. At the time of the Spanish Conquest (1519–1521) they had a stratified society with centralized power and state-level institutions: laws, taxes, a complex administrative organization, an army, and police powers. They also had a strongly hierarchical institutional religion, which retained many of the shamanic religious traits that characterized their earlier hunter–gatherer society.

The society was stratified into several levels: The top level was made up of nobles, then came long-distance merchants and luxury artisans, next the majority of the population, made up of commoners organized into land-holding groups based on a kinship structure, and finally the lowest stratum, composed of slaves. It was possible for a commoner to rise to the rank of noble through bravery in combat, and this bravery was demonstrated by the number of sacrificial prisoners he captured. Slavery was not permanent, and the children of slaves were free. There was a ruler who was assisted by a Council of Four, and all political matters were supervised by a supreme council composed of 15–20 distinguished nobles who advised the ruler and the Council.

Steward and Faron (1959) suggested that fierce warfare served several functions: (1) to supply religious leaders with victims for the blood sacrifice they believed was demanded by the gods; (2) to afford individual warriors an opportunity to gain status through the display of human trophies, a motivation also emphasized by Hassig (1992); (3) to allow warriors to acquire supernatural powers through cannibalistic rites; and (4) to enable male warriors to add captive women to their households as concubines and food producers, thereby enhancing their economic and social status as well as their RS.

Kurtz (1978) noted that the Aztecs had extremely harsh laws, with the death sentence being common. Executions were public and most frequently carried out in the marketplaces; people were executed for theft, drunkenness, fornication, and adultery. Davies (1984) remarked that those most often sacrificed were war captives, slaves, women, and children—that is to say, precisely those who had few, if any, rights of their own. It was noted by Robicsek and Hales (1984) that a special custom during a sacrificial ceremony was to promptly sacrifice a musician—in lieu of the originally intended victim—who missed his beat on the drum while celebrating the ritual of human sacrifice. Their comment (p. 57) was: "Undoubtedly, some of our symphony conductors would love to revive this tradition." I hope the remark is directed not against all of us musicians but at drummers only.

Intensive accounts were compiled by Spanish monks who interviewed Mexican Indians who had witnessed the various Aztec sacrificial rites. The first account was that of the Franciscan monk Fray Bernardino de Sahagun (1932) who arrived in Mexico in 1529, mastered the language, wrote a vocabulary, and has been characterized as not only the first great historian in the New World, but the first true ethnologist (Wissler, 1932). He wrote in the manner in which the Indians spoke, and his history has been characterized as that of the Mexican Indian, told in Indian fashion. The history was completed in 1569, with 12 volumes published by 1578. He spent his life in Mexico, dying in 1590 in Mexico City.

Sahagun described the sacrificial rituals and their symbolic meaning in extensive detail. A festival occurred in each of the 18 months of the Aztec calendar—each month being 20 days long. No useful purpose would be served if each of the sacrifices is described; they were accompanied by extensive pageantry with fixed ceremonial ritual, dedicated to one of the various gods, were excessively brutal, and resulted in the deaths of thousands of people (mainly captives who were slaves).

The usual practice was to tie a sacrificial victim to a large stone, kill him with knife thrusts, and tear out the beating heart. The body was thrown down the temple steps, carried to a chapel, cut to pieces, and distributed to be eaten. A particularly brutal ceremony occurred in the tenth month, dedicated to the god of fire. Captives were thrown alive into a pit of live coals, allowed to burn for a while, then pulled out while still alive, their breast opened, and the heart torn out. On some occasions men, women, or children from the community were sacrificed in small numbers (often a single man or woman who represented the image of a god or goddess, and sometimes children, who were sacrificed to a god to obtain whatever benefits the god could bestow).

Another extensive account of the sacrificial rites was proved by the Dominican monk Fray Diego Durán (1994), who was born in Seville in 1537, was schooled in Mexico, entered the order in 1556, and died in Mexico in 1588. Durán had contact with Indian informants old enough to have experienced events prior to the Spanish conquest. He had a strong command of the native language of the Aztecs, and also interviewed Spanish eyewitnesses to the conquest. He both admired the good organization of the Aztec world and expressed horror at the practices of human sacrifice.

Of particular interest is his description of the first sacrificial ceremony known to have been held. The Aztecs invited the lords from all of the lands and all the noblemen from the surrounding areas that they could. The guests were given lavish presents, feasted, and assigned to festively decorated booths to watch the proceedings. Prisoners were brought out and each in turn was tied to the sacrificial stone, engaged in a mock duel with his executioner, was vanquished, was held down, and had his heart torn out by a priest, as described above.

Durán noted that the guests were shocked and bewildered by the proceedings, and returned home filled with astonishment and fright. This caused many of the nearby cities and provinces to cease rebellion and to avoid conflict with the Aztecs. Given the way they treated their enemies, it was sound policy to be on good terms with them. Not only did this ceremony terrify and subdue neighbors, it was followed by a feast at which local noblemen and those who had distinguished themselves in war received fine gifts, which left them pleased and proud. Warriors were allowed to eat the body of the captive they had taken, with the head placed on the skull rack and the bones placed on poles in his house as a sign of prestige. This latter action was calculated to remove the fear of the dead and of ghosts. These practices made it easier to entice soldiers to fight wars because they were allowed material plunder from conquered peoples and had honors bestowed on them at the various festivals.

Durán accepted claims that in that first festival, which lasted 4 days, 80,000 prisoners were killed, but Heyden (1994) considered this a gross exaggeration. He suggested that the Spanish were always prone to exaggerate the number of sacrificial victims to justify the conquest, and that the correct number was "only" 20,000!

Human sacrifice and cannibalism were integral to the Aztec religion, which was an ecclesiastical state institution with a hierarchy of priests, training schools, and state-sponsored rituals. Rituals were coordinated with agricultural and solar cycles, often designed to request rain and agricultural fertility and to give thanks for harvests. Other ceremonies sought success in war or were intended to maintain the universe by "feeding" the sun and the earth.

Graulich (1988) drew on a variety of sources, ranging across mythic, calendric, and iconographic (the latter two being primary records made at the time), and concluded that sacrifice had a dual aspect. Prisoners of war were sacrificed to different deities, and these sacrifices always had two steps— the extraction of the heart followed by decapitation. The heart was removed by the high priest, who opened the chest of the restrained victim and tore out the heart. The steaming heart was lifted toward the sun and then cast in the face of the idol of the sun god. The heart symbolized movement, and was considered to be the preferred food of the Sun, the presentation of which propelled it on its daily course, keeping the succession of night and day and of rainy and dry seasons.

A second aspect was the beheading, which was done as an offering to the god of the earth; the earth was irrigated with human blood to allow it to bear fruit. In this manner, the sacrifice was directed to both gods simultaneously. The head was then taken as a trophy and displayed on the well-known skull racks. Graulich (1988, p. 404) believes the sources "clearly indicate the prisoners of war were 'killed' twice, first by extraction of the heart and next by decapitation."

There seems little disagreement that the Aztecs engaged in ritual sacrifice of captured victims and slaves, and Ingham (1984) hypothesized that these sacrifices were both a symbolic equivalent to payment of tribute and an instrument to politically repress neighboring peoples. Helmuth (1973) believes the reasons for cannibalism included things such as aggression, ridicule, revenge, preventing revenge, and simple appetite. The sacrifice to the gods was a metaphor for tribute to the state, while the sacrifice of captured warriors was an effective form of persuasion to intimidate any neighbors who would resist or rebel. In this view, Aztec militarism is vital to the economic welfare of the society in order to maintain the tremendous traffic flow of foodstuff into and manufactured articles out of the city.

Nutritional Hypotheses Hassig (1992) agreed that subsistence problems were partially solved through military expansion, exacting tribute, and expropriating land. To maintain internal support from the people it was necessary to generate increasing amounts of tribute from neighboring states—which caused considerable hardship for commoners of those states, who now had the burden of supporting the Aztecs as well as their own ruling class. It was burdens such as these that Hassig believes led to the defeat of the Aztecs by the Spanish; neighbors were quite willing to assist the Spaniards in defeating the exploitive Aztecs.

Turner and Turner (1999) remarked that the Aztecs are universally regarded to have been the most bloodstained and violent of American Indian groups, performing sacrificial killings, victim mutilation, and cannibalism on a scale known nowhere else in the Americas. Harris (1979) asked not why the Aztec sacrificed and ate people, but why they sacrificed and ate more people than anyone else, why it continued for so long, and why it became the main focus of their ecclesiastical rituals. He argued that there were not enough wild sources of meat to supply sufficient animal protein and there were few domestic birds or dogs sufficient to compensate for the absence of cattle, sheep, goats, horses, pigs, guinea pigs, llama, or alpaca, making it necessary to engage in ritual butchering of captives for the purpose of distributing their flesh. This habitat depletion, combined with frequent and devastating crop failures and famines, was followed by intense periods of warfare and prisoner sacrifice.

Sahlins (1979), in reply, maintained that Aztec cannibalism was not intensive enough to have made a difference—there usually were only 20,000 or so sacrifices a year in the Valley of Mexico, which had a population of two million. This small amount of meat was not distributed equally among the members of the population (the nobles having high priority), and even if an elite 25% of the population received it all, Sahlins maintained that this would have provided an insignificant amount of nutrition for each—on the order of one mouthful of hamburger a day.

Harner (1977) noted that the corpse was tumbled down the steps of the pyramid, where elderly attendants cut off the arms, legs, and head. At least three of the limbs were normally the property of the captor, who hosted a feast at his quarters, of which the central dish was a stew of tomatoes, peppers, and the limbs of the victim. The torso apparently went to the royal zoo to feed the animals. If this description is accepted, Sahlins' arguments seem reasonable. Only a chosen few would benefit from the meat obtained from such sacrifice, and it would hardly be enough to sustain a starving population.

Garn and Block (1970) estimated the amount of protein a man would provide, and concluded that one man would serve 60, skimpily. They concluded that human flesh could serve as an emergency source of both protein and calories, but that it was doubtful regular people-eating ever had much nutritional meaning. Turner and Turner (1999) cited two estimates: one that a 100-pound person would provide roughly 30 pounds of meat from muscle and connective tissue, about 15 pounds of fat, and several pounds of organs, blood, and skin, and another that an average human adult would provide about 66 pounds of edible meat. White (1992) remarked that if protein and fats were at the shortages suggested by Harner, the archaeological signature that he, Turner and Turner, and others have found for instances in which there was cannibalism should have been present—and they were not.

The arguments of Harner and Harris were considered by Garn (1979), who once again performed calculations that led him to conclude Aztec cannibalism was not motivated by nutritional need, and that its style would be practicable only when there was a caloric surplus. He defended this latter conclusion after considering the rather large energy costs that would be involved in catching people, bringing them back, and then pen-feeding them for a period of time. Garn (1979, p. 903) concluded: "ritualized cannibalism may have existed for ceremonial and gustatory pleasure, but (like truffle-hunting) scarcely for caloric profit." Although this conclusion might be appropriate in regards to the Aztecs, Dornstreich and Morren (1974) presented calculations that led them to conclude that cannibalism in New Guinea could have had considerable nutritional value. These arguments will be considered in Chapter 6, where instances of cannibalism in New Hebrides are discussed.

One of the most succinct and comprehensive discussions of nutritional matters is contained in the book *Aztec Medicine, Health, and Nutrition* by Ortiz de Montellano (1990). He thoroughly analyzed the population levels and carrying capacity of the Mexico Basin, as well as the nature of the Aztec diet. One of his premises was that conclusions about the adequacy of the native diet depended on the size of the population just before the Spanish Conquest, assuming that the larger the population the more difficult it would have been to maintain levels of adequate nutrition. He concluded that the estimates of population levels on which Harner and Harris relied are too high, and presented detailed analyses of these levels, rainfall distribution, and corn yields in Chapter 3 of his book. The Mexico Basin contained about 1,200,000 people at that time and this population level was within the carrying capacity of the resources of the Basin. Following brief periods of famine there was an intensification of agriculture, as well as increased military activity to conquer new areas for potential tribute. The direction of expansion was toward high fertility areas with greater rainfall. These areas were the ones in which, during times of one of the worst famines, Aztecs had sold their children to obtain food.

Ortiz de Montellano presented a rebuttal of the specific arguments of Harner and Harris regarding cannibalism, and I will briefly review these points. The first argument was that the Aztecs lacked domesticated herbivores as a source of protein. His response is that they had available an extraordinary range of wild animal protein (peccary, pronghorn antelope, tapir, agoutis, and muscovy ducks), and that they also consumed domesticated turkeys and dogs.

Another argument was that a corn diet does not contain all the essential amino acids and must be supplemented by either meat or beans, a combination that must be eaten together at the same meal. His reply is that the customary Aztec diet satisfied all nutritional requirements, including vitamins and minerals. They retained a highly diversified food procurement system, never abandoning their earlier hunter–gatherer dietary habits, and practiced intense agricultural cultivation. The major dietary item was corn in the form of tortillas, which were treated with a 5% lime solution. This is an important step, because it enhances the quality of the protein by altering the relative amounts of different essential amino acids—making both niacin and its precursor, tryptophan, more available for absorption, as well as greatly increasing the calcium content of the corn. Corn was supplemented by the desert plants amaranth, mesquite, and maguey, which were readily available; they provided a higher percentage of protein when compared to wheat and other grains and had an excellent balance of amino acids, such as lysine, which corn lacks. To these basic foods they added cultivated corn, beans, squash, and chilis. Altogether their diet was adequate, balanced, and tasty.

The Aztecs ate a wide variety of living things: armadillos, pocket gophers, weasels, rattlesnakes, mice, iguanas, fish, frogs, salamanders, fish eggs, water beetles and their eggs, dragonfly larvae, grasshoppers, ants, and worms. The consumption of this wide range of critters made a significant contribution to the Aztec diet, contra Harner and Harris.

A third argument was that the Basin was subject to frequent droughts and famines, and these, combined with increased population pressure, led to human cannibalism to remedy a shortage in protein. Ortiz de Montellano replied that the regional rainfall—temperature pattern tended to make droughts local rather than widespread. He noted that famine in Mexico was less frequent than in the famine belt of the Old World, where cannibalism was not prevalent. Another problem is that the practice of sacrifice incorporating cannibalism reached its peak at harvest time when food would be at its most adequate levels.

Based on this evidence Ortiz de Montellano (1990) concluded that the Aztecs lived in a resource-rich environment, exploited a complete variety of foods that was adequate, and which, even in small amounts, would have remedied all the shortcomings of an exclusively corn diet. He emphasized that the Basin of Mexico was not populated near the limit of its carrying capacity, and the people were neither malnourished nor suffering from protein or vitamin deficiencies. Aztec life expectancy has been estimated to be longer than that for France at the end of the eighteenth century. Weather-induced famines tended to be local in nature, and the Aztecs would have been able to supplement diets for those in stricken areas with foodstuffs obtained from highly productive areas they controlled that did not suffer great rainfall variations. After their early experience with famines, the Aztecs began active military campaigns, and acquired these rich areas from their neighbors, over whom they exercised harsh and repressive control, exacting massive amounts of tribute.

The evidence supports the conclusion that Aztec cannibalism was ritualistic, to maintain autocratic control of their neighbors, and to make it possible for civil and religious leaders to control the citizens through the agency of the gods. Ehrenreich (1997) added that the local spectators would have witnessed the power of their own leaders over individual life and death, which would lead them to mind their manners. Hassig (1992) noted that captives, indeed, were needed for religious festivals, but their numbers turned on political considerations. The practice of cannibalism to supplement the diet was probably of little nutritional value.

It has been suggested that my analysis is faulty because even a bite of hamburger a day could have tremendous nutritional significance in times of stress if it increased fitness in the face of natural selection, favoring those individuals who received that supplement. I have suggested several reasons to doubt such a supplementary nutritional hypothesis, and will review them here.

First, the majority of sacrifices took place around the time of harvest when food supplies would be most adequate, not during times when food would be most scarce. Second, famines were local in geographic distribution, and foodstuffs could be brought in from neighboring regions. Third, there is evidence that following famines the Aztecs aggressively conquered neighboring regions that had rich agricultural resources, and effectively exacted tribute from these conquered people. Fourth, the distribution of human flesh was such that the Aztec have-nots would be unlikely to receive any—it went to priests, officials, and warriors, with some even to feed zoo animals (hardly suggesting that there was a large starving human population). Fifth, there is no evidence that the standard diet lacked essential elements. Sixth, it does not appear that the Aztecs were malnourished, and their life expectancy was not short when compared with that of other parts of the world at that time. Seventh, it is doubtful that it would be cost effective to conduct warfare to obtain captives for a minimal nutritional benefit, given the major costs involved in conducting war, taking captives, keeping them, and feeding them until the time of sacrifice. Finally, there are strong reasons to believe that there were a number of political and theological reasons that justified the sacrifices and the subsequent cannibalism. Considering the above seven points and the fact that there is a strong alternative explanation for the practices of sacrifice and cannibalism, the nutritional hypothesis appears suspect.

It is interesting that some anthropologists are willing to concede that human sacrifice of the most brutal sort took place, but are unwilling to accept the fact that ritual cannibalism took place. They can accept the proposition that these people horribly tortured and mutilated living captives, but not that they took a bite afterward. For some, the act of cannibalism appears to be justifiable if it was necessary for people to survive, but not if it was part of the theater of life.

OSTEOARCHAEOLOGY

Neolithic Cannibalism Clusters of human and animal bones found in Neolithic levels (between 3000 and 4000 BC) of the Fontbrégoua Cave in southeastern France were studied by Villa et al. (1986). They addressed the question of whether these bones provided evidence for dietary cannibalism—the use of humans by humans for food. It was assumed that if it is known that the remains of animals were processed as food items it would support, by analogy, the argument that human remains, which had been subjected to identical processing and bear the same markings, were also eaten. Four lines of evidence were needed to support the hypothesis of dietary cannibalism: (1) similar butchering techniques in human and animal remains, (2) similar patterns of long bone breakage that might facilitate marrow extraction, (3) identical patterns of postprocessing discard of human and animal remains, and (4) evidence of cooking that indicates comparable treatment of human and animal remains.

White (1992) regarded the Fontbrégoua evidence (as well as that found in the Anasazi sites to be discussed next) as meeting the criteria necessary to conclude that it had high-intensity historical integrity. This level of integrity requires that both artifacts and their contexts are products largely or exclusively derived from past human actions. In addition, the evidence must withstand fine-grained analyses, in the sense that the archaeological record is the product of a limited number of events or episodes. In one of the French sites that had not been subjected to disturbance, Villa and his colleagues found the bones of six individual humans that had been processed and discarded at the same time. They also found human bones that originally had been deposited together at two other sites, but had later been displaced vertically and horizontally by other agents. There were no graves at the site, which suggests these bones were not mortuary remains, because it is known that during this time period in Provence each of the dead was buried individually.

The pattern of butchering for the human bones corresponded to the pattern of butchering found for bones of wild animals that were found at the same sites. Cut marks showed features suggesting they were made shortly after death, being typical of those found when animal bones have had fillets removed from them. All marrow bones were broken into several fragments, which would facilitate removal of the nutritionally valuable marrow. They concluded that the meat had been filleted and not cooked on the bone, based on the microscopic morphology of the bone surfaces, which had not been subjected to temperatures high enough to cook meat. Rather, the uncooked bones were discarded after filleting and marrow fracturing. They concluded (p. 233): "Our inference that animal and human meat was eaten is based on the evidence of ordinary butchering practices and unceremonial patterns of discard in a domestic setting."

Paleolithic Cannibalism

Defleur et al. (1999) found, in a cave in southeastern France, convincing evidence of cannibalism that took place 100,000 to 200,000 years ago. There were bones of a minimum of six individuals that showed abundant and unequivocal evidence of hominid-induced modification. These bones met the rigorous criteria required to conclude that the bones were defleshed and disarticulated, and the bone marrow was extracted. This study provides the best evidence that some Neanderthals not only practiced cannibalism, but also had fire, given the signs of burning or roasting of the bones.

Commentators concluded these findings indicate Neanderthals were capable of considerable sophistication in their behavior patterns; usually they buried their dead in a fetal position in simicircular graves, but in this instance they engaged in cannibalism. This is a clear indication of multidimensional behavior that mirrors the behavior of more modern people. It was concluded that cannibalism is very old in human evolution (Culotta, 1999b).

Anasazi Cannibalism

White (1992) and Turner and Turner (1999) have amassed convincing evidence that cannibalism occurred among the Anasazi, who were ancestral to modern Pueblo Indians. The Anasazi inhabited much of the Colorado Plateau, and their cultural relics are best represented in the Four Corners region of the southwestern United States (the geographic point at which the states of Utah, Colorado, New Mexico, and Arizona meet). The best archaeological evidence for prehistoric cannibalism has been assembled from this region, and the well-preserved and carefully analyzed specimens are among the most securely documented examples of prehistoric cultural evolution in the New World.

White accepts the usual definition of cannibalism as the conspecific consumption of human tissue, and endorses the ideas of Villa et al. (1986) that it is necessary to present the four lines of evidence listed above to verify the presence of cannibalism in an archaeological context. He concluded that the evidence provided by his Anasazi specimens meets those criteria.

Turner and Turner (1999) adopted a more rigorous set of criteria to accept the cannibalism hypothesis, based on the postmortem distribution and modification of bones, what is known as taphonomy. It is possible to determine whether damage occurred prior to death (antemortem), at death (perimortem), or after death (postmortem). An antemortem wound, such as a compound fracture of the bone of a living person, will show a bone reaction and surrounding infection, which means it must have contained its full organic component, which prevented it from shattering the way weathered bone does. An impact that shatters a bone into multiple small rectangular pieces indicates that the binding organic component of the bone was low, and would be interpreted as a postmortem event. Perimortem damage differs from antemortem damage by the lack of any infection, or healing of the bone structure, and from postmortem damage by the lack of shattering that is characteristic of weathered bones.

They required a minimal signature containing six features of perimortem damage (damage that occurred during the brief transitional phase at or around the time of death). The six criteria are (1) a high proportion of breakage among the bone samples, (2) cut marks, (3) anvil abrasions, (4) burning, (5) many missing vertebrae, and (6) pot polishing.

As mentioned above, the Anasazi archaeological sequence is one of the most securely documented examples of prehistoric cultural evolution in the New World. It has been established that the early Anasazi were hunter—gatherers who later came to depend on the cultivation of maize— with corn composing 70–80% of their diet. This transition to agricultural food production based on maize became the dominant mode of subsistence well before AD 1000. Such high reliance on a single crop would make them vulnerable to fluctuations in food supply, and weather patterns in the southwestern United States support the idea that such fluctuations would have occurred frequently.

Turner and Turner (1999) favor the hypothesis that the cannibalism known to have occurred in the Anasazi regions was due to ritual cannibalism following violence and was motivated by the desire to strike terror in the local residents and perhaps to further ritualistic ceremonies. They believed that the cannibals were Mexican Indians who entered the Chaco Canyon from northern Mexico. The reasons they prefer this interpretation will be discussed below.

One of the earliest archaeological reports of killing, mutilation, and probable cannibalism in the southwestern United States was provided by Turner and Morris (1970). A multiple burial site dating to about AD 1600 was found at Polucca Wash, and it contained bones of at least 30 Hopis. These bones were those of all age groups, ranging from a 1-year-old infant to an elderly adult, and included some bones that probably belonged to at least three women. The age and sex composition of this group of individuals were not characteristic of Hopi salt-gathering or trading expeditions or of a courting party, being more similar to that of a migratory extended family. Because the burial site was located 10 miles from major habitation ruins, the small number of bones of women and children suggests that the party was waylaid by assailants who killed the men and captured most of the children and women. Turner and Morris concluded that these individuals met their death at the site at which the bones were buried.

Fewer than 10% of the bones of these 30 individuals were unbroken; every skull was smashed, mainly from in front with the teeth broken, probably while still covered with flesh. That every skull had the brain exposed, the burnt condition of the bones, the extent of dismemberment, and the pattern of damage to long bones are consistent with the assumption that cannibalism took place. It is not possible to know whether this cannibalism was done for food or as a ritual. An interesting aspect of this finding is that its location and time of occurrence correspond nicely with a Hopi myth that has been in the oral tradition for 10 to 12 generations. Myth has it that Hopi warriors from five villages raided a large village on the top of a mesa, roughly in the region of the burial site. The warriors put to death, dismembered, and horribly mutilated the captive men, and the women and children were taken to the captors' villages. Turner and Morris remarked that archaeological evidence has seldom shown a better fit to legendary events.

More evidence for Anasazi cannibalism was published by Flinn, Turner, and Brew (1976). The site they studied was on Burnt Mesa in northwestern New Mexico, and the decorated ceramics found dated the site at about AD 900–950. One pit house contained a disarticulated mass burial of at least 11 persons, all deposited at the same time. The presence of the bones of women and children suggests the mass burial was of a family or residential group, rather than some other type of culturally defined group, which would have been composed solely of adult males. There was no evidence of animal scavenging—no canine puncture marks or parallel incisor grooves from rodent gnawing. None of the bones had been left exposed after death and later deposited on the pit house floor. There were cut marks, patterns of skeletal destruction, and charred bones, all of which are consistent with cannibalism.

Turner and Turner (1990) examined remains found at two other Pueblo sites, one of which contained the remains of 19 children and adults. These bones showed extensive damage due to carnivores, and it was concluded that the individuals probably had died of sickness, the site had been abandoned, and carnivores chewed on and consumed the remains. The remains finally were gathered up and deposited in the room not too long after the death-causing episode, and once buried neither carnivores nor rodents could gain access to the skeletal remains. This evidence does not support the cannibalism interpretation; it does provide evidence that it is possible to decide the cause of death by the state of bones.

In the same report, Turner and Turner discussed a study of 2,000 antelope bones and fragments found in the Pueblo trash. The pattern of damage to these bones was considerably different from those in the preceding ones. They contained cut marks, stone anvil or hammer abrasions, and massive long-bone midshaft breakage. The ends of the bones had been gnawed, as typical of rodents, and there were carnivore tooth punctures. It was concluded that these bones had been butchered, dismembered by joint cutting, the meat stripped, and shafts smashed to expose the marrow. The flesh and bones with flesh attached had been boiled and then discarded. Village dogs chewed the bones and remaining gristle, with wood rats working on any remaining tissue. They assumed that the whole pile was covered with sand and other trash soon after being discarded, because the bones showed few signs of weathering. The differences between the damage to the antelope bones and to the human bones of people who had died from natural causes led Turner and Turner to conclude that these people had not been cut, wounded, or harmed by other humans.

In another room, located about 10 miles northwest, the bones of four individuals were found, all of which contained evidence of violence and possible cannibalism. There were signs of stone tool cut marks, impact fractures, anvil and hammerstone abrasion, marrow exposure, burning, and other intentional damage by humans. It was concluded that the individuals had suffered violent deaths, were unceremoniously abandoned on the floor, and the jumbled and smashed remains of the individuals were deposited in a storage pit, suggesting they were victims of social pathology, either in the interests of revenge or cannibalism.

White (1992) meticulously studied a bone assemblage from an Anasazi Pueblo in Mancos Canyon, located in southwestern Colorado. There were 2,106 bone fragments, of which only 114 were not human. These well-preserved bones were assembled through controlled excavations, and there was little evidence of pre- or postdepositional disturbance. It was estimated that there were about 18 people per pueblo in the early period of habitation, and about 12 later. The bones were from about 29 individuals of both sexes (17 adults and 12 children), deposited during the same time period. There was no sign of carnivore disturbance, and little weathering. Most individuals died in the prime of life, which is unlike the pattern for collections based on cemetery populations. Many of the individuals showed signs of nutritional stress, had died from human agency, and showed no sign of embedded projectile points as would be expected from battle wounds, and the pattern of processing and discarding the remains varied greatly, suggesting the cause was primarily nutritional and not ceremonial. White had blind examinations made of bones, and found that examiners were able to discriminate readily between cuts made with stone tools and those that resulted from gnawing by carnivores. These tests indicated it is unlikely carnivores modified the Mancos bone assemblage.

Through exhaustive analyses of the detailed characteristics of each bone fragment, White concluded there was extraction of meat, blood, brains, marrow, grease, juice, sinew, bone, and viscera through activities that included skinning, evisceration, dismemberment, defleshing, bone breakage, as well as marrow, brain, and bone-grease extraction. To test the idea that the human bones had been cooked in pots, several mule deer bones were broken into splinters that had ends that would articulate. This bone fragment assemblage was submerged in water in a replica of a corrugated Anasazi cooking vessel. The pot and its contents were heated on a gas stove at full heat for 3 hours, which brought it to a slow boil. A wooden stick was used to stir the contents from time to time, as would probably have been done if they were being prepared for consumption. The pattern of modification of these bones closely replicated in all respects that found on the archaeological specimens. White considers that the similarity of the human bones to these cooked deer bones strongly indicates that the Mancos assemblage was due to cannibalism rather than mortuary ritual. It is also likely that the spongy bones were crushed and directly consumed, roasted in bone cakes, or cooked in stews that containing crushed bone.

White noted that the bones showed evidence of human-induced tool marks that resulted from defleshing, disarticulation, and percussion. There was evidence of thermal alteration (as noted above), minimal evidence of geological alteration, and no evidence of alteration by nonhuman mammals.

White's (1992, p. 364) conservative conclusion is: "These observations support the inference that human cannibalism occurred in the prehistoric Mancos Canyon." The bodies were partially or entirely skinned, segmented, defleshed, and roasted. White suggested there may have been no evidence of carnivore gnawing of bones because the village dogs had already been consumed. He was careful to point out that it is not possible to know who consumed the people of the starving pueblo: friends, relatives, or acquaintances, whether the victims were strangers who had died of starvation, or if the victims had been eaten after they had died of starvation, or had been killed and eaten. It is possible that the Anasazi may have killed and eaten enemies, or been killed and eaten by enemies. The idea that the cannibalism was due to a need to survive is strengthened by the fact that there was no evidence that any of the human bone splinters had been fashioned into artifacts.

Salmon (1995) drew a negative conclusion regarding these results, remarking that all of our earliest ancestors were not cannibals. Salmon suggested that cannibalism is not a normal cultural practice, but is something bordering on psychotic behavior. However, there is no reason to assume that all of our ancestors necessarily had to be cannibals for any of them to be. The point is that cannibalism is in the human behavioral repertoire, and probably is exhibited for a number of reasons—a common one being severe and chronic nutritional deprivation. A behavior might be exhibited only under extreme circumstances and still be a part of our biological heritage, and the fact that its course follows a systematic pattern argues against the hypothesis that it is psychotic in character.

Another rather bizarre objection to the work of Turner and his colleagues as well as that of White was offered by Bullock (1998), in a letter to the editor of *Science,* in which journal a news article had appeared describing the archaeological research concerning the Anasazi. Bullock maintained that the theories of prehistoric cannibalism remain only theories, select material taken out of context, apply forensic methods subjectively, and that their differentiation between human and scavenger action on bone is suspect. Of course, most science is based on "only" theories—conceptual models developed to advance the understanding of a range of different observations. These theories are used to develop predictions that are then tested against reality, and their value depends on a number of converging operations that support the same conceptual model, and support it better than they do alternatives.

Bahn (1992a) in a review of White's book complained that the conclusion that cannibalism is the behavior most likely responsible for the archaeological evidence is mere inference, and fretted that archaeological evidence is always ambiguous. The charges by Bullock and Bahn are reminiscent of the objection made by creationists to Neo-Darwinian evolutionary biology—that it is only a theory. So what? The establishment of an encompassing general theory is one of the goals of progressive science in any discipline.

Gifford-Gonzales (1993) made much the same objection to this "only theory" line of reasoning in a review of White's book. She stressed the importance of having multiple, independent lines of evidence to strengthen the case for the likelihood of a specific inferential option. She noted that White's analysis of the bones had provided such independent lines of evidence: cutmarks, fire-related damage, hammerstone and anvil marks, evidence of pounding, pot polish, and chewing marks. All of this evidence exactly parallels damage to animal remains handled by humans in other Anasazi site contexts at which it is accepted that there was butchery and culinary processing. She concluded (p. 332): "Taken together, these and the context of deposition all point to consumption of the Mancos people by other humans." She also remarked that those who suggest this is mortuary processing rather than cannibalism would have to stipulate why the people handling the Mancos bodies emulated food consumption processing in every detail but the actual eating. This general point will be discussed at the end of Chapter 7, where I will wonder why the fact that people have been tortured horribly is acceptable, but not that anyone took a bite of the dead or dying individuals.

Bullock raised the objection that Turner and White did not consider aspects of culture and human motivation when they drew their conclusions. To the contrary, they made an impressive effort to evaluate various explanations of the physical aspects of the bones they studied; the converging lines of evidence they bring to bear lend strength to their hypotheses, and they carefully consider alternative explanations. The interesting aspect of Bullock's letter is that it repeats more lengthy charges he made earlier (Bullock, 1991, 1992), which Turner and Turner (1992) refuted at length. These charges and their refutation will be discussed in detail in Chapter 7, where I will consider them and try to understand the attitudes of some members of the anthropological community regarding the issue of cannibalism.

Turner and Turner (1999) published a magnificent book entitled *Man Corn*, which is the literal translation of the Aztec word *tlacatlaolli*, referring to a "sacred meal of sacrificed human meat, cooked with corn." They examined prehistoric cannibalism in the southwest on a regional scale, rather than site by site, and demonstrated that it was possible to distinguish between bones processed for consumption and all other forms of bone damage and mortuary practice. The massive amount of evidence they surveyed indicates that cannibalism was practiced for almost four centuries in the southwest, beginning about AD 900, particularly by people in the Chaco Canyon area of the Four Corners. They argued that cannibalism in the southwest originated in Mexico (our friends the Aztecs) and dates back at least 2,500 years.

The Turners examined 76 claims for cannibalism or violence in southwestern sites that were found between 1893 and 1995. There were 48 claims of cannibalism, and they personally examined the human remains of 29, finding that 24 of them satisfied their rigorous six taphonomic criteria, and five did not. They found the original analyst's descriptions and illustrations so convincing that they agreed that cannibalism had occurred in another 10 cases. In 18 other claims they personally examined the remains or evaluated the analyst's presentation, and concluded that violence had occurred without evidence of cannibalism. The evidence for the rest of the claims was either negative or needed restudy to reach a conclusion. However, it is unlikely that much study will take place in the southwestern United States given the state of Indian–archaeologist politics; many in the Indian community object to the disturbance of the remains of their ancestors that would be caused by further excavations. Many archaeologists are concentrating their efforts elsewhere as a result, much to the loss of a better understanding of Anasazi culture and religion.

Turner and Turner (1999) examined the bones of 870 individuals from 165 sites at the Museum of Northern Arizona, and found that at least 68 (almost 8%) from four sites had been cannibalized. They emphasized that the vast majority of all southwestern burials show abundant evidence of consideration and concern for the dead, deflecting the charge that they were depicting the Indians as cruel savages.

Although it is impossible to know for sure who ate whom, and for what reason, Turner and Turner (1999) believe the cannibals were groups of Mexican Indians who migrated northward, bringing with them their warrior—priesthood tradition. They used human sacrifice and cannibalism to terrorize the local populace into submission, as the Aztecs had done. The evidence for cannibalism and human body processing in Mexico indicates that human sacrifice rarely occurred in Mexico without cannibalism, and the Mexican bone assemblages have the taphonomic signature found in the southwest. That cannibalism in Mesoamerica is known to go back at least 25 centuries indicates that human sacrifice and cannibalism are much older in Mesoamerica than in the southwest. These considerations led them to suggest that vanquished Toltec warrior cults migrated northward, arriving in the southwest sometime around AD 900, and these immigrants terrorized and subjugated the local residents.

An evolutionary hypothesis cannot be evaluated because there is no way to know if enemies were eating the residents, or if it was kin, friends, relatives, slaves, or strangers eating one another. One hint regarding the dynamics that drove cannibalism can be gained by examining the sex ratio of victims; the sites with cannibalism have nearly identical frequencies of adult males and females (which would be consistent with the hypothesis of either survival or ritual cannibalism), whereas those in which there was only violence had remains of more than twice as many adult males than females. This suggests that when only violence occurred houses were destroyed, men were slaughtered or suffered ritual sacrifice, and women were taken captive.

Although the Turners doubted there was survival cannibalism, it is difficult to reject the idea that it never occurred, but it probably would have been a rare event. Turner and Turner noted that in other areas of the region in which the winters were even more harsh there should have been starvation emergencies, yet no evidence of cannibalism could be found. They suggested that when food supplies ran low most people simply moved away. The evidence for cannibalism among the Anasazi, for whatever reason or by whom, is overwhelming.

The archaeological evidence provides overwhelming support for the proposition that cannibalism was common throughout human history, and there is little doubt that the Paleolithic and Neolithic record will be strengthened as further specimens are uncovered in existing digs.

BASIC HUMAN NATURE

The archaeological record satisfies the rigorous criteria necessary to support the argument that survival and ritual cannibalism were practiced in prehistoric times. Now, what have behavioral and biological theorists concluded regarding the characteristics of human nature based on analyses of such things as the archaeological record? I have provided an overview of ideas regarding the nature of the first human societies in Chapter 2 of *Darwinian Dominion* (Petrinovich, 1999), and that presentation can be consulted to provide detailed information, references, and arguments.

Archeological evidence indicates that between 2 and 3 million years ago tool-using hominids were cutting up the carcasses of large mammals, probably after scavenging carcasses of animals that had been killed by other carnivores (Heinzelin et al., 1999). Although meat might have provided only a minor proportion of the diet of these people, it would have been advantageous to be able to chase away animal killers in order to obtain carcasses for themselves, and to develop tools and techniques to dismember those carcasses. Tim White (Culotta, 1999a) noted that the recent evidence indicates that these people had the ability to butcher animals using stone tools. These early hominids had unusually large teeth, and the tools they were using enabled them to dismember large mammal carcasses, such as those of antelopes and horses. It has been suggested that this dietary breakthrough—the ability to get at a whole new world of food—bone marrow—may have resulted in the dramatic increase in brain size that took place at about this time.

Drastic changes in behavioral styles were caused by extreme shifts in the fauna in various parts of Africa, probably due to a climate shift produced by polar glaciation. The climatic changes probably caused a fragmentation of previously continuous populations of humans, producing ideal conditions for speciation to occur. It generally is agreed that more than one humanoid species existed at the same time, with many isolated breeding populations. Tattersall (1995) noted that the variety of Pleistocene fossils supports this idea, and that during this time stone tools began to appear, which suggests that the hunted *Australopithecus* was replaced by the hunting *Homo*.

About 1.5 million years ago handaxes and cleavers began to be used, and there is evidence of a successful technological development of such tools. Human societies would have been composed of relatively small groups of individuals, most of whom were kin who survived primarily by gathering and processing plant materials, supplemented increasingly by meat provided by successful male hunters. Thus, the bases for human cooperation were established and strengthened, as well as those for competition and aggression among males to sequester resources.

Accumulating evidence from intensive field studies of present-day hunter–gatherer societies indicates that members of early *Homo* hunter—gatherer communities probably were highly sophisticated in the use of ecological resources, and when compared to agriculturists of the time they did not die young, often worked less and had more leisure time, ate better, and suffered fewer periods of famine (Bettinger, 1991; Hill & Hurtado, 1996). Analyses of cross-cultural data suggest that the transition from hunter–gatherer to agricultural societies enhanced the necessity to fight in defense of resources. Whereas a hunter—gatherer band could always pick up its portable belongings and move to more productive foraging and hunting areas, or flee in the face of an enemy, agriculturists and herders were stuck. They had relatively numerous possessions, immobile and labor-expensive houses, and stores of foodstuffs. If they fled they would lose everything and risk starvation. The best way to survive and prosper would be to fight at the slightest provocation and to act in such an aggressive manner that a reputation for unrelenting fierceness is established. Nisbett and Cohen (1996) referred to this tendency to do battle in lawless frontier regions in terms of the development of a Culture of Honor—with honor meaning if me or mine are insulted or threatened in any way, I will defend my honor by fighting and killing the offender.

As discussed in *Darwinian Dominion* (Petrinovich, 1999), two positions are commonly adopted regarding basic human nature: One is that human nature is beastly, savage, and red of tooth and claw; the other is that human nature rests on capacities to cooperate, communicate, and trust. Both are probably correct, and are involved when the costs and benefits on which survival depends enter into the life history ledger. There is much to be said for the idea that there were aspects of behavior that typify the proverbial Noble Savage, as many early humanists and cultural anthropologists have maintained. However, there also is a darker side; it was advantageous to those who selfishly protect kith and kin against outsiders in order to reproduce successfully and accumulate goods. This need to protect members of the family and community led to a distrust and fear of strangers, who probably could and would kill, rape, and pillage, if given the chance.

It is helpful to consider the characteristics of the environments of evolutionary adaptation (EEAs) that would have influenced patterns of behavior that would lead to successful reproduction. Humans share many characteristics with other mammals, particularly those characteristics concerned with details of sexual reproduction. We also have many characteristics in common with nonhuman primates, and some of these influences have been conserved, and probably provide the bases out of which human nature was constructed.

Diamond (1997) argued that the earliest human community structure was that typifying the hunter–gatherer band: a small society, typically of 5 to 80 people, almost all of whom were close relatives by birth or marriage. He characterized these groups in terms of one or more extended families, and believes that all humans lived in bands until at least 40,000 years ago, with most still living so as recently as 11,000 years ago. Such a societal structure would have had profound influences on evolved human nature, and Bettinger (1991) maintained that no anthropological theory can lay credible claim to generality until tested against evidence found for hunter–gatherers—evidence he believes represents one of the cornerstones of anthropology.

These hunter–gatherer bands had no regular economic specialization except by age and sex, and all able-bodied individuals assisted in foraging for food. There were no formal institutions, such as laws, police, or treaties that could resolve conflicts between bands. These bands were, therefore, essentially egalitarian, with no formalized social stratification, no formalized or hereditary leadership, and no formalized sources of information or decision making. They operated in a manner similar to what is found for nonhuman primates (gorillas, chimpanzees, and bonobos), which also live in bands. Although there might be egalitarianism within the band, members of other bands would be distrusted and feared, and would either be eliminated or avoided.

The next stage beyond the band is what Diamond called a tribe, which is larger (composed of hundreds rather than dozens of people), usually living in fixed settlements. These tribes consisted of more than one kinship group, and they tended to exchange marriage partners. In this type of society everyone still tends to know everyone else and the society can still be predominantly egalitarian. When communities became this large, settlements began to appear and agriculture started to develop. Diamond believes these tribes lacked economic specialists and did not have slaves, because there were no specialized jobs for a slave to perform.

As a community becomes larger than the tribe, ranging from several thousand to several tens of thousands, it becomes necessary to centralize control in order to resolve conflicts between strangers. Ruling chieftains make their appearance, and Diamond suggested that chiefdoms arose by around BC 5500 in the Fertile Crescent of the Near East and southwestern Asia, and by around BC 1000 in Mesoamerica and the Andes. These chiefs were recognized officially, their position was sustained as a hereditary right, and one of their important functions was to resolve conflicts and develop ways to encounter strangers regularly without first attempting to kill them. Economic specialization had taken place by this time, chiefs required servants as well as skilled artisans, and this requirement created jobs that could be filled by slaves, making it profitable to capture people from other societies.

If this analysis of societies has merit, and it seems reasonable to assume it does, then basic evolved traits might be expected to appear whenever those aspects that characterize large societies are no longer operable. The foundation of human nature evolved during the thousands of years humans operated at the level of hunter–gatherer bands. When the authority and laws that were developed to regulate the chieftain societies we now live in are no longer of use it would be expected that those of the hunter–gatherer would come into play. And this seems to be the case when people face starvation; the consumption of living things that normally are not eaten begins, and finally the unthinkable cannibalism begins, and beings are eaten as would be expected based on the relative importance of the community and kinship organization that would have been prevalent in the days of hunter–gatherers.

Some Thoughts about War

Keeley (1996) analyzed primitive societies and concluded that warfare is a human universal, given that 90 to 95% of known societies have engaged in it. He suggested that primitive societies were more savage than peaceful. The archaeological evidence is that homicide has been practiced throughout human existence, and warfare can be found to have existed for every well-studied region throughout the past 10,000 years. Those small-band societies that did not engage in warfare instead had very high homicide rates—there was either warfare or homicidal feuding. He concluded that although pacifistic societies have always existed, they were rare and require special circumstances.

Ehrenreich (1997) suggested that the development of warfare was not based on the experience of hunting, but of being preyed on by animals that initially were more skillful hunters than humans and also were more numerous than humans. As she expressed it (p. 40): "Before, and well into, the age of man-the-hunter, there would have been man-the-hunted."

Keeley's book consists of extensive documentation of the prevalence of violence and warfare throughout prehistoric times and during recorded history. He noted that in primitive societies, warfare against outsiders ("them") was more relentless and uncontrolled, often without rules, and was aimed at annihilation. The precipitating causes of most wars were acts of violence that provoked immediate defense and retaliation. These acts of violence often were intended to pacify dangerous neighbors through intimidation, expulsion, or annihilation, and to acquire additional food, mates, valuables, labor, and territory by plunder, capture, and physical exclusion of victims. Keeley (1996, p. 175) concluded: "Primitive war was not a puerile or deficient form of warfare, but war reduced to its essentials: killing enemies with a minimum of risk, denying them the means of life via vandalism and theft (even the means of reproduction by the kidnapping of their women and children), terrorizing them into either yielding territory or desisting from their encroachments and aggressions." The picture that will emerge in Chapter 6 indicates that this characterization helps us to understand many cannibalistic societies.

Keeley discussed casualty rates from ancient and modern battles that indicate an average of 70% of the men who engaged in ancient battles were killed or wounded, as compared to only 60% of the men in the bloodiest modern battles. The proportion of war casualties in primitive societies almost always exceeded that in even the most war-torn modern states. Warlike practices of "primitive" societies can be just as sophisticated as those of "civilized" ones, and in small-scale societies the matter is one of "my relations, right or wrong," whereas in larger ones it is "my country, right or wrong."

In his discussions of warfare among the Iroquois, Snow (1994) suggested what he considered the necessary, but not sufficient, conditions for the practice of torture and cannibalism. He believes that there are at least six cultural conditions that always are present: (1) prominent militarism and intergroup conflict, (2) the taking of prisoners as an important objective of conflict, (3) a great social emphasis on conformity, compliance, and generosity, which displaces aggression to outsiders, (4) a personalistic world view, by which he means all everyday occurrences are regarded as the doings of supernatural forces or other humans, (5) a sacrifice to supernatural elements as part of regular religious observance, and (6) an intensive group competition for scarce resources, with great uncertainty about outcomes.

Snow rejected the suggestion that human beings are fundamentally nonviolent by nature, expressing the worry that pious pronouncements about the inherent amiability of humans could blind us to the warning signs of extreme behaviors. If we accept the idea that there are violent and warlike tendencies within human nature, then whenever certain combinations of conditions occur, such as the six enumerated above, we would be at risk if we ignore such signs.

War has always been universally condemned, with peace being preferred. Keeley posed a question: Why, given this universal attitude, is warfare universal? This discrepancy between attitude and reality makes it difficult to argue that values and attitudes play a significant role in promoting peace or war—if they did war should be rare and peace common, instead of the opposite being the case. If this argument is accepted, it suggests that it will be difficult to reach the Eden of Social Justice, given the basic demonic, warlike nature of humans. There is, however, hope that by understanding this evil nature, we shall overcome.

The prehistoric record indicates that early people engaged in almost continual conflict to protect themselves, the members of their community (usually kin), and their possessions. This conflict is based on strong nepotistic tendencies to provide support and succor to kith and kin, and this positive cooperative base leads both to the positive love and regard for kin, friend, and neighbors, and to a distrust of outsiders. Both tendencies can be exploited by demagogues and ideologues to control and manipulate people in the community. In the next chapter the examination of cultural traditions moves to more recent historical times.

6

Ritual Cannibalism

Cannibal, n. A gastronome of the old school who preserves the simple tastes and adheres to the natural diet of the pre-pork period.

—Ambrose Bierce (1911)

The history discussed in this chapter represents some of the classic information regarding ritual cannibalism that has been described throughout the world. The Caribbean area is where the term *cannibal* was first applied to the culinary practice of eating other people. Most of the narratives were provided by explorers, missionaries, foreign military administrators, police and judicial personnel, foreign merchants and farmers, and cultural anthropologists. There has been concern over how much of these narratives were justifications for territorial conquests developed to support the notion of the "white man's burden"—a justification for the exploitation and enslavement of native populations. It is true that such justifications have been made, and I will discuss the general merits of these arguments in Chapter 7, after presenting examples of ritual cannibalism in this chapter.

I have made no attempt to provide a comprehensive survey of the extensive literature that is available regarding ritual cannibalism. Indeed, as Kim Hill (personal communication, 1999) noted, there must be hundreds of societies that practiced ritual cannibalism that I have not considered. Hill also pointed out that it is important to consider where and how often cannibalism occurred as a normal practice, and why it occurred in some places and not others. He considers these to be the most interesting and important considerations, and I agree that they are of central importance. However, I am not an anthropologist, and my interests and background do not qualify me to undertake those important challenges. I hope this book might whet the appetite of a qualified anthropologist to take on those intriguing tasks. Here, I will touch on only a few representative cases that have been documented, and will array them by the different major geographic regions in which they occurred.

In the last chapter, I sided with those who considered cannibalism among the Aztecs to be primarily ritualistic rather than nutritional, and a similar pattern seems apparent in many of the cases considered here. I mentioned the two major types of cannibalism described by Harris (1985) for these cultures: the peaceful acquisition of the body of a relative who is consumed in the course of a mortuary rite or whose body is used to conduct therapeutic ceremonials (endocannibalism) and the acquisition of humans through hunting and killing, with the goal being to eat these humans, who were almost always members of other cultural or social groups (exocannibalism). The former is done as a mark of respect for and honor to the consumed and the latter to intimidate and drive fear into would-be enemies, to acquire desirable powers possessed by those enemies, to achieve high status in the home community, or to exact revenge on outsiders who have harmed community members.

THE CARIBS

I will start with the Caribs in honor of the fact that the word *cannibal* was derived via Spanish to refer to the practices of members of these nonstate societies in South America. I will conclude that cannibalism indeed was practiced quite widely by the Caribs. The Caribs, today, are represented by remnant communities living in Venezuela, Guyana, Surinam, French Guyana, and the Lesser Antilles (Whitehead, 1990). There has been considerable confusion over the actual identity of the Carib, who Whitehead noted were originally Arawakan. There is general agreement that the Caribs were fierce, and they presumably drove the resident Arawakan population from the islands of the Lesser Antilles about a century before the arrival of the Spaniards (Steward & Faron, 1959).

Whitehead believes the Spanish intentionally caused confusion regarding tribal identity, using the word *caribe* as a political category to designate groups that most fiercely resisted conquest, rather than as a culturally appropriate designation. The Spanish characterized the Carib as members of a bloodthirsty, cruel, and ruthless nation who were addicted to the capture of slaves, the joy of battle, and the eating of human flesh. There was political value in fostering the cannibalistic and slave-taking stereotypes to justify conquest and "pacification" as well as economic isolation of the Caribs. The issue was further complicated by conflict between the Dutch and Spanish who were competing for resources and ultimately for slaves.

Lestringant (1997) noted that the Caribs did not slaughter women, but captured them and used them for breeding stock. The Brazilian cannibals believed it was the male alone who had the power to engender, making it unreasonable to eat a child, even if it was born to a captive mother. In 1501, the Spanish Queen Isabella issued a royal decree declaring that war against the Caribs was a just war, and that prisoners could be sold as slaves. It was necessary only to tie the cannibal label to the most peaceable of Indian tribes to justify its enslavement, even though that might lead to its annihilation. The attribution of the practice of infanticide to tribes was used as a powerful indictment of non-European peoples in general, particularly to justify English imperialism.

Although the reasons Caribs originally developed such ferocity are obscure, they were described as fierce and warlike from the time of the earliest contact with Europeans. The legends of other Amerindian groups cast them in this same warlike light (Whitehead, 1990). The major purposes of warfare were to obtain status as a warrior (a rite of passage), to capture young women for wives, to capture boys to replenish the population, and, Steward and Faron (1959) added, to avenge previous raids. A peculiar feature of the language of the Lesser Antilles is that Carib was spoken only by men, while women spoke Arawak. This probably was because the Arawak had been the principal victims of Carib raids, with male captives being killed and the women taken as wives. These sex differences in language could have persisted because the sexes were segregated, with women consigned to a slavelike status.

Whitehead believes the Tiger Dance that is executed prior to an attack is intended to awake the Tiger-Spirit, who will take possession of the warrior and enable him to kill ruthlessly, as the tiger kills. However, it was considered necessary after battle to rid oneself of the Tiger-Spirit by tasting the blood and flesh of the dead enemy. If an attack was successful, some of the enemy corpses were eaten on the spot, with captive men brought home, bound for 5 days, and then killed according to a fixed procedure, which included several means of torture by both men and women (Steward & Faron, 1959). They were killed by being shot with arrows, beaten to death with a club, and cooked. Courageous warriors received the heart and other men ate the remainder of the body, with the fat being presented to the chiefs, who preserved it for later use.

The Dutch "civilized" the Caribs by teaching them new strategies and tactics that were more effective to hunt slaves. The Dutch complained, in 1767, that they were able to persuade the Caribs to refrain from killing their victims, and to bring them back alive, only by promises of double payment for each live captive. Whereas the Caribs had been able to form an alliance with the Dutch against the Spanish, the Dutch finally reached a détente with the Spanish in order to maintain their capital- and labor-intensive sugar plantations. The Spanish, however, regarded the Dutch with derision, noting that the Indians embraced the company of the Dutch because

both were barbarians lacking the constraints of making tributes, performing labor, or accepting the sweet yoke of the Gospel (Whitehead, 1990).
When the British supplanted the Dutch, in 1803, they found that Carib warriors were being used as bush-police against black slaves, a practice the
British abolished.

Given the abundant and constant sources of protein available to the
Caribs, Tannahill (1975) suggested it is unlikely they practiced cannibalism
out of nutritional necessity, because both the islands and sea offered a rich
and endless variety of many abundant foods. The Island Carib cultivated
more fruit crops than was common in other tropical forest areas—growing
pineapples, papayas, and guavas. Rather, cannibalism seems to have more
of the ritualistic character already described for the Aztecs. There is little
doubt they were fierce and cannibalistic, but the ends served appear to be
those of conducting successful warfare and exacting revenge on neighboring enemies rather than meeting nutritional requirements.

AFRICA

Another region of the world to which the term cannibal was applied, as
early as 1544, is Africa (Lestringant, 1997), where all peoples were described as cannibals in early chronicles. Most of the accounts of cannibalism were provided by Belgian and British missionaries, government
officials, and those involved in commerce, and they should be considered
with full recognition of those filters kept in mind.

Zandelande One of the more interesting and comprehensive sur-
veys of African culture is that of F. Giorgetti Gero
(1970), an Italian missionary who spent 38 years
among the Azande, arriving in the region in 1926.
The Zande nation includes what was known as the Central Africa Empire,
Zaire, and part of the Sudan, including the Bantu and Sudanese people.
Gero was linguistically sophisticated, published a phrasebook and a small
dictionary, and mastered several of the languages of the region. He noted
that each of the tribes had its own dialect, yet understood each other per-
fectly.

One of his major interests was to refute the charge that all of the Azande,
individuals and groups, were cannibals. There had been a history of cannibalism among some groups, and this cannibalism persisted in restricted
sectors after the Avongara tribe moved in on the resident peoples and established what is known as Azande. By the turn of the century, the victorious warriors fed on enemies slain in battle, which made it possible for
them to survive and return home, even though lacking adequate logistic

support for a war party. Cannibalism was rare when Gero first arrived in 1926, and had disappeared by 1930. He was aware that many of his informants belonged to some of the most cannibalistic clans, but he balanced their reports with accounts by others who were not so deeply involved, hoping to sketch a reasoned account.

The Niam Niam group of the Bantu people lived in small groups of about 30–40 persons, and early in their history cannibalism was practiced to eliminate isolated members of any neighboring clan; when a man of the group died, an enemy village was raided in order to kill a man or kidnap a boy to be raised as one of their own—in that way preserving the balance of numbers. He believed cannibalism may have occurred originally because people were driven to it by hunger, noting that they had always suffered hunger throughout their early history. After the Avongara prevailed, they established a stable political and economic system, improving the economic condition to a level that made survival cannibalism no longer necessary. Neither the Arabs nor the European colonizers initially inspired the Azande to repress cannibalism; rather, the presence of colonizers indirectly strengthened the activity because the natives wanted to enhance an impression of their ferocity in order to repel the European invaders.

Prior to the arrival of the Avongara, the Niam Niam group was among the most aggressive. It was reported that cannibalism was practiced by adults and young of both sexes, often to punish those who committed adultery, practitioners of the evil eye and black magic, kleptomaniacs, those killed in war, prisoners, unfaithful wives, lesbians, and unsuccessful rainmakers (guess they didn't have enough bad drummers or musicians to go around).

Petty thieves had their ears cut off and eaten. Captured small children were nursed and brought up as members of the clan, whereas adults were kept as slaves and eaten when food became scarce, with those attempting to escape killed on the spot and eaten. When available, women were considered choice food, their flesh being more tender and containing more of the valued fats. Gero (1970, p. 46) wrote: "I was told that human flesh is very sweet, even more so than monkey meat, which, they say, tastes very much like human flesh. For obvious reasons I could not try human flesh, but I tasted a morsel from a (*Colobus*) monkey, which I found to be very appetizing, though much too sweet, much more than pork." At this time corpses of the dead were used to supplement and enrich the usually far too frugal fare.

After having become Azande, the Niam Niam were characterized by Gero as a happy race, more cruel than cannibal. Gero (1970, p. 183) concluded: "It is unjust to insult with an infamous and undeserved name a conquering people who was perhaps cruel in war, but now is famous only for laboriousness, gentleness and amiability to such a degree that anybody who contacts them loves them." This is hardly a remark made by a moralizing missionary seeking to justify barbaric treatment of black savages by the white man.

Another anthropophagic group was the Apambia, who Gero believed ate human flesh under conditions of dire scarcity, with the victims being criminals, war casualties, prisoners, solitary wayfarers, and (for some clans) corpses. These people had no groundnuts, sesame, bananas, or maize. Gero described the national dish of the Apambia to be spinach with fat from a woman's breast. In this tribe a woman's task was to tend the home and till the field. The men spent most of their time outdoors hunting small game and a variety of monkeys, with an occasional ambush of a solitary wayfarer.

After the arrival of the Avongara, maize, millet, sugar cane, groundnuts, sesame, various types of banana, and manioc were introduced. These domestic crops provided a steadier supply of food, and nutritional cannibalism occurred only during rare periods of famine. Cannibalism was, however, still used from time to time as a strategic war weapon that would terrorize opponents into meek submission.

Sierra Leone   Sierra Leone is located on the coast of West Africa, with the seat of government located in the chief port at Freetown. It had fertile plantations of Indian corn, cassava, oil palm, and rubber, the cultivation of which was controlled by the British, requiring a large labor force. Our interest in Sierra Leone is centered on its terrorist cults—particularly the Human Leopards and Human Alligators—men whose object was to catch people, then kill and eat them. Kalous (1974) assembled about 1,000 colonial papers and published about one-third of them. These documents provide a first-hand glimpse into views of English administrators and native officials. The compiler acknowledged that the papers undoubtedly contain errors and exaggerations, but they give a true picture of one view, the official one, of the past. Because the purpose of the papers was to provide an official record, and to issue orders and instructions regarding policies to be enforced, they probably contain a minimal amount of falsification, although clearly they represent the official European perspective. MacCormack (1983) cautioned against using this material without examining it in the light of other anthropological information. She used archival material in her discussion of cannibalism in Sierra Leone, but supplemented it with historical accounts based on 10 years of intermittent fieldwork. Her conclusions support the ones described below.

In addition to Kalous's material there is a less reliable book by Captain K. J. Beatty (1915), a circuit judge in Sierra Leone, which presents a few judicial cases, and reflects the paternalistic, condescending, and negative view that many white colonials had of natives. In a preface to Beatty's book, Sir William Brandford Griffith (1915) stated the rather astounding belief that there were numerous half-human chimpanzees in the bush that issued maniacal shrieks and cries—supernatural spirits striving to bridge the animal and the human. He considered (pp. viii–ix) most of the people to be "highly intelligent, shrewd, with more than the average sense of humour, and with the most marvelous faculty for keeping hidden what they did not wish to be known—the result probably of secret societies for countless generations." His opinion was that the only way to eliminate these "objectionable societies" was to introduce the four R's, with the fourth being Religion, which was required to supersede the native "crude beliefs." His opinion was that the Human Leopards were men of mature age who believed the flesh of victims, particularly the fat and blood, would increase their virility.

The people believed that Human Leopards were witches, who actually transformed themselves into leopards. It appears that murders were committed by men dressed to resemble leopards, armed with two three-pronged "leopard" knives (one in each hand) and possessed of a medicine packet know as "Borfima," which would make the owner rich and powerful. This packet contained things such as the white of an egg, the blood, fat, and other parts of a human being, the blood of a cock, and a few grains of rice. To retain their effectiveness, these contents must occasionally be anointed with human fat and smeared with human blood. The wounds that were inflicted on victims were made to resemble those of a leopard's claw. Beatty (1915, p. 32) stated that the flesh was either eaten raw on the spot or taken away and cooked—"some like it raw, some roast, and some prefer it boiled with rice." A first-hand description by a member of the Leopard Society described the treatment of a victim, who was killed and divided up among the members; each member who received a share was bound to supply another victim to be killed and divided among the members, all of whom eat their shares.

Among the documents published by Kalous was a petition filed in 1898 by 28 British subjects living in Sierra Leone. They urged the British government to abolish the titles of tribal Chiefs, to deal a death blow to their barbarous customs and institutions, and to replace these customs with peace, order, and good government. The petition was prompted by a massacre of over 400 British and Sierra Leoneans by the Chiefs, who objected to British rule. Throughout these documents there are references to the inherent lethargy of an ignorant race of people (because of their objection to a tax "raised in their interests to be expended upon improvements in their country") and to their indolence and superstition. References to cannibalism were numerous, and it was considered to represent the need to gratify unnatural cravings as well as to celebrate tribal occasions. It was agreed that natives could not be allowed to indulge in practices such as slavery and cannibalism, which are contrary to the British ideas of humanity, and that British tribunals should be established to dispose of any such cases. Executions were to be done according to the method of civilized nations, not by burning or torture.

A number of the documents were written by the District Commissioner, T. J. Alldridge, who reported on a punitive expedition in which he led troops in the burning of eight towns. He suggested that it might be desirable to have all of the abundant rice crop destroyed as well. This white man certainly did have a heavy burden.

There are several accounts from the Congo that indicate the low esteem in which natives were held. Captain Guy Burrows (1903) wrote that the natives think there is no harm in cannibalism and that it is as natural for them to eat the flesh of a human being as it is for Europeans to eat beef or mutton. He remarked that they found the flesh of man to be superior to that of other animals, and that they prefer the flesh of the white man to the black, because Europeans are accustomed to the habitual use of salt. His account was accompanied by an enlargement of a photograph showing prisoners in chains with human body parts tied around their neck.

An interesting anecdote regarding the Belgian Congo is presented by Pakenham (1991), who claimed that a child raised as a slave by the Arabs impressed them so much by his exploits in battle that he was given his freedom. After that he served as a lieutenant hunting slaves and ivory, as did others loyal to the Arabs, with a pack of "obedient cannibals." Pakenham claimed that troublemakers were distributed as rations. There was a story that following an extensive battle, the freed slave's troops prevailed, killed the opposing leader, and remarked, when asked of the whereabouts of that leader, that "We ate him the day before yesterday." The Belgian officers remarked that cannibalism following a battle in which hundreds were killed was horrible, but exceedingly useful and hygienic. It was claimed that there were thousands of men smoking human hands and human chops on their camp fires, enough to feed the army for many days. It is most likely that these stories are highly exaggerated, used to justify the autocratic rule and gross exploitation by the British and the Belgians. They make for hair-raising tales of savagery, and probably stimulated many movie scripts and a great deal of pulp fiction.

Kalous (1974, p. ix) wrote that historians should avoid a benign variety of paternalism toward Africa, and should not gloss over unpleasant facts: "Africans are just poor big children who must not be told [the] harsh truth about their past—that would be harmful to their mental health. . . . A typical 'progressive' historian of Africa would certainly condemn Nazi atrocities, . . . yet when dealing with . . . human sacrifices, . . . cannibalism or African domestic slavery he would probably do his best to make them morally neutral and to some extent at least 'acceptable' for his readers. The result is a falsely positive, positively false picture of African past." Obviously, Kalous had little regard for either Africans or Africanists.

The Belgian Congo

One of the cruelest instances of exploitation, to the point of genocide, occurred in the Belgian Congo, which was the exclusive colony not of Belgium, but of King Leopold II of Belgium. Hochschild (1998) chronicled the appalling slaughter of the native population that took place in the Congo for the purpose of extracting the rich resources of that region—particularly ivory and rubber.

The Belgian colony was larger than England, France, Germany, Spain, and Italy combined, and more than 76 times the size of Belgium (Hochschild, 1998). There were more than 200 different ethnic groups speaking more than 400 languages and dialects. This fragmented population made it relatively easy to divide and conquer the local tribes. Hochschild characterized some of the Congo peoples, such as the Pygmies, as admirably peaceful. Some tribes practiced slavery and ritual cannibalism, and sometimes severed a head or hand as proof that an enemy had been killed in battle, a practice that Leopold's agents continued during their exploitation of the region.

If serious resistance appeared, armed warriors of a chief allied with the regime would destroy villages and kill all in sight. One report noted that the right hands of those killed were cut off to show the authorities how many had been killed—and there were 81 in one instance. The indigenous way of tallying victims was used effectively by the warriors who collaborated with Leopold's regime.

These mutilations led to an interesting reversal of the whites' obsession with black cannibalism; a myth circulated among the natives that the cans of corned beef seen in white men's houses did not contain the meat of animals, but chopped-up hands. This is reminiscent of Africans' worries about widespread white cannibalism. They worried that the large, smoking copper cooking kettles that could be seen on sailing vessels were used to turn captives' flesh into salt meat, their brains into cheese, and their blood into the European red wine (Hochschild, 1998, p. 16).

The extent of mass murder was just as great in those sections of the Congo controlled by Portugal, France, and Germany. And matters came to be little better when independence finally came to the Congo, given that little had been done to ready the people for self-rule. The story of the Belgian Congo represents one of the worst cases of the exploitation of a native people by white economic interests—a case that has been documented carefully. There were many heroic people among the native people, missionaries, and some who were repelled by the policies and actions of the white exploiters, but the overriding message is one of greed, brutality, and general unconcern among "civilized" people for many years, until the world was forced to pay attention to the genocidal slaughter.

SOUTH AMERICA

Tupinamba of Eastern Brazil
The Tupinamba were located along some 2000 miles of the eastern coast of Brazil, and their cannibalism has been discussed extensively. They subsisted through intensive farming, hunting, and fishing (both coastal and in the vast system of tributaries of the Amazon), which provided sufficient nutrients to support a dense population with unusually large villages. They have been characterized as fierce warriors whose raids were conducted to avenge wrongs and to take captives for cannibalistic rites and as human trophies, practices that allowed warriors to gain prestige.

Viveiros de Castro (1992) considers Tupinamba warfare to be motivated by blood revenge. Although the preferred victim was an adult man of valor, the Tupinamba killed and ate anyone who fell into their hands. It is the extent and nature of this cannibalism that are of primary concern here. The classic descriptions of their cannibalism were provided by Hans Stadden in mid-sixteenth-century accounts of his experiences among the Tupinamba of the Rio de Janeiro region. These accounts have been challenged and rejected by Arens (1979), and his challenge has been rejected by Forsyth (1983, 1985). This controversy will be discussed in Chapter 7 when some of the problems anthropologists face when trying to reconstruct historical reality are considered.

Before the start of an attack, magical rights were performed, after which warriors set out, accompanied by their women. They first besieged an enemy village, shooting incendiary arrows at the houses, and finally facing them with bows and arrows and clubs. If the raid was successful they cut off the heads and genitals of the killed enemy and brought captives back to the home village. Everyone who was captured was eventually eaten. The men were eaten after a few days; the women were taken as wives or concubines, but after a few years they, too, would be eaten; any children the captive women had did not become free tribal members, and after several years their ultimate fate was to be eaten.

Captive warriors did not attempt to escape because having been captured, their status in their home village was ruined. A drinking bout was held by the captors at the time the victim was to be sacrificed, and the portions of the victim to be eaten were allotted to various people in advance. The prisoner was decorated festively, and joined the villagers in general singing and dancing, which included a ritual verbal duel with his executioner. Viveiros de Castro described the dialogue that took place between the killer and captive. It opened with a harangue by the executioner, who asked the captive if he was indeed one of those who had killed members of the tribe, and if he was prepared to die. The captive affirmed his status as a killer and a cannibal, recalling the enemies he had slain in circumstances the same as those in which he now found himself. He demanded the vengeance that would strike him down, with the warning, "kill me, so my people may avenge me; you shall fall in the same way." He was promptly obliged, being killed using a special club.

The executioner did not participate in the goings on after that; he withdrew to his home, fasted, and maintained absolute silence throughout the days of drunkenness that followed. Women prepared the beer that fueled the event, and they were described as voraciously participating in the consumption of the flesh, getting priority to the genitalia of the executed enemy. If an enemy warrior had been given a village woman as a wife, she wept during the killing, but then joined the cannibalistic banquet. The victim's blood was drunk, and the flesh was eaten by everyone except the executioner. The skulls and names of the victims were given to the men who had captured the enemies; the heads were considered to be valuable trophies, proving the old adage that one way to get ahead was to get a head.

Interestingly, enemies could get a pardon if they were good singers or musicians. The Tupinamba highly esteemed men who were skilled in discourse or song, and these talents could confer immunity from consumption (Viveiros de Castro, 1992). It clearly is much better to be a musician here than in Aztec-land—if you even missed a drum beat there you had had it.

One view of the ritual significance of all this fierce warfare, sacrificial ritual, and cannibalism is that there is a strong funereal aspect to the sacrificial events; the sacrificed victims were used as a means of communication between the living and dead—both to avenge recent dead and to commemorate mythic ancestors. These sacrifices were required to avenge deaths, whether they were caused by enemies or to satisfy the spirit of a forebear. The ancestors imposed on the living the imperative to obtain revenge, and there was also a transference of energies—a recuperation of the vital essence of a dead relative.

A dissenting view of the relative importance of the different factors was developed by Balée (1984), who emphasized ecological factors. In his view, the primary factor was acquisition of rich lands and access to rivers through military action. He discounted the importance of nutritional factors because the sacrificial cannibalistic rites involved only one or a few captives, with hundreds or thousands of consumers to be fed. He also noted that some prisoners were kept for long periods of time before being sacrificed; this practice would not be good resource management. It could be that the pur-

pose of military conquest was to obtain resources as well as to intimidate
enemies, exact revenge, and enhance the status of warriors within the community. The Tupinamba will be discussed further in Chapter 7.

**The Jivaro
of Equador**   The Jivaro of Equador lived in a fairly rugged terrain
on the eastern flank of the Andes where game and
fish were not abundant (Ross, 1984). The Jivaro are
well known for their practice of making shrunken
whole heads of war victims as trophies. The custom originally seemed to
be motivated by revenge and a belief that the trophy head gives the taker
supernatural power (Steward & Faron, 1959). Raiding parties attacked villages and developed elaborate methods to preserve and shrink the heads
of victims. Between 1916 and 1928 the barter in shrunken heads was a major factor contributing to an escalation of warfare among the different Jivaro groups.

The heads were eagerly sought by whites, particularly North Americans,
who offered a rifle to tribesmen for each head trophy (Ross, 1984). In addition to the supernatural motivation, the acquisition of guns soon became a
material goal of head-hunting raids. These guns provided them with security, allowing them to compete with other tribal groups in the hostile country. The head taking led to a large number of revenge killings, and Ross
estimated that about 59% of adult males and 27% of adult females were
shot, either in revenge for a previous killing or to avenge supernatural dis-
ease-related deaths supposedly caused by their enemies. Twelve percent of
children were killed during the course of intercommunity revenge raids.

The Jivaro, although exceedingly fierce, did not practice cannibalism,
but hunted heads for trophies as recently as 1959–1960, when as many as
80 persons perished in a circumscribed region before hostilities were
brought to a halt by authorities. Would the Jivaro be considered to be more
cruel if, after killing and beheading their victims, they took a bite of them
as well? I suspect they would be; Europeans had a strong enough fascination with the practice of shrinking heads to buy them as souvenirs, but the
explorers, missionaries, and tourists did not partake of any cannibal feasts.
It is acceptable to kill or use people for decorations, but not for consumption, regardless of the cruelty of the violations of victims.

**Cauca Valley
of Western
Colombia**   The chiefs of the Cauca Valley kept their communities on a warlike footing, much as did the Caribs. As
with the Caribs, the purpose of warfare seemed to be
to take prisoners, most of whom were killed and eat-
en outright, although some were sacrificed to the god of war before being
eaten, doing double duty, as with the Aztecs. Women accompanied men

into battle, carrying arms, fighting, and taking human trophies (Steward & Faron, 1959). Prior to an attack the warriors shouted insults, and to intimidate enemies threatened to devour them; they blew trumpets made from the long bones of slain enemies and beat drums, the heads of which were made from skin flayed from victims (Carneiro, 1990).

Men, women (no matter how young or attractive), and children were slaughtered. Those taken prisoner were eaten; some were decapitated in the field, cooked, and eaten, but most were taken home to be killed, quartered, cooked, and eaten. Williams (1859) claimed to have seen victims who had their limbs cut off while still alive, with these being cooked and eaten as the victim looked on. Bodies were either roasted or boiled, and the fresh blood was drunk. Carneiro cited one report of a chief who preferred to smoke-dry the entire corpse of an enemy in order to preserve it, and it was noted that when the site was first visited by the Spanish it contained the smoked and stuffed bodies of some 400 enemy warriors. Although commoners were allowed to partake, it was the chiefs and warriors who were first in line. Once again, the primary purpose of cannibalism seemed not to be nutritional (given their protein-rich diet), but was to attain status, exact revenge, drive fear into the heart of a potential enemy, and perhaps incorporate the martial virtues of a dead warrior into oneself.

The Guayaki of Paraguay
A French anthropologist, Pierre Clastres, lived with the Guayaki Indians for 1 year, beginning in February 1963. He published a book in French in 1972, and an English translation appeared in 1998 (Clastres, 1998). He presented a fascinating ethnology of two tribes that had been in contact with the white world for only a few months, and that had for the most part been limited to dealings with one Paraguayan farmer. When the emergence of the members of these tribes became known to ethnologists, there was great interest in studying them. Clastres received funds from the French Centre National de la Recherche Scientifique, spent 4 months becoming acquainted with the language while in Paris, and familiarized himself with what was known about the tribes. When he arrived at the Indians' camp he was able to understand and speak a few sentences and establish some form of rudimentary communication.

The story of these tribes is quite typical. Toward the end of the first half of the sixteenth century, Spanish Conquistadores mounted an expedition to the interior looking for gold and silver. They encountered the fierce Indians of the Chaco region, and after enduring considerable hardship and adversity, gave up the dream of conquering a land of riches. As Clastres put it, they abandoned themselves to debauchery in the arms of their beautiful Indian mistresses. They allied themselves with the Guarani, and soon there was a large population of half-white, half-Indian children. Although the Spanish managed to subdue some of the Guarani tribes, there were many more in the forests (among them the Guayaki) who were never seen except when they stole food from gardens. If the Guarani men were able to get prior warning of the approach of a forest tribe, they might fight them off. If so, they would kill those they captured and hold a great banquet, at which they ate the prisoners in revenge for those the forest warriors had killed.

At the beginning of the seventeenth century, Spanish soldiers arrived, followed by Jesuit priests who set up mission settlements and treated the Indians decently. The Indians were caught between the Spaniards of Ascencion and the Portuguese of São Paolo, both of whom cherished the Guarani tribes as an inexhaustible source of slaves. Although the Jesuits were able to convert these Guarani to Christianity, they were unable to reach the Guayaki Indians in the forest. The Jesuits, with the help of the Guarani, succeeded in capturing 30 Guayaki and brought them to the mission. The Jesuits had mastered their language, studied their customs and beliefs, albeit from the perspective of Christian views, and established an archive of materials. Later, Father Pedro Lozano published a book, *The History of the Conquest of Paraguay*, that contained these materials. Clastres (1998) remarked that the picture Lozano painted, although incomplete, was very accurate as far as he was able to verify based on his observations.

In 1953, the white settlers became annoyed by the fact that one forest tribe, the Ache (which means "the people"), often killed isolated horses and cows. [Clastres (1998) refers to the tribe as "Atchei," but I will use "Ache" following Hill and Hurtado (1996).] There was also considerable profit to be made in selling live Indians. The whites surprised most of the Ache, killed some, and captured 40. These people represented an extraordinary profit for these Indian hunters, particularly if a child could be sold. This child would become a slave of the family that bought it, because it would be forced to work for that family for nothing all its life. The only satisfying aspect of this sorry episode is that the white hunters put the Indians in a cattle corral to hold them before sale and they all escaped during the night. Although a government decree was passed protecting Indians and making it a crime to kill one, it was ineffective due to an inability to enforce it.

During this period, a clever Paraguayan farmer had acquired two adult males of the Ache tribe and treated them well; because the farmer demonstrated more goodwill than other whites, the Indians decided it would be in the best interests of the whole tribe if they joined them. The farmer's interest was to obtain cheap labor, to receive subsistence payments and supplies for the Indians from the Paraguayan government (some of the goods he sold to local people), and to take advantage of the young girls in the tribe. The forest was becoming ever smaller, the Indians were coming into contact with whites more often, and the retaliation of white men for the killing of cows and horses was becoming increasingly brutal. At this point, the two Indians disappeared, appearing several weeks later followed by the whole tribe seeking help and protection in the white man's world.

These forest tribes of Guayaki Indians had been in hiding for centuries, being descended from the ancient Guarani tribes. In addition to the Ache, another fierce band will enter the story—the Iroiangi, who had been their neighbors. The two tribes coexisted peacefully because they kept to their own territories for fear of reprisals if they crossed the border—they each feared the other tribesmen were cannibals!

The farmer was interested in accumulating more people because his shipment of supplies was based on the size of the Indian population. He enlisted the Ache to help him find the Iroiangi and convince them that it would be in their best interests to join his settlement. The party captured an old man and his daughter, brought them to the settlement, treated them well for 3 weeks, and sent them back to their tribe with gifts and the promise of more to come. The Iroiangi came out of the forest and joined the camp on the same day (February 23, 1963) that Clastres arrived. Although the Guayaki Indians managed their short-term survival by joining the community, it was not an advantage in the long run. When Clastres arrived there were about 100 Indians, and when he left a year later there were about 75. The others had died due to illness and tuberculosis, combined with a lack of proper health care. The last word Clastres had in 1968 was that only 30 were left, which he took to indicate that they were condemned to extinction as a people.

The Ache are a fierce group of hunter–gatherers; they have an extensive set of spiritual rituals that seems to alter the sex ratio in favor of men, which leads to polyandry. When Clastres drew up genealogies of the present-day Ache he noted that just about as many girls as boys were born, but many of the girls disappeared. When a man dies in the prime of life it is believed that he must have a companion to go with him on his voyage to the home of the spirits; otherwise he will demand revenge from the world for the offense he has received. In such cases one of his children is killed, almost always a girl. Therefore there were almost twice as many men as women, as was the case during the times about which Father Lozano wrote.

There is strong attachment between mothers and children and between neonate and family group. Clastres emphasized that at birth the group shows concern for the neonate, and accepts responsibility for keeping it healthy and protecting it from the presumed nocturnal forest dwellers who lie in wait to locate and kill it. The bands within a tribe have friendly relations because they share a number of blood relatives. Visits between groups are for the purpose either of war or to exchange wives peacefully—in both cases the object is to get women.

Men are permitted to marry anyone except their mother, sister, daughter, godmother, and goddaughter, with the latter two not being very serious prohibitions. The rules that are enforced depend on the distribution of the sexes. If circumstances are such that there are few women, then a more permissible system is adopted, which allows a woman to have more than one husband. If the sex ratio is more balanced, then monogamy is the general rule, with only chiefs permitted to have more than one wife.

The major reason for discussing aspects of the history and social structure of the Guayaki is that there appears to have been a great deal of cannibalism, at least in their recent past. If so, this challenges claims that cannibalism is only a relic of the remote past of humankind, providing yet another instance of cannibalism in the latter part of the twentieth century. This cannibalism probably did not serve an important role in nutrition given its infrequence, but is yet another instance of ritual cannibalism.

Clastres devoted an entire chapter to a discussion of cannibalism, and noted that Lozano believed it was occurring at the time he wrote. Clastres noted that the Iroiangi had no doubt the Ache were cannibals (which Clastres considers to be the case), and the Ache made the same accusation regarding them (which probably was not true, as they buried their dead). He interpreted this to be an instance of people slandering enemies in every possible way (p. 311): "They are ugly, cowardly, stupid, do not know how to speak, and, above all, are eaters of men. . . . The cannibal is always the Other!" Such demonization of others as savages also characterized the attitudes of whites in South America, who labeled tribes as cannibals in order to justify their exploitation or extermination.

Clastres performed useful functions for members of the tribes, and became a trusted familiar to them. He gained an understanding, particularly from conversations with children, that certain lines of questioning were not permissible, and realized that it was best to listen and follow along with conversations, rather than steadfastly moving forward on a topic that seemed to evoke resistance. He began to be impressed with the number of independent descriptions of instances of cannibalism, all of which fit a pattern. If a child from another tribe was taken by the Ache it was not only killed, but was roasted and eaten, according to several accounts. He claimed that once the Ache were sure he knew of their cannibalism, not one of them tried to hide it from him, although they would not talk of it in the presence of the Paraguayan farmer.

The pattern was one of both endo- and exocannibalism. Children of the tribe could be killed and eaten to protect against the spirits of the dead, and adults were consumed to provide their bodies a final resting place and to free their spirits. The exocannibalism, according to Clastres, occurred when men killed enemy men in order to take their women. The purpose of the attack was to take women, and the cannibalism was gustatory—to partake of a meal of delicious human flesh, as long as it was on hand.

Clastres claimed the dead were eaten by all present, except by close relatives of the deceased. A father and mother do not eat their children and children do not eat their parents or each other. A brother never eats his sister, a father his daughter, or a mother her son. In fact, they do not eat anyone they are forbidden to marry—the prohibition against incest and cannibalism is part of a single unified system. The penis of a man is boiled and given to the women—to pregnant women first—in the belief that they will give birth to a boy. In general, cannibalism was a method of fighting against the souls of the dead. To eliminate a soul, the body must be eaten, and if it is not, the soul stays near the living ready to act against them and to kill them.

Hill and Hurtado (1996) noted that one of the four groups of Ache studied by Clastres, the Ypety group, was shunned by its neighbors because it practiced cannibalism and was a long-standing enemy of the northern groups. Hill and Hurtado noted that this group is still called *Ache ua*, "those who eat Ache," and Clastres reported that they practiced regular cannibalism through 1963.

Kim Hill (personal communication, 1999) kindly made available to me some unpublished observations he has made during the 23 years he worked with the Ache. He interviewed members of the cannibal group in the course of his splendid demographic studies, and was able to verify the events reported by Clastres. He noted there were dozens of cases of cannibalism in the second half of the twentieth century that were described to him in great detail *by the individual who did the killing and eating* (his emphasis). Hill remarked that he knew these people very well and obtained independent corroboration of the events from several different informants working separately, and who had no knowledge of what the others had said.

Hill made the following remarks regarding his informants' reports.

> The Ache Ua group regularly ate (1) all killed enemy Ache and outsiders; (2) most members of their own group who died of natural causes; and (3) some children who were killed to be eaten. They considered the bodies to be excellent fat meat, and their descriptions of the process are so nonchalant and nutritiously attractive that at least a few members of a non-cannibal group participated in some of the last known cannibalistic events (when multiple groups of Ache lived at the same reservation). Importantly, these cannibals are not extinct! There are at least a dozen or two of the "ex-cannibals" still alive, who could be interviewed to verify the accounts of Clastres and myself.

Although neither Hill nor Clastres directly observed the eating of a body, Hill noted that neither Clastres nor he ever saw a club fight either, and all anthropologists accept the fact that the Ache participate in club fights; there are hundreds of interviews about the events from participants, and it is known that many other South American groups hold club fights.

Hill draws the astute conclusion that just as Ache club fighting is a well-established ethnographic fact, so too is Ache cannibalism.

I found the ethnography provided by Clastres compelling and convincing. It is consistent with what earlier observers reported and what Hill subsequently has found, and the patterns of behavior described seem reasonable in terms of what we know of similar cultures. There is always a problem when assessing the adequacy of an ethnographic account of a group of people who are difficult to reach and study, or who no longer are in existence. All that can be done is to evaluate the adequacy and consistency of the description, and consider the study in terms of methodological norms. These problems are not unique to the field of ethnography, but have been encountered by ethologists who study exotic species of animals in remote locations, particularly if the environment is becoming so compromised that the species either become extinct or their behavior patterns are disrupted as they face the altered challenges to their existence. There will be more discussion of these concerns at the end of the next chapter.

Helmuth (1973) considered the Indian groups in South America to determine whether endocannibalism was related to the social structure of hunter–gatherers, who he typified as having a lower social organization, and exocannibalism was related to a farming economy and a more sedentary settlement life. He chose these groups because there is a sufficient amount of information regarding both types of cannibalism—16 tribes are classified as having practiced endocannibalism and 38 exocannibalism. He found that endocannibalism was significantly associated with hunter–gatherers and exocannibalism with farming. Because he considered hunter–gatherer economies to be more primitive than farming ones, he argued that endocannibalism is older than and primary to exocannibalism

NEW HEBRIDES

Cannibalism has been widely documented in the New Hebrides, and five groups will be discussed in this section: Fiji, Maori, Bimin-Kuskusmin, those living on Malekula Island (who are particularly ferocious, killing and eating captives taken in warfare), and the Fore, whose mortuary cannibalism is of particular interest because it has been linked to the deadly kuru outbreak, which appears to be a form of Creutzfeldt–Jacob disease.

Fiji and Maori   The Fiji were highly successful agriculturists, growing among other things yams, taro, bananas, sugar-cane, and papaya. Thomas Williams (1859), a Wesleyan missionary who spent 13 years in Fiji, published a book that contained first hand accounts of their cultural activities. He estimated that the population at that time was about 150,000. He commented on the wide range and plentiful amount of foods that could be gathered with little difficulty, and noted that tribesmen were successful fisherman. They were fine potters, gathered feathers for trade, and made canoes, also for trade.

Although his account is full of Christian moralizing regarding the cruelty of their warfare and the disgusting nature of their cannibalism, on balance his accounts seem plausible. For example, he writes (p. 84):

> Dull, barren stupidity forms no part of his character. His feelings are acute, but not lasting; his emotions easily roused but transient; he can love truly, and hate deeply; he can sympathize with thorough sincerity, and feign with consummate skill; his fidelity and loyalty are strong and enduring, while his revenge never dies, but waits to avail itself of circumstances, or of the blackest treachery, to accomplish its purpose. His senses are keen, and so well employed, that he often excels the white man in ordinary things. . . . In social diplomacy the Fijian is very cautious and clever.

Again, these are not the pious ranting of a religious zealot who is determined to characterize the Fijians as savages with few redeeming features.

Fiji men have been considered to be among the more fierce cannibal groups of the New Hebrides Island group. Williams (1859) considered revenge to be the main reason for cannibalism in Fiji, and Carneiro (1990, p. 202) believes intimidation of the living that took place prior to the ingestion of the dead was also part of the aim, writing: "Certainly one could hardly show greater hatred and disdain towards an enemy than by eating him." A man who clubbed an enemy to death was accorded honors and could attain high rank by distinguishing himself in battle. If the man he killed was of distinguished rank, the slayer was allowed to take his name, and warriors of rank received proud titles.

Sahlins (1983) believed there were several important reasons they engaged in cannibalism: revenge, a gourmet appreciation of human flesh, political ambition, masculine bravado, and fear of the chief. Victims were generally acquired in battle, were rebellious subjects, or were taken from previously conquered peoples. Sahlins cited estimates that indicated cannibalism had been frequent in the nineteenth century: One missionary's estimate was that during a 5-year period in the 1840s, over 500 people had been eaten within 15 miles of his residence; massacres of more than 300 people were known to follow the sacking of large towns; another missionary was shown evidence (in the form of an alignment of stones, each one representing a victim) that one chief had eaten 872 people.

They most often used surprise to attack enemies, but sometimes made open attacks that began with an exchange of insults and threats. The Fijians almost always brought their war captives home before eating them, and carried drums that were beaten as they approached their village, giving advance notice to friends and relatives of their success. Sahlins (1983) concluded that women were brought back as wives, which he believed served the interests both of exogamy and avoidance of incest within the village. In this way, Sahlins (1983, p. 86) believes "the Fijians were able to invent a solution that would satisfy all appetites by marrying out and dining out."

Williams remarked that when captives were taken they were treated with incredible barbarity before being killed. The corpses were offered by a priest to the war-god before being cooked. The butchering of a captive's corpse was done by a man skilled in wielding a bamboo knife, with which he cut off the several members, joint by joint, according to Williams (1859), who claimed to have witnessed these events. Reverend Lyeth, who was also a physician, provided a meticulous anatomical description of preparation for the oven, to which he was an eyewitness (Sahlins, 1983).

The blood of the victim was caught and drunk fresh, the body parts were baked in a special oven, and sometimes were boiled. Sahlins (1983) claimed the victims generally were cooked overnight in underground ovens and consumed the following day. Williams wrote that the heart, thighs, and arm above the elbow were the "greatest dainties." Carneiro noted, as did Sahlins, that although the primary motivation for cannibalism was to exact revenge or attain status, some of the warriors also seemed to have developed a gastronomic taste for human flesh—they just liked it.

Human bodies were eaten in connection with civil occasions, such as building a temple or launching a large canoe. Usually an enemy was the preferred provender, but when this was impracticable a common man at hand was acceptable, and there were blacklists marking those who could be taken. Williams doubted that a body was ever eaten raw. This description of warfare and cannibalism is quite similar to that for the Malekula (described below).

The Maori have also been described as a fierce cannibalistic group. Bowden (1984, p. 82) wrote that they engaged in exocannibalism for purposes of revenge: "to kill and eat a man was the most vengeful and degrading thing one person could do to another." Most of the man-eating took place on the battlefield after the losers had been routed. Victims would be butchered on the spot and cooked in simple steam ovens. Bowden noted that there was agreement that the bodies of slain enemies were never used as common food, and that women were rarely, if ever, permitted to eat human flesh. In his view the idea of food was central to their cannibalism, but its major significance was symbolic not dietary. Lewis (1986) agrees that Maori cannibalism was an aspect of ritual warfare that has been well documented in contemporary nineteenth-century eyewitness accounts.

**Bimin-
Kuskusmin**

The Bimin-Kuskusmin are located in the West Sepik interior of Papua, New Guinea, and were studied by Poole (1983), who witnessed numerous acts of mortuary cannibalism. About 1,000 people dwell in a rugged, ecologically diverse, mountainous region. They indulge in extensive warfare and practice mortuary cannibalism in the belief that the powers of both male and female victims are acquired through eating certain parts of certain kinds of people. An interesting aspect of Poole's report is that he, an anthropologist, was able to witness cannibalism in several different contexts.

Warriors never consumed women, children, or burial cadavers. They consumed only small morsels of the female parts of slain human warriors—female parts being the flesh and fat, but not the muscle, of the thighs and upper arms. Poole witnessed mortuary cannibalism on 11 occasions, and on some occasions he noted there was reticence and ambivalence on the part of the participants, which he suspected might have been shaped by the knowledge that European officials and missionaries were strongly against such practices. Customarily, male lineage agnates of a deceased man, but not his direct descendants, ate morsels of his bone marrow (which is considered a male substance)—and Poole witnessed this act on five occasions. Parents, their children, and other direct descendants may not consume parts of each other in mortuary cannibalism. Poole noted there is the same pattern of prohibitions against sexual intercourse with members of the community—another instance of the similarity between oral and sexual taboos.

Poole witnessed five instances in which female kin ate morsels of a deceased woman's lower belly fat, a practice that is believed to enhance and perpetuate the deceased woman's reproductive power by increasing the consumer's. He witnessed four events in which the husband of a deceased woman, who had been sexually active, ate raw fragments of flesh from her vagina. On two occasions male elders of the clan ate parts of a deceased male ritual elder's raw heart tissue.

In addition to these customary rituals of mortuary cannibalism there was a complex rite that reportedly occurred only once every generation, but that Poole never witnessed, the last one believed to have taken place in the late 1940s. This rite involves the active participation of all adult, fully initiated men and women, and takes place in two episodes: one at the beginning of a major, semiannual harvest of nuts (which requires an adult male victim) and the other at the end of the second semiannual harvest (which requires an adult female victim). These victims were captured during raids on neighboring villages.

The male victim was bound to the center of a great log, with his face upward. He was dressed in the regalia of a male ritual elder, fed on strong male food, and at dawn of the following day had arrows driven into his thighs and upper arms. Efforts were made to prolong his agony until dusk, a practice that was thought to strengthen his male substance. When he was dead, female ritual elders butchered the body, and parts were appropriately distributed to different categories of participants in the rite, with these parts steamed, quickly roasted, and then eaten.

The female victim was bound to a log on her side, with face downward, fed on female foods, similarly tortured, and butchered by male ritual elders. Again, parts were appropriately distributed to the ritual participants. The purpose of both rites was to produce an abundant crop of nuts, which would produce strong sons. Poole remarked on the complex articulation of the ritual acts, and noted that the people do not have a single term for "cannibalism" but have terms that emphasize different dimensions of the practice.

Malekula

Malekula (which became the country of Vanuata in 1980), the second largest island of the New Hebrides group, is divided into a number of districts that function as distinct units characterized by differences in dialect, social structure, economics, and ritual life (Deacon, 1934). One of the earliest, and probably least trustworthy, chronicles of Malekula was provided by the explorer, photographer, and filmmaker Martin Johnson (Johnson, 1922). Imperato and Imperato (1992) characterized Johnson and his wife, Osa, as products of the vaudeville circuit who were traveling for adventure and profit. They had little sense of the science of anthropology, nor did they understand the local culture, characterizing the Malekulans as a cross between apes and men—"monkey people"—a missing link, who had abandoned their villages for a life in the trees (Imperato & Imperato, 1992). Johnson (1922) remarked on their great slobbery mouths that seemed to bespeak many cannibal feasts. The Johnsons were traveling to make films to entertain and amuse the American public. He was an excellent photographer, and his 1922 book contains wonderfully clear photographs of the island and its people, but his narrative is centered on his intent to observe and photograph an act of cannibalism. He claims to have done so, but the purported photographic evidence is far from convincing, consisting of some natives dancing around a fire on which human flesh supposedly was being cooked. It is impossible to tell from the photograph what they had been cooking. Johnson (1922, p. 187) remarked that he suspected the nature of the cooking meat, which "certainly was not much different in appearance from pork. But some sixth sense whispered to me that it was not pork." So much for his evidence of cannibalism.

Harrison (1936) spent 2 years in the New Hebrides, one of them on Malekula, and noted that the diversity of cultures found on the island was remarkable, with at least 26 different language types. Harrison knew several of the dialects, and could use pidgin when he encountered a strange one, so he is immune from the charge that he had to rely on informants because he was not acquainted with the language. He had the benefit of information contained in a book by the anthropologist Arthur Bernard Deacon (1934), who had spent a year on Malekula, died there, and his voluminous notes compiled and published by colleagues. Harrison wanted to record information, not to act, and to use all of his experience to obtain the confidence of and maximum information from "these difficult people," who were powerfully armed. At the time he studied them there were several regional tribes, among them the Small, Middle, and Big Nambas. The Small Nambas consisted of several tribes in two dozen small villages that were rapidly becoming extinct. The Middle Nambas consisted of six villages populated by vigorous fighters who were cannibals and "very antiwhite man." The Big Namba consisted of one tribe with one dialect and one culture, with a population of about 2,200. The high chief was hostile to all whites, and Harrison remarked that this chief was the only man in the area with whom he was never able to establish any sort of friendliness.

Deacon (1934) described the principal occupation of the people as gardening, with their diet being predominantly vegetarian, yams being the staple food. Some fish were caught by the coastal villagers, everywhere wild pigs were hunted, and they also kept domesticated pigs. Harrison (1936) concluded that men exerted pressure on women to have children, because a man's afterlife depended on sons to attend him in death and to respect his spirit. The first domestic duty of a wife was to her husband's pigs. Women tended not to be killed in raids because the marriage system involved patrilineal local exogamy, which meant that the married women in any village would have been born in other villages. Thus, a woman in an enemy village could well be one of your own group by birth. Deacon stated that if someone was killed during a fight, and one of the killers had a friend or kinsman among the opposing force, then that member of the opposing force acted as an intermediary, procuring a safe passage for the dead man's clansfolk to come and remove the body.

Harrison described war in the prewhite days as a game with rules and no cheating. War is really manhunting, and its essence is ambush and surprise, with the goal being to bring back a corpse to be eaten. Deacon (1934), however, characterized two types of warfare: In one a man is killed primarily so that he may be eaten (as described by Harrison); in the other he is killed for purposes of vengeance or to punish him for some heinous offense, and is then eaten in a gesture of mocking contempt. Of course, this can result in feelings of trepidation; he who eats a man today may in revenge be himself eaten tomorrow. Although villagers can be ordered to be killed by the chief, only enemies are eaten.

Harrison (1937) noted that during the year he was among the Big Nambas, 30 men were killed, and about 7 were successfully taken back and eaten. After arriving in the village, the corpse was hung on the largest drum, which had been hollowed out from a whole teak trunk, and the men danced all night. Toward dawn the hanging body was beaten by strokes from sharp-edged hardwood clubs, breaking the bones. It was taken down, cut into large pieces, wrapped in leaves, and cooked in an oven, but never cooked inside a house. Every man must eat a portion, and Harrison (p. 404) reported: "The taste is like that of tender pork, rather sweet." He noted that some men are noted flesh-lovers, and eat as much as a whole limb, adding that such men have "a peculiar greasy look about the eyes." The inner part of the thighs and the head were the greatest delicacies.

Because all must partake, Harrison believed that a vague "power" is thereby added to the whole community at the expense of the spiritual and ideal life of the enemy community, and this stealing of power constitutes a supreme insult to the enemy. Only men may eat the bodies of men, according to Deacon, but women were allowed to consume the bodies of women. Parts of the bodies were sent out to other villages on all occasions of cannibalism, and the recipient of a portion was expected to reciprocate or lose face—which could cause more wars should they fail or be unable to reciprocate.

The journalist Mike Krieger (1994) visited Malekula and interviewed some of the old villagers, who confirmed stories that it was common to eat dead or wounded warriors. They stated that the practice had been on the decline since the 1920s, but persisted to some extent until World War II. His interviews supported the idea that enemies were eaten as a traditional part of a victory celebration.

The cannibalism of the Malekulans, once again, probably had no nutritional or survival value, but was purely of ritual significance. Ehrenreich (1997) proposed that given the fact that such peoples lived amid plenty, women could single-handedly grow crops, leaving no indispensable and unique occupation for men. So they engaged in warfare—one of the most rigidly "gendered" activities know to humankind. Gregor (1990) remarked, as did Keeley, that all peoples almost everywhere deplore war and desire peace, but that it is not easy to find relatively peaceful societies. It seems that war is a routine, typical, and (unfortunately) normal human activity, and that this has been the case throughout the existence of humans— for "primitives" and "civilized" alike.

The Fore   The situation is somewhat different for the Fore compared to the other tribes discussed. The Fore are the southernmost branch of the tribes found in the East New Guinea Highlands. They live in villages of 70 to 120 people (Durham, 1991), and in 1969 were reported to have a population of about 13,000 (Glasse, 1969). Environmental resources are generally adequate and the people make good use of them. They were first contacted by missionaries and government officials in the 1940s. At this time, it was reported that death was commemorated through a cannibalistic mortuary feast that brought together kin, coresidents, and allies in a feast of respect. This is quite unlike the preceding instances in which the major justification of cannibalism was to exact revenge, maintain order, and terrify potential enemies.

Cannibalism was spread to the South Fore from the north shortly after the turn of the century, and Glasse (1969) suggested that it became firmly established only after the supply of pigs declined substantially. There was some warfare because one way a man could prove his virility and courage was to slay an enemy. Before the cessation of warfare the people probably went hungry from time to time despite the abundance of the land, partly because warfare preoccupied the men and kept the women from their gardens and partly because there were occasional fluctuations in rainfall.

Much attention has been devoted to the Fore because their form of cannibalism has been linked to a deadly clinical disease state called kuru. Gillison (1983) noted that kuru was present in a neighboring group, the Gimi (with whom she was in the field for 2 years), and these women and children also practiced mortuary cannibalism. Richard Rhodes (1997) reviewed the kuru episode in a clear and informative book, and I have drawn extensively on it, as well as on the treatment by Durham (1991).

Kuru is a degenerative disease of the central nervous system found almost exclusively among adult women and young children of both sexes, with about 2,000 documented deaths by 1957. The word "kuru" was taken from the Fore term for trembling. The affliction begins with a failure of motor coordination and an athetoid tremor involving the trunk, extremities, and head, with the tremors accompanied by an unsteady gait; by the second month speech becomes blurred and by the third month the victims are unable to walk or stand. Just prior to their inevitable death, victims lose the ability to swallow, urinate, or defecate, and die of thirst and starvation if they have not already succumbed to pneumonia.

Early in 1957 the microbiologist Carleton Gajdusek entered the Fore region and found that every Fore village had a history of recent deaths from kuru. He began analyzing the epidemiology of the cases, examining patients and taking tissue samples. For this program of research he was awarded the 1976 Nobel Prize in Physiology/Medicine. His group estimated that the disease annually afflicted about 1% of the total Fore population of about 30,000, and in some villages the incidence rate reached 5–10%. Arens (1979, p. 107), who questions the cannibalistic hypothesis, mentioned in passing that accounts of Gajdusek's findings failed to mention that the report was published in "a respected but regional medical journal." Arens failed to mention that this regional medical journal is *The*

New England Journal of Medicine; although regional in title it is arguably the premier medical research journal in the United States.

Mathews, Glasse, and Lindenbaum (1968) believe that kuru probably developed in the North Fore as early as 1900, but did not reach epidemic proportions until it spread to the South Fore, a region in which cannibalism became very prevalent. Many of the Fore believed that sorcery was causing the disease, particularly because it was primarily women who were dying; the men believed this was because women were bewitched with kuru. The women also entertained hypotheses of sorcery, but believed that men were doing it in order to eliminate women. Rhodes (1997) described a series of medical hypotheses that were entertained and rejected, with Gajdusek concluding that kuru was transmitted orally through the consumption of partially cooked brains of kuru victims by women and children. It was difficult to establish the cause because the incubation period of the virus is at least 4 years, with a significant number of people developing the disease only after more than 10 or 20 years.

Cannibalism was suppressed in the 1950s, and kuru progressively declined according to a person's age cohort; it ceased to be found among the age group 4–9 by 1968, 10–14 by 1972, and 15–19 by 1973. Deaths had declined by more than two-thirds by 1972 (Rhodes, 1997). Mathews et al. (1968) noted that in those areas in which there was no tradition of cannibalism there was no kuru, unless there was a tradition of intermarriage with the Fore, which could introduce infected individuals into the area.

Women and young children were the main consumers of brains; men consumed most of the pork available at a mortuary feast; if they consumed humans it was only the red meat, and they never ate a woman who had died of kuru. The women did not eat lepers or those who died of diarrhea, but women who had died of kuru were considered to be the victims of sorcery not disease, and could be eaten safely. According to women informants, this meat, which was described as tasty and sweet, constituted an appropriate revenge against the men who claimed the best parts of any available pig. When, largely by coincidence, kuru declined as a result of the cessation of cannibalism there was a social quarantine of communities thought to contain many sorcerers (given high rates of kuru), and the Fore took this coincidence as a sign that their antisorcery efforts had finally succeeded (Durham, 1991).

Endocannibalism has been identified as the likely mode of transmission of the deadly virus, and the pattern of cannibalism explained the sex and age distribution of the disease. The cohort of children growing up free of kuru also had grown up in a community now free of endocannibalism. The disease was not transmitted vertically from infected mother to child unless the child had direct exposure during mortuary rites. Gillison (1983) noted that among the Gimi, whose women, but not men, engaged in mortuary cannibalism, kuru was also present; however, it ceased when the people turned their attention to domestic pig production. She believes that the women were allowed to have adequate amounts of pork from that time on and ceased their mortuary cannibalism.

Steadman and Merbs (1982) denied the importance of cannibalism, insisting that kuru was transmitted as a result of other general mortuary practices; women handled infected corpses, became infected when they wiped their eyes or rubbed open sores, and in turn affected their children in the same way. It was noted that the women seldom washed their hands, and always had their children with them.

The histological pattern of brain damage was unusual, and was the same for kuru and Creutzfeldt–Jakob disease (CJD). Both show a similar pattern of brain degeneration in the cerebellum, which (among other things) regulates motor movement, but CJD, unlike kuru, damages areas of the cerebrum as well. The most plausible explanation regarding its mode of introduction is that it resulted from a sporadic case of CJD, given the near identity of the two diseases. Microscopic examination disclosed widespread neuronal degeneration with the development of vacuoles around neurons, giving the gray matter a sponge-like quality—called a subacute spongiform encephalopathy.

There is a similar disease, called scrapie, that afflicts sheep, causing them to stagger, develop tremors, go blind, fall down, and eventually die. Veterinarians took tissue from a sheep infected with scrapie, and after a long incubation period about 30% of healthy sheep injected with it showed symptoms of the disease and died, as did 100% of injected goats. It was concluded that kuru probably was transmitted by people eating contaminated brain tissue, and scrapie by sheep eating afterbirth of infected sheep. The next step was to inject the brain of chimpanzees with kuru and with CJD virus taken from human victims; symptoms and brain degeneration were similar to those found for humans. The epidemiological and medical patterns of transmission ruled out any simple genetic theories of transmission.

Another related disease is transmissible mink encephalopathy, which develops when mink are fed infected sheep carcasses. It is then transmitted from mink to mink through bites during fights. A similar virus was found to cause the mad-cow disease [bovine spongiform encephalopathy (BSE)] that appeared in Britain and that was believed to be the result of the consumption of hamburger that had cattle brains ground up in it. To use all of a slaughtered animal profitably, a meat and bone meal was made from material taken from the slaughterhouse. This stuff includes cooked and dried remains of dead animals, including cattle that had fallen before slaughter and had to be killed, as well as sheep that died of undiagnosed disease. Problems suddenly appeared when the British lowered the processing temperature used in production of the meal and stopped using solvents to dissolve fat, thereby producing the meal more effectively and cheaply. Epidemiologists concluded that these changes protected the virus and led to spread of the disease. This disease also has a long incubation period (perhaps as long as 25–30 years), and great alarm was caused worldwide when it was realized it could be transmitted from animals to humans. Rhodes noted that Gajdusek concluded that kuru had begun with a single case of CJD that was spread through the Fore by cannibalism, and BSE was being spread cannibalistically in cattle through infected meat and bone meal.

The nature of the virus has been identified in research with mice, and the causative agent in all of these cases acts in similar ways. It is likely that CJD and BSE are caused by aberrant proteins called prions. Recent evidence indicates that BSE has been transmitted to people through eating beef, and that BSE and a new variant of CJD are caused by the same particle (Blakeslee, 1997). This new particle has been transmitted across species— to a pig, a goat, sheep, and mice. The existence of cross-species transmission supports the idea that BSE was spread through eating beef products that included infected offal; the practice of including offal was banned from human food in late 1989 (Almond & Pattison, 1997).

There have also been reports of cannibalism in the Samoan Islands of the South Pacific, but they will not be considered here. Freeman (1983) discussed several instances of cannibalism on several different islands, usually to exact revenge on prisoners of war or to avenge the killing of kin.

NUTRITIONAL VALUE OF CANNIBALISM

Before leaving the New Hebrides I will discuss an analysis by Dornstreich and Morren (1974), who examined the question of the possible nutritional value of cannibalism. They began with the assumption that cannibalism never served as the predominant source of meat, or even that it was a regular or frequent activity among those groups practicing it at one time or another. They also assumed that human flesh is nutritionally comparable to all other sorts of animal food, and that it was a savory food equated by the New Guineans with other kinds of meat, particularly pork.

Their analysis was based on the reasonable assumption that a typical New Guinea population might consist of about 100 people, about 46% of whom would be 20 years or older, with each of them weighing about 60 kg. They then assumed that the above group kills one 60-kg man in a cannibalistic raid, and that this victim yields 18% protein with a digestibility of 95%—all seemingly reasonable in light of nutritional studies. There would be about 10,260 g of protein, and a 60% dressing-out proportion would yield 6,156 g of protein. They used a daily protein requirement of

0.71 g/kg body weight, meaning that the yield of protein from one 60-kg man would provide each of 60 adult eaters with about 102.6 g/day of protein, assuming the group ate a man per day, 14.6 g/day of protein if they ate one man per week, and 3.4 g/day of protein if they ate one man per month. One man per week fulfills about 35% of the group's protein requirement, one man per month about 8% of the requirement, and 10 men per year about 6% of the requirement.

Dornstreich and Morren (1974, p. 9) estimated the amount of protein that would be obtained from eating pork, and concluded: "a group of 100 people (46 of whom are adults) which obtains and eats some five to ten adult victims per year would get as much meat from eating people as it does from eating pork . . . a marginally well-nourished New Guinea population would essentially resolve its protein insufficiencies." Providing 5–10% of the total protein requirement with human flesh suggested that there could be a nutritional benefit of cannibalism, and they recommended that the sort of detailed data they used in this analysis be collected before concluding otherwise. Although this analysis may make sense with small populations such as those found in the New Hebrides, it seems inapplicable in the case of large states, such as the Aztec.

ROASTED OR BOILED?

Claude Lévi-Strauss (1966) argued that cooking can be considered to be a language that has an unconscious structure. In the case of cannibalism, he believed that the way in which people are cooked is indicative of the structure of their society. He proposed a culinary triangle, with "raw" at the apex, "cooked" at one of the two lower angles, and "rotted" (boiled) at the other. Roasted food is directly exposed to fire, therefore having an unmediated conjunction, whereas boiled food is doubly mediated by the water in which it is cooked and the receptacle that holds the contents. From this he reasoned that roasted is on the side of nature (associated with ingroup solidarity), whereas boiled is on the side of culture (associated with food served to guests). He further reasoned that eating a relative (endocannibalism) would involve boiling and eating an enemy (exocannibalism) would involve roasting.

Shankman (1969) analyzed the cross-cultural literature bearing on what I have characterized as ritual cannibalism, eliminating instances of survival cannibalism that would be driven by necessity and not choice. He found 60 cases that qualified, could be considered reliable, and for which both the identity of the edibles (who it was that was being eaten—relatives or enemies) as well as the mode of preparation (which he classified as boiling, roasting, baking, smoking, raw, and other) were specified.

Shankman (1969, p. 61) succinctly described the outcome: "the exclusive focus on the roasted and boiled has been spoiled by the natives who have discovered a veritable smorgasbord of ways of preparing people." Twenty of the 60 societies prepared the same kind of person in more than one way, different groups within the same society may prepare the same kind of person in different ways, only 17 of the societies boiled anyone (and only 6% boiled exclusively), and roasting was slightly more frequent than boiling. There was no difference in the frequency of roasting or boiling related to endo- or exocannibalism. So, the hypotheses of Levi-Strauss were not supported by this study, and another neat dichotomy bites the dust.

I believe it is safe to conclude from this review of observations and studies that cannibalism has been found in a wide variety of circumstances and cultures. I also believe it is not reasonable to assume that all, or even many, of the observations presented here are the result of an underlying motivation to demonize the participants as savages beneath contempt. Certainly, many of the early observers had a systematic bias, given that they were interested in converting people to Christianity, exploiting them, or both. However, agreement in the details of these reports of ritual and revenge cannibalism lend credence to the idea that they are valid. In addition to a purely ritual significance, it is reasonable to believe that cannibalism might provide a useful nutritional advantage in some circumstances.

7

Myth in Anthropology

"Don't threaten me, Thagerson! My cousin's an anthropologist, and she can make your life *hell!*

> Cartoon by Gary Larson (1998) depicting a next door suburbanite addressing a cave man neighbor over a fence.

Some anthropologists (e.g., Arens, 1979; Salmon, 1995) have questioned the evidence indicating that widespread cannibalism has been practiced in many human societies, arguing that such support is based on only hearsay and biased evidence. Salmon (1995) expressed doubts that cannibalism ever was a culturally sanctioned practice in any society, and believes that accusations of cannibalism have always been loaded with political motives to discredit and dehumanize members of other societies. She mentioned the Andes plane crash incident (described in Chapter 4), but dismissed it with the comment that it was based on journalistic reports. Why journalistic reports should never be accepted as veridical was not explained. Could it be because such reports invade anthropological territory—a territory that should be entered only by those who have had anthropological hands laid on?

The Donner Party incident (discussed in Chapter 2) was not mentioned by either Arens or Salmon, although it is one of the better documented events in which cannibalism occurred on several occasions. Incidentally, the data regarding the demographics of death by starvation for the Donner Party and the Mormon Willie Handcart Company were published by a bona fide anthropologist, Donald Grayson (1990, 1993, 1996, 1997). Salmon failed to consider any of the numerous incidents of lifeboat cannibalism (discussed in Chapter 3), which are well documented through accounts of survivors, records of inquiry boards, and court records on those few occasions when prosecution was mounted (Simpson, 1984). Nor does she discuss the extensive cannibalism that took place during more than one time period in both Russia and China in the twentieth century (considered in Chapter 8).

Extensive archaeological research was discussed in Chapter 5, which Salmon dismissed as inconclusive: the only conclusive evidence, in her view, would be human remains found in the human gut. Bahn (1992b) also believes that definite evidence, such as human remains inside preserved human feces (coprolites), is required. Incidentally, it has been reported that evidence of coprolites containing human tissue has been found and identified. The results will soon be published in a technical journal according to a journalistic account (Preston, 1998).

Salmon discounted the importance of survival cannibalism on the grounds that it is not a normal cultural practice, but borders on psychotic behavior. I have examined the incidents of survival cannibalism in Chapters 2, 3, and 4, will consider other instances in Chapter 8, and do not believe this to be a reasonable objection. I made no attempt, particularly in the case of shipwrecks, to present an exhaustive analysis of all known cases of survival cannibalism, but included only some of the best known, adequately documented ones to develop and support generalizations regarding the occurrence of cannibalism. Those generalizations were to the effect that patterns of behavior proceed in an orderly manner according to expectations based on evolutionary considerations, rather than resembling those of individuals who have been reduced to a chaotic, psychotic state.

As I read this literature, I was struck by the fact that Arens' (1979) book, *The Man-Eating Myth,* has had considerable impact on writers from many fields, often being cited as a convincing demonstration that instances of cannibalism can be found only in those rare instances when survival cannibalism occurred. For example, Bahn (1992a) remarked that Arens's book shattered many illusions by revealing that there is almost no reliable evidence for the custom of cannibalism, other than in extreme cases for survival. As I pursued the voluminous literature regarding survival cannibalism, and then turned my attention to ritual cannibalism, I was struck by the fact that neither type was rare, nor should they be categorized as the unfolding of bizarre, psychotic events. The Arens book has been reissued in paperback; the printing I have was the sixth, which means that it has enjoyed wide distribution and is still widely cited.

Needham (1980), in a generally positive review of Arens' book, made the accurate prediction that once in paperback the book will be a popular and almost indispensable title in anthropology courses, and that it is likely to attract attention far outside university circles. Because of the impact Arens has had I will expend some effort in challenging the adequacy of his arguments and scholarship. I will first present some of the claims Arens has made, then consider some reviews of the book that have appeared both in anthropological journals and in general scholarly and journalistic publications, and finally will present some detailed rebuttals that have been made of his factual claims, particularly regarding the Tupinamba (discussed in Chapter 6) and the Iroquois (which will be discussed below). I consider the preceding discussions of cannibalism among the Aztec (see Chapter 5) and the Fore (see Chapter 6) to be sufficient to establish that there is adequate evidence for ritual cannibalism in those cases. I have not presented an exhaustive survey of the descriptions of cannibalism in all of those cultures and locations in which it has been described. I chose the ones I did because they are representative of the circumstances and types that have been described, there is adequate documentation, and they have been the subject of considerable discussion and analyses. I agree with Kim Hill (personal communication, 1999) who wrote: "If anthropologists don't want to believe in evidence for regularly-practiced, culturally-sanctioned cannibalism it is because they are purposely avoiding the evidence."

Some of the objections to the type of biological theory I espouse are based on a basic misunderstanding of evolutionary mechanisms. There is also a political reaction against the idea of what has been referred to as "biological determinism," a stance that developed in opposition to early arguments favoring eugenics. In addition, there is the puzzle of why it is politically incorrect to suggest that groups of people are cannibalistic, even though there seems to be no problem in characterizing them as brutal and warlike. I will also discuss problems that field workers, including anthropologists, face when conducting intensive field studies of the behavior and structure of other cultures.

THE MYTHS

Arens stated that he had a dual purpose in writing his book: to assess critically the instances and documentation for cannibalism and to examine this material and its theoretical explanations to arrive at a broad understanding of the nature and function of anthropology throughout the twentieth century. At the outset he wrote (p. 9) that he was "dubious about the actual existence of this act as an accepted practice for any time and place. Recourse to cannibalism under survival conditions or as a rare instance of antisocial behavior is not denied for any culture. But whenever it occurs this is considered a regrettable act rather than custom." He continued (pp. 9–10): "I propose that anthropology has not maintained the usual standards of documentation and intellectual rigor expected when other topics are being considered. . . . Instead, it has chosen uncritically to lend its support to the collective representations and thinly disguised prejudices of western culture about others."

I have reviewed an extensive number of cases, drawn from many independent sources, presented by specialists from many different endeavors and disciplines, and collected in a wide range of different regions and cultures. I find it difficult to reject all, or even many, of these instances, and believe the objections Arens has raised should be questioned. Either a considerable number of otherwise reliable observers have made invalid observations over and again, or Arens is just plain wrong.

It is difficult to assume, as he does, that all explorers, conquistadors, missionaries, traders, and colonizers (p. 18)—as well as many anthropologists, historians, and journalists—have inaccurately, and perhaps dishonestly, represented the instances of cannibalism they claimed to have witnessed, and for which physical evidence has been found. As he noted, many of the accounts reveal a similar pattern. These similarities led Arens to charge that either there has been massive collusion, or the chronicles are instances of plagiarism from one purported authority by another (which he charges directly in the case of Hans Staden, to be discussed below).

I believe the charge of collusion springs from his political agenda: that white, male, Christian, European paternalists have collectively presented the thinly disguised prejudices of western culture about others as facts about human nature (p. 10). Arens suggested that one way to demonize members of another culture is to apply collective prejudice (p. 145) and to accuse them of being mindless savage cannibals (pp. 38, 129), thereby justifying the practice of pacifying, subduing, enslaving, exploiting, and Christianizing them. He regarded statements that women and children have sometimes been the primary cannibals (for example, in the case of the Fore and Tupinamba) as representing a symbolic position regarding females in cultures renowned for sexual antagonism and opposition (p. 110). Earlier (p. 26), he considered references to the vile nature of "the opposite gender" to represent instances of stereotyped cultural sexual antagonisms that are little more than prejudicial depictions of the unsavory nature of a minority, with little if any bearing on empirical reality.

When considering characterizations of the Carib made by Staden, he suggested (p. 29) that images of nakedness, indiscriminate sexual liaison, and cannibalism are meant to convey the idea that Indians are more akin to animals than culture-bearing human beings. He continued this (p. 140), stating that the charge of cannibalism places "those" people outside the pale of culture, relegating them to a category with animals. Could there be an underlying idea of the Noble Savage versus the wickedness of European civilization lurking in his attributions of scheming on the part of those who find evidence for cannibalism?

The phraseology Arens used throughout the book is calculated to demonize those who discuss cannibalism in other cultures. He accused those chroniclers of precisely that tactic when he complained (p. 129) that much of the literature on "the natives" defines their actions as rituals, whereas our own behavior is referred to as "customs," which in his view implies a more rational purpose driving our behavior. He considered that the attribution of cannibalism to the Caribbean and to Africa constitutes nothing more than an amusing racial slur (p. 115), and in the cannibalism book, as well as in his book on incest (Arens, 1986), he accused those who discuss different cultural patterns of "tribe-trotting."

He characterized sociobiology as a new synthesis that analyzes anthropophagy in terms that can be seen as the ultimate in "human nastiness." He continued (pp. 129–130): "this new discipline rests upon only the very little that is known in the quest for the vast unknown, rampant human cannibalism is merely assumed." In this book, as well as the one on incest, he betrays a dislike for, and a general misunderstanding of the basic ideas involved when Darwinian evolutionary ideas are applied to understand human behavioral patterns, usually lumping all such applications under the label "sociobiology." I will discuss these matters later in this chapter when I discuss our old friend, the nature–nurture issue.

He wrote (p. 21): "I have been unable to uncover adequate documentation of cannibalism as a custom in any form for any society . . . the sustaining ethnography is lacking." A rather curious analogy was suggested (p. 166): "Like the poor, cannibals are always with us, but happily just beyond the possibility of actual observation." The evidence I have discussed to this point makes many of his statements appear curiously wrong, the result, I believe, of distorting and ignoring much of the evidence that is damaging to his case. By the way, regarding his statement concerning the poor, I can with little difficulty make it possible for him to actually observe the poor in any part of the world, including any major U.S. region or city of his choice.

Arens (1979, p. 181) concluded that the positive contribution of his survey regarding ritual (particularly mortuary) cannibalism is "that despite an extensive review of highly recommended and generally accepted basic sources, it was not possible to isolate a single reliable complete first-hand account by an anthropologist of this purported conventional way of disposing of the dead." As I have indicated here, and as several reviewers noted, there was abundant evidence, including first-hand observations by anthropologists, that mortuary cannibalism had been widely practiced throughout human history at the time he wrote.

Even more unfortunate for Arens, subsequent evidence on many fronts has shown that his views are becoming increasingly weakened as new data and analyses have become available since the original publication of his book. In his book on incest (1986, p. vii) he remarked: "I concluded with fervor, but not without some trepidation, that there was little if any evidential reason to accept the prevailing folk and anthropological notion that man-eating was once a widespread human custom." In a research news article in *Science* (Gibbons, 1997, p. 635) he admitted that the case for cannibalism has become stronger: "I think the procedures are sounder, and there is more evidence for cannibalism than before." Yet he permits the book to. go through several paperback editions without adding any material acknowledging that his case is being weakened or suggesting that it is probably wrong.

REVIEWS

To counter the argument that my views are those of an idiosyncratic, wild Darwinian who is not an anthropologist, I will discuss a few reviews by anthropologists of Arens' book. Kidd (1988) made the interesting observation that *The Man-Eating Myth* has been reviewed intermittently for several years, with those reviews written by anthropologists negative and those written by journalists (in largely upscale periodicals) relatively favorable.

Among the early anthropological reviews was one by Wagner (1979), who challenged several of Arens' conclusions and methods. Wagner thought it was bias that led Arens to disregard his own advocacy of high standards, and objected to his style, which he characterized as cavalier and more reminiscent of a pamphleteer with an ax to grind than that of a scholar. He also suspected that Arens had selectively chosen data to further his case. Another point Wagner made (that I want to echo) is that ordering people into groups of "us" and "them" is a tendency that is well known by most anthropologists (as well as evolutionary biologists); I suggest it might be an unhealthy aspect of a moral universal—an evolved tendency that originally served the interest of survival and furthered the reproductive efforts of individuals within the community.

The anthropologist Vincent Crapanzano (1979) reviewed the book for the *New York Times Book Review*, remarking that it is poorly written, repetitive, and snide, which he believes lessens any impact it could have—would that had been the case. He worried that Arens capitalized on denying the existence of cannibalism much in the same way as Harner and Harris capitalized on it.

Another reviewer, Springer (1980, p. 148), regarded the major difficulty to be that Arens is almost certainly wrong because he used faulty methods of evaluation, and that his "critical attitudes amount to little more than a refusal to believe any statement regarding the existence of cannibalism, combined with a variety of impeachments of the motives of those who report it." He remarked that the refusal to accept evidence of mortuary cannibalism unless there is a first-hand account by an anthropologist, if applied to other areas, such as Plains Indian warfare, would lead to the denial that such warfare had ever occurred, and there is complete agreement that it did occur. He concluded (p. 150): "In sum, the book does not advance our knowledge of cannibalism."

The eminent University of Oxford anthropologist P. G. Rivière (1980) referred to Arens' catastrophic failure to take account of well-authenticated cases of cannibalism, specifically citing that of the Tupinamba. He concluded (p. 205): "Bad books do not usually deserve long reviews, and I have given this one more attention because it is also a dangerous book. With little work and less scholarship, it may well be the origin of a myth."

In a lengthy review article, Brady (1982) remarked that Arens had relegated cannibalism as physical fact to the same graveyard that claimed the Easter Rabbit and Santa Claus. In a more serious vein, Brady worried that Arens never pursued the problem of how anthropology has come to know what it does about anthropophagy in any strict historical or epistemological sense. He accused Arens of setting standards so high that purported cannibals might be suspected of just "mouthing" their victims unless positive proof of swallowing could be obtained—shades of the demands made by Salmon and by Bahn that archaeologists must find human remains in the gut or in the feces of their specimens for the evidence to be compelling.

He concluded that Arens' review of much of the literature is problematic. On the positive side, he considered the controversy to have some value if it prevents anthropologists from leaping to conclusions regarding the subject. Brady (p. 606) faulted Arens' arguments for their lack of "methodological and philosophical sophistication, their substantive accuracy, or their utility in resolving the very problems he identifies."

Needham (1980) concurred with these points regarding lack of methodological sophistication. Although first-hand accounts are desirable, there is nothing inherently unacceptable in using circumstantial evidence to draw an inference. Such circumstantial evidence is not an inferior substitute for direct sensory evidence; it is the very foundation of knowledge. All scientists, philosophers, and historians analyze converging lines of evidence to arrive at a theoretical conclusion, and then refine the theory by looking for other lines of evidence that would confirm or disconfirm their conclusion. Brady (1982) remarked that many things that are observable in principle, such as masturbation in monasteries and homosexuality in the Army, may not be readily accessible to direct observation.

Despite this barrage of criticism, journalist Gina Kolata (1986), writing a news article in *Science,* accepted much of Arens' argumentation, including his interpretation of the Tupinamba case, the claim by Steadman that there is no evidence of cannibalism in New Guinea, because no "solid reporter" has ever witnessed it, and that kuru could have been transmitted by mortuary practices that did not include cannibalism. She is skeptical of archaeological claims for cannibalism, but did not include any mention of the Anasazi findings. I have discussed some of these points in earlier chapters, and find her views unsatisfactory.

SUBSTANTIVE ANALYSIS

Tupinamba

Arens opens *The Man-Eating Myth* with an attack on the accuracy and honesty of the writings of Hans Staden, who visited the South American coast in the mid-sixteenth century as a common seaman on a Portuguese ship. He was captured by the Tupinamba, and several years after his return to Europe wrote of his experiences. Arens noted that we are not dealing with the work of a single individual (he was assisted by a university professor of medicine in the writing), nor was he trained in the craft of ethnography (how many were at that time). Arens concluded (1979, p. 31): "the peculiar content of the published material, taken together with the linguistic problems involved, leads to the conclusion that plagiarism is the simplest and most likely explanation for the consistency of the data."

Forsyth (1983, 1985), an American anthropologist, presented a reanalysis of the basic material, and offered a rebuttal to the attack made by Arens. He wrote (1985, p. 17): "when his arguments questioning Tupinamba cannibalism are examined against what his sources actually say and against corroborative data, Arens' revisionist thesis fails to meet the basic criteria of adequate ethnohistoric interpretation." Forsyth (1983) begins by discussing the role of Jesuit missionaries in Brazil; he noted they spent much of their time in Indian villages, learned the language, and attended to the medical needs of the Indians without charge. These behaviors contrasted sharply with the treatment Indians received from settlers, which greatly impressed those Indians who had contact with the Jesuits. The linguistic ability of the Jesuits was sufficient to allow one of them to begin translating and transcribing selected parts of the Bible, as well as chants and prayers, into the Tupian language. Another wrote a grammar of the language, and all Jesuits were required to study the Tupi language in order to communicate with the Indians. Some had many years of experience among the Indians, and one of them was once an Indian slaver who spoke the language fluently, abandoned his previous occupation, and became a lay brother.

The fact that the Jesuits spoke the Tupi language, wrote dictionaries and grammars, and lived in Indian villages for extended periods of time leads Forsyth to accept many of their eyewitness accounts of cannibalism, to believe accounts that they confiscated bodies to prevent them from being eaten, and that they had successfully rescued prisoners before they could be killed and eaten (or at least attempted to baptize a victim before execution).

Forsyth wondered why the missionaries should waste their time trying to eradicate cannibalism if the practice did not exist. He wrote (p. 172):

> If the Tupinamba did not practice cannibalism, numerous experienced and knowledgeable Jesuits lie outright. They lied in their letters to friends and associates. They lied in their letters to their superiors. They lied in reports to their order. They even lied in their letters to one another. And they did so consistently, without qualification or exception, over more than half a century.

He noted that other aspects of the Jesuit's account of Tupinamba behavior are well accepted, and he questioned how we can possibly believe anything the Jesuits say about polygyny, that descent was traced through the male line, and that the Indians maintained extended households, slept in hammocks, and ate fish. It is agreed that most of these descriptions are accurate. Concerning the behavior of Indians, are the Jesuits inaccurate only on the issue of cannibalism, or are we to disregard everything they described? There are a large number of independent descriptions confirming Staden's account, and Forsyth concluded that the nature and quantity of the Jesuit sources make Arens' arguments untenable, and I agree. Forsyth admitted that there may be distortions, because these were Catholic missionaries whose goal was to convert the Indians not to study their culture. However, Indian society was observed in depth and at length, cannibalism was observed with a sense of horror, and attempts were made to stop it. He agreed with Arens that the Europeans subdued the Tupinamba and destroyed their culture, but those facts do not negate the accuracy of the Jesuits' day-to-day observations.

Clastres (1998) agreed with the above assessment, noting that the Jesuit archives essentially constituted an encyclopedia of America, accumulated over the decades. He concluded that he was able to verify the accuracy of many of the statements made by Jesuits in the course of his own fieldwork with the Guayaki Indians.

So much for the Jesuits—what about Hans Staden? Without going into lengthy detail, I will summarize the essential points made by Forsyth (1985) in opposition to the analyses by Arens. The first is the complaint that Staden spent less than 12 months among the Tupinamba, which Arens did not consider sufficient time to observe the whole process of raising, killing, and eating captured children. Forsyth believes this is an irrelevant objection, pointing out that if this same logic was applied to the work of contemporary ethnographers, any description of the life cycle in a society would be suspect if the ethnographer did not remain in the field for 50 or 60 years to observe an entire life cycle—and certainly would challenge any study conducted over less than a year—such as was the case in the pioneering research of Margaret Mead. This is another instance of setting an unrealistic standard beyond what is demanded in other areas of anthropology; what is accepted in most instances is to gather information from different informants at different stages in the contemporary process, and then to reconstruct the sequence of events to understand the life history.

Second, Arens raised questions about Staden's knowledge of the Tupi language. The evidence presented by Forsyth indicates that Staden spoke the language quite well (in addition to his native German, Portuguese, and probably a bit of Spanish), that Tupi was the *lingua franca* of Brazil at this time, and that Staden had spent 2 years shipwrecked along the coast of Brazil before being captured by and forced to live among the Tupinamba. This seems an adequate time to gain a sound understanding of the language.

Third, Arens accuses Staden of considering the Indians to be outside the realm of civilization, placing them with animals. As evidence that Staden overemphasized their animal nature to the detriment of other traits of "real" human beings, he cited Staden's statement that they were not able to count beyond five, consequently having to resort to their fingers and toes. Forsyth notes that Staden's statement concerning Tupinamba enumeration is correct; ancient Tupi had no terms for numbers beyond four, with larger numbers expressed in circumlocutions, often involving fingers and toes. Arens seems to have forgotten the concept of social relativity; it is possible for different symbolic forms to exist in different cultures, and for these forms to permit sophisticated functioning given normal circumstances.

Fourth, Arens makes the serious charge that other sources of information on Tupinamba cannibalism were plagiarized from Staden, which is an even more serious indictment in light of his claim that this plagiarism was from a disreputable source. The charge of plagiarism is based on the fact that Staden and several later chroniclers, in describing the scene in which victims are executed, use similar phraseology in quoting the two sentences exchanged between executioner and victim. As Arens described the ritual (p. 28), the executioner tells the prisoner: "'I am he that will kill you, since you and yours have slain and eaten many of my friends.' The prisoner replies: 'When I am dead I shall still have many to avenge my death.'" Forsyth finds this evidence to be insufficient to justify the charge of plagiarism, any more than plagiarism would be charged if different independent observers used the same words to describe the Pledge of Allegiance, which is, after all, repeated with considerable similarity throughout the United States.

The exchange between executioner and prisoner is a highly ritualized exchange at the very climax of the sacrificial ceremony, and such exchanges have been described for many sacrificial situations in many different geographic locations. An analogy would be the Roman Catholic recitation of

"Hail Marys"; different independent observers would record the same ritualized prompt and response, and this would not be an instance of one observer plagiarizing from another. Forsyth noted that the short time
sequences over which different writers would have had to plagiarize these
utterances from one another, and the rate at which they would have had to
be transmitted from writer to writer, make this charge extremely unlikely.
Forsyth (1985, p. 31) drew a harsh conclusion:

> Arens' treatment of Tupinamba cannibalism is an example of poor ethnohistoric
> scholarship . . . because his methods do not meet the basic standards of histori-
> cal analysis . . . is marred by inadequate control of chronology, selective use of
> data to make his case (while ignoring data which contradict his thesis) . . . and
> a totally deficient treatment of the corroborative data available.

Other experts have tended to agree with the above criticisms. Viveiros
de Castro (1992) wrote: "I do not believe it necessary to discuss . . . the 'dis-
coveries' of Arens (1979), who reveals a profound ignorance about the
Tupinamba." Lewis (1986, p. 75) concluded: "Although Arens has attempted to discredit this picture of Tupi cannibalism by questioning
the evidence . . . the cumulative testimony is overwhelming and very
convincing." White (1992) remarked that Arens has effectively set the cannibal ledger to zero, and in so doing has challenged the academic communities to raise the standards of their evidence and scholarship—which,
incidentally, both Turner and White have met convincingly in their discussion of the osteoarchaeology of the Anasazi.

Iroquois Arens (1979) considered the claims for cannibalism
among the Iroquois to be yet another example of in-
terpretive reporting that exploited preset images the
popular media had provided of these tribes. He developed his point with reference to an essay by Tuck (1971a), which he
characterized as having originally appeared in "a magazine for the non-
specialist" (the *Scientific American*—hardly your ordinary popular periodical), remarking (pp. 127–128):

> Unfortunately, this opportunity to communicate with the general reading pub-
> lic all too often convinces an author of the necessity to jettison scientific stan-
> dards along with jargon. This sort of patronizing attitude, more than anything
> else, is a disservice to both the readership and the discipline, not to mention the
> history of those who are the subject of the study.

In a rebuttal of the points made by Arens, Abler (1980, p. 309) commented:
"Parsons should behave as they preach." Abler, who characterized his re-

buttal as applying to Arens' sloppy scholarship not cannibalism, noted that all the material he presented had been available to Arens, and concluded that Arens failed to meet the standards he expects of others.

While delivering this patronizing sermon, Arens neglected to mention that the archaeologist Tuck (1971b) published the primary account of this material in a scholarly book with Syracuse University Press in the same year. This book summarized the results of excavations carried out in Onondaga County, central New York State, during the summers of 1965 through 1967, as well as the subsequent study of collections made by other archaeologists before and after that time.

Tuck (1971b) discussed the physical evidence that suggested there was cannibalism at a site called "Bloody Hill." Incidentally, Arens objected to the name Bloody Hill, claiming that a single instance of Iroquois activity is described using the pejorative phrase the "Savage Ritual of Bloody Hill." Abler (1980) observed: "'Bloody Hill' is not an appellation created by [a] sensationalistic archaeologist to excite a sadistic reading public . . . this location was thought in local folklore to have been the site of a battle. Thus the name is an old one . . . [applied] at the turn of the century." It is a historical name, not an anthropological attribution.

Abler (1992) believes the case for cannibalism among the Iroquois in early historic times is so strong that it cannot be doubted, referring to an extensive primary literature. He referred (p. 167) to several instances of cannibalism, in one of which Mohawks ambushed a Seneca village and captured two old men who were "cut into Pieces and boyled to make Soop."

There is no doubt that the confederation of Woodland Indian tribes that lived near Lake Ontario (near modern Syracuse) spoke the Iroquois language. All sources have acknowledged that the Iroquois confederacy (originally five nations: Mohawk, Oneida, Onondaga, Cayuga, and Seneca) contained fierce warriors. Tuck (1971a) estimated that the five tribes of the confederacy never had more than 12,000 members, with only about 2,200 fighting men, yet they crushed the nearest of their traditional Algonkin-speaking enemies and destroyed Iroquois-speaking tribes that did not belong to their confederacy. The confederacy sided successfully with the British during the French and Indian Wars, and fought for the British in the American Revolutionary War, an alliance that led to the eventual destruction of the confederacy by the victorious American Revolutionaries.

Cadwallader Colden (1727), an early British administrator, characterized the Iroquois as a poor barbarous people who had, however, a bright and noble genius, and recommended to the Governor of New York that everything should be done to gain their cooperation, lest the French use them in battle. This view constitutes a grudging admiration for and fear of the capacities of the Iroquois.

Archaeological evidence supporting the idea of Iroquois cannibalism consisted of several fragments of human long bones and two human teeth discovered in a layer of topsoil. When the site was excavated, a solid layer of large fire-cracked granite rock was revealed, and beneath that numerous charred logs with three to four inches of ash. More and more human bones that bore the marks of a knife or butchering marks were encountered as excavation progressed. Tuck (1971b) suggested that "the pit was first dug to its present dimensions, a large and very hot fire was kindled within, large cobbles were used to cover the fire to form a roasting platform atop which game or other food could be roasted." He suggested that, at least some of the time, the victim of these feasts was not an animal but a human being, with the remains found at Bloody Hill being those of one such unfortunate individual. He qualified this suggestion by remarking that whether it was cannibalism or merely a ceremonial stripping of the flesh from a corpse in a mortuary ritual cannot be determined, but he favored the interpretation of cannibalism in light of the tribal narratives of the time period and the oral histories that contemporary Iroquois provided. Abler remarked, and White (1992) agreed, that the evidence of cannibalism Tuck presented is not an isolated find, given that such evidence has appeared in the archaeological record in sites dating to about AD 1300, and continues into historic times.

Snow (1994), an archaeologist/ethnohistorian, discussed Iroquois cultural history, and also is convinced there is evidence of ritual cannibalism. He placed the practice within the context of warfare, and believed it was intended to obtain power and prestige within the community, to exact revenge against neighbors for actual harm or because they had influenced supernatural agents to cause epidemics, and to take captives—females for consorts and men either as slaves or for torture and, on occasion, to be eaten.

Much of the evidence on which anthropologists have depended was based on first-hand narratives by Jesuit missionaries, the type that Arens rejects on the grounds that none of these narratives contains eyewitness descriptions of cannibalism—which several commentators have pointed out is not the case. Abler maintained that it is most unlikely Iroquois anthropophagy is simply Jesuit propaganda. Once again, there is an immense amount of material written by many Jesuits who lived for several years among the Iroquois. These accounts were collected in 40 volumes, several of which report eyewitness accounts of cannibalism by Jesuits. Harris (1985) quoted a number of these accounts to refute Arens' contention that although the Jesuits often referred to Iroquois cruelty and cannibalism, they did not present eyewitness descriptions of cannibalism.

The evidence against Arens' assertions is convincing, just as in the case of the Tupinamba, in light of consistent details concerning many aspects of

160

Myth in Anthropology

Iroquois behavior and various independent accounts of Iroquois customs. There are also corroborating accounts provided by European settlers as well as the content of myths and oral histories of contemporary Iroquois. Once again, it seems unreasonable to suppose that the Jesuits were preferentially unbelievable: descriptions of the warlike game of lacrosse, at which the Indians spent considerable time and energy and still play today, are believable, but descriptions of cannibalism are not.

Among pieces of physical evidence that testify to the fierceness of the Iroquois are a large number of severed finger bones and other evidence of torture found in village refuse middens. Many captives were adopted and became full members of their adoptive nations, often being given the names of a recently lost relative the captive was to replace, or a name selected from a set of traditional names owned by the clan—practices I have mentioned earlier for other tribal groups.

Edward Westermarck and Incest

Arens' views regarding biological influences on human behavior typify those of many in the social sciences. Because I consider these views of human nature to be mistaken I will examine them further. Arens criticized the views of Westermarck on the subject of incest (Arens, 1986), and the reasons he rejects those views will highlight some of the problems I see. Degler (1991) described Westermarck (a sociologist with both a Ph.D. and LL.D.) as a self-taught Finnish anthropologist who was a confirmed adherent to Darwin's conception of human evolution. Westermarck (1906, 1908) published two large volumes entitled *The Origin and Development of Moral Ideas*, and in the second volume he summarized the ideas for which he is best remembered—the origin and development of the incest taboo. Arens (p. 67) characterized Westermarck as "overwhelmingly impressed by evolutionary biology, and in particular Darwin's." Westermarck's central idea regarding avoidance of incest was that human erotic feelings were weak within families, which he attributed to an instinctive aversion to sexual intercourse between persons who have been living closely together from early youth, with this aversion the result of natural selection.

Many of Westermarck's theoretical views regarding incest have received considerable research support in recent times. For example, Wolf (1980) found that in China, when a young son and a resident daughter of the same age were raised together, the marriages generally were reproductively unsuccessful, the couples hated the marriage, and divorces were four times greater among these couples compared to those not reared together. In Israel, a number of studies involving hundreds of young people raised in kibbutzim revealed that there were no marriages and very few extramarital sexual liaisons among members of the same peer group (Shepher, 1983). In this case, the aversion was voluntary, there being no enforcement of marriage rules, although the children's parents often encouraged marriage (Parker, 1976). Another compelling study was done by McCabe (1983) on arranged marriages in Lebanon between a son of one brother and the daughter of another brother, with the couple raised in close proximity; divorces were four times more frequent and there were 23% fewer children than in marriages between unrelated persons. An interesting aspect of this study is that the success of marriages between cousins who did not grow up with each other was similar to that found between unrelated persons, which indicates that the operative factor is familiarity rather than genetic closeness.

Degler suggested that one reason Westermarck occupies an obscure place in the history of cultural thought is that he did not assume a sharp discontinuity between the behavior of animals and human beings; he explained the incest taboo in such a way that it places human beings in the Darwinian continuum of natural beings and processes. And this tendency has drawn the ire of many social scientists, particularly cultural anthropologists.

Ford and Beach (1951), in their classic book *Patterns of Sexual Behavior,* suggested that incest taboos have arisen and persisted during societal evolution not only for genetic reasons, but because they provide a protective device against disintegration of the nuclear family. These taboos minimize intrafamilial sexual jealousies and conflicts within the nuclear family—the basic cooperative reproductive unit in human society. They noted that close inbreeding has unfortunate biological consequences as well.

Arens (1986, p. *xi*) wrote: "I am extremely wary of both implications and errors of what has come to be known as sociobiology. . . . I place greater emphasis than usual on the role of culture, in the form of human inventiveness, with regard to an understanding of incestuous behavior." He endorsed the view that if there were no natural inclinations to commit incest, then why would a prohibition against incest exist? Westermarck's views regarding the development of a nearly universal taboo, even though the practice is selected against, are much to the mark. As Degler (1991) pointed out, good analogies to incest are suicide and murder, both of which are selected against and widely prohibited. Even though the social rules are redundant with the outcome of selection, they still are universal. Degler (1991, p. 264) noted that "culture and biology worked in the same direction, namely, to enhance reproductive success."

Arens describes Westermarck's position as such a glaring fallacy of reasoning that it is hard to imagine how it could have gone unconsidered by Westermarck. Arens (1986, p. 74) suggested, quite correctly, that Westermarck's "relative neglect can be deduced primarily to the contemporary rejection of his dismal view of human nature. This outlook on humanity became exceedingly more unfashionable with the rise of the social sciences, whose concerns and answers provided more positive contrasting images."

Arens (1986, p. 78) offered a weak explanation of the research findings cited above: "[Wolf failed] . . . to note some other variable embedded in the . . . arrangement that could affect the quality and outcome of the union." However, he did not specify what that other variable is or how it might have affected the union. Of course, there could always be a confounding variable that might have influenced the outcome of any study, but unless it and its influence are identified, such a suggestion amounts to little more than a refusal to accept the conclusion.

Arens considers this research to offer only tentative support to the aversion hypothesis in other ethnographic settings, and that the notions of contemporary sociobiology, with its new vocabulary to replace worn-out notions of instinct and sentiment, often evoke an emotional and acrimonious response. He concluded (p. 81): "Linking animals to humans has never been an attractive equation in social science, while the study of animal behavior for clues to humanity is looked upon with even more disfavor."

I believe Arens is correct in his assessment of the tactics and strategies of many in the social sciences, and consider the development of these tactics to be a primary cause of the lack of success social scientists have had in developing adequate general theories of human behavior. In addition, Westermarck's views were not in accord with those developed by Freud regarding the central core of the incest taboo, and the dominant role psychoanalytic thinking assumed for many social scientists might well have pushed him into the background. I have analyzed at considerable length the problems and issues involved in using general evolutionary principles to understand the similarities and differences between behaviors and social structures in humans and in other animals, and refer the interested reader to that extensive discussion (Petrinovich, 1999).

Westermarck and Cannibalism   Westermarck devoted an entire 29-page chapter to cannibalism in his second volume, which Arens did not mention in *The Man-Eating Myth* (1979). Either he had not read the book in 1979, when the *Myth* was published, or he read it later and has neglected to mention that fact anywhere. Westermarck's discussion is comprehensive, citing a huge literature that was available at the turn of the twentieth century describing all types of cannibalism: for survival, revenge and humiliation, mortuary, religious, and to obtain the powers of friends, relatives, and enemies. His views are strikingly modern in the sense that they emphasized many of the points regarding natural selection now accepted by evolutionary biologists. Arens is probably correct that Westermarck has not been accorded more recognition, given his belief that laws applying to the rest of the animal kingdom, as well as to plants, should apply to man.

Abler (1980) hinted at the political agenda behind many of Arens' views, and considered it dishonest to discuss Iroquois torture and cannibalism without acknowledging its cruelty. However, Abler stated (p. 315) that it "pales beside the cruel injuries and deaths inflicted on military and civilian populations through the socially approved use of 'legitimate' weapons by 20th century 'civilization'. . . .It is not that the seventeenth century Iroquois were inhuman, but rather they were like the rest of us, all too human in their treatment of other men." A similar sentiment was expressed by Montaigne (1580), who commented that we emphasize the horrible savagery of things such as cannibalism, although we are blind to savagery of our own, such as tearing by the rack and torture of a body still full of feeling—and all of it under the cloak of piety and religion. It is to the political agenda and to the misconstrual of arguments regarding an evolved human nature to which I will now turn.

SUSTAINING MISCONCEPTIONS

Throughout this book I have discussed misconceptions that sustain the arguments of those generally opposed to biological explanations of complex human behavior. These basic misconceptions seem to satisfy those who espouse the standard postmodernist position that emphasizes the importance of cultural relativity (Osborne, 1997). I believe this position is based partly on acceptance of the notion that "primitive people" were noble savages whose nobility was diminished and finally eliminated through the actions and policies of representatives of "civilized society." This belief system persists despite the numerous disclaimers offered by those tarred with the brush of "sociobiology."

The issues that concern this chapter can be illuminated by considering the methodological and ideological stances endorsed by many cultural anthropologists. Much of the evidence regarding cannibalism has been gathered by both cultural and physical anthropologists. The mainstream methods and ideologies of these two anthropological disciplines differ radically. One dominant view within cultural anthropology, based on the beliefs of Franz Boas, emphasized the importance of cultural influences. These views were promulgated in an even more extreme form by his many colleagues and students, including Ruth Benedict and Alfred Kroeber. The views within physical anthropology, influenced strongly by evolutionary biology, were espoused by those who studied primate behavior and archaeology. Not only did the basic views differ, the methods and standards of objectivity required differed as well.

These two faces of anthropology have barely managed to coexist; many (but certainly not all) cultural anthropologists reject evolutionary explanations, considering them to be little more than "a plug for biological determinism," as Eleanor Leacock (1992, p. 4) characterized Derek Freeman's (1983) criticism of the Samoan research of Margaret Mead (1928).

Biological Determinism Revisited   I have discussed the nature of evolutionary mechanisms in Chapter 2 of this book and in greater detail elsewhere (Petrinovich, 1995, 1996, 1999). The charge of biological (genetic) determinism still leveled against "sociobiologists" (a label that seems to encompass anyone stressing the evolutionary continuity between complex aspects of the behavior and social structures found for humans and those of other animals) makes little sense as anything other than pejorative attribution.

Serious investigation of the interplay of the large number of factors involved in the development of complex behaviors makes it clear that there is no such thing as a genetic or biological determinism at work in the thinking of current "sociobiologists." There are inherited physical and behavioral characteristics and predispositions, and these are influenced, from the moment of conception, by physiological and environmental factors. It can only be hoped that some day people will stop arguing whether biology or culture is the more important—as most of us with a sociobiological orientation have long ago ceased to do. Such a question is no more sensible than asking whether the height or width of a rectangle is more important in determining its area. Ehrenreich (1997, p. 88) expressed the issue nicely:

> But those who value human freedom have little to fear from genetic types of explanations anyway. Even in an environment favorable to their expression, the existence of inherited predispositions does not condemn us to enact them. If it could be shown, for example, that humans have an innate taste for male domination, or for bloodshed, or any other form of nastiness, we could seek to order our social arrangements so as to counter this tendency.

A few of Arens' (1986) statements regarding incest are interesting examples of a faulty characterization of evolutionary theory and also misrepresent biological data. [By the way, I do not disagree continually with Arens' construal of biological issues because his views are particularly bad. I use his phrasings as examples because his views are germane to the particular issues of cannibalism and incest with which I have been dealing.] When discussing questions regarding the effects of inbreeding and outbreeding, Arens remarked that this is an issue that has compelled the attention of anthropologists and sociologists, but not of biologists and geneticists as much. This is a mind-boggling statement. Any elementary or advanced textbook treatment of evolutionary mechanisms considers problems that arise as the result of intensive, close inbreeding. In fact, avoiding these effects and maintaining the desired genetic variability in a breeding population from generation to generation are considered to be among the reasons sexual reproduction is the dominant mode used by most plant and animal species. There are numerous specialized technical treatments of these issues, including any of the general textbooks on evolution cited in the references: Bell (1997), Mayr (1970), or Sober (1984).

The distinction between proximate and ultimate factors in evolutionary explanations continues to be one of the most difficult for many to grasp. The ultimate factor, in evolutionary terminology, is differential reproductive success (RS), expressed in terms of contributing genes to succeeding generations of offspring, who are able to continue the process through the generations. Natural selection, however, does not influence genes directly; selection is at the level of the physical characteristics (phenotype) of individual organisms. If the selection of certain characteristics is strong enough, if these characteristics are heritable, and if possessing them gives individuals an advantage in the game of reproduction, then those characteristics will become more frequent in the breeding population, other things being equal. When this is the case, the individual members of the population should be able to cope more successfully with the demands the environment poses, and those genes involved in the inheritance of phenotypic characteristics will become fixed at high levels in the population.

Avoidance of incest enhances the RS of individuals by making it possible to avoid the deleterious effects of inbreeding, and also makes it easier to maintain a cooperative and supportive nuclear family unit, given the absence of destructive competition between nuclear family members for mates. This family can be extended to encompass others in the community, and the population will come to contain more individuals who avoid incestuous matings, with the important proviso that these tendencies are heritable.

Is the failure to understand this issue a problem? For Arens (1986, p. 98) it is: "a rule against sex or marriage characterizes human society, and such regulations can be expressed in a variety of ways as the result of the creation of elaborate social categories having little or nothing to do with biological considerations." Rules regarding sex and marriage are intimate to the game of reproduction, and although the rules may vary from culture to culture, they must not lead to the defeat of the ultimate goal—reproductive success—if the society is to remain viable. Arens continued: "Apparently anything is possible when the human mind contemplates sexual or marriage prohibition." Maybe any scheme is possible, but some will be less successful than others, will fail the test of ultimate RS, and thereby suffer in the competition with others for the resources that sustain life. True, many kinds of rules, regulations, and customs will work, so there will be great variability from culture to culture, and even from group to group—but they all have to serve (or at least must not defeat) the ultimate end in a satisfactory manner. Arens (p. 100) just does not understand this, as evidenced by his belief that "Culture and, thus, incest have been features of our existence for some time, resulting in a potential greater tolerance for inbreeding among humans in comparison to other species, which follow the dictates of nature." Hardly any animal species blindly follows "the dictates of nature," and humans are not freed from constraints regarding basic physiology, the pressures of natural selection, or the relative merits of different modes of reproduction.

It is generally agreed that human language is an inherited capacity, and that possessing a language confers a competitive advantage to humans who have it compared to other animals (Pinker, 1994). There is a wide variety of elaborate languages and dialects found throughout the world, but this does not mean language has little or nothing to do with biological considerations. It means only that the inherited ability to develop language is a generalized capacity on which auditory inputs of many different types can be mapped within an appropriate developmental sequence. The ultimate selective advantage can be realized through the development of various proximate forms, but any true language provides an advantage, and this advantage enhances RS, albeit in a number of different ways.

Arens and Cannibalism Revisited   Arens (1979) has difficulties deciding what to make of conclusions regarding the existence of cannibalism based on anthropological evidence. On the one hand (p. 8) he worried that anthropophagy is one of the unchallenged "facts" of anthropology that guides "some basic anthropological assumptions about human nature which have managed to ingratiate themselves within the discipline." He continued (p. 9): "I propose that anthropology has not maintained the usual standards of documentation and intellectual rigor expected when other topics are being considered." He complained about (p. 10) the "thinly disguised prejudices of western culture about others."

On the other hand, he later (p. 109) complained: "cannibalism has a sporadic revival whenever there are no anthropologists to observe . . . if it ever existed, cannibalism was no longer extant when the ethnographers were present." Here it appears that we should require the testimony of these flawed observers, their thinly disguised prejudices and all. He questioned (p. 119) the findings of paleontologists, physical anthropologists, archeologists, and prehistorians who "stray from their realms of expertise, begin to muse on the primal nature of the beast and attempt to drape the bones and stones with a cultural mantle." He suggested that "they have little choice but to draw on the work of their colleagues in social anthropology who study more contemporary primitive man." Social anthropologists are now the good guys, but a few pages later (p. 133) he suggested that archeologists and paleontologists arrive at some of their more indefensible deductions due to "their unsuspecting reliance on the contributions of social anthropologists whose research methods are not as rigorous." His views regarding the reliability and validity of the observations of social anthropologists seem to vacilate: At times he considers them the best source of information; at other times he says that they use research methods that are not rigorous, which results in the presentation of thinly disguised prejudices as fact. Wagner (1979, p. 269) also expressed concern regarding this ambivalence in her review of Arens' book: She remarked that he challenges the idea that cannibalism ever existed because there are no first-hand accounts by anthropologists; but she considers much of the book to be "a very heated attack on both the discipline of anthropology and his colleagues in this field."

This discussion is not intended to be an attack on the methods of cultural anthropologists. Rather, its intent is to highlight some of the problems that plague any attempt to understand a foreign culture—be it human or nonhuman. As Popper (1979, p. 342) reminded us, observation plays a decisive role in science, but it is a process in which the observer plays an active part. We do not "have" an observation, we "make" an observation, and we make it with an expectation. "An observation is always preceded by a particular interest, a question, or a problem—in short, by something theoretical." Given that even the most primitive observation always presupposes the existence of expectations, it is important to consider the reliability of observations of different people at different times, and to search for possible biasing influences on those observations. If this is the case for simple observation, then it is an even more serious consideration when making complex observations of the entities that characterize a culture.

Our goal should be to develop strong observational methods to use when conducting field studies. Just as important as questions regarding the quality of observational data is the necessity to use converging lines of evidence to assess the realities of interest. Here, I refer to the examination of mythology, historical records (including archaeological, whenever it is pertinent), direct observation, and statements of various kinds by informants. In the studies of cannibalism in different cultures, when these lines of evidence converge to give a similar picture, matters become much more convincing. I conclude that the anthropological, historical, mythological, and archaeological evidence converges, making the story of cannibalism more than a myth.

8

Political
Famines and
Starvation

To taste the sea all one needs is one gulp.—

Aleksandri I. Solzhenitsyn (1974)

Doubts have been expressed as to whether cannibalism still exists anywhere in the world, and even if it ever existed. Of course, it is difficult to observe something directly if it no longer exists. Using a similar logic doubt has been expressed as to whether the holocaust took place, because there is a paucity of eyewitness accounts of people being gassed. If the only acceptable evidence regarding natural occurrences is direct observation, we would have little to study in the realms of evolutionary biology or archaeology, and would have to abandon historical disciplines that rely on amassing circumstantial evidence to speak to an issue. Care must be taken if reconstructions of the past are used to develop theories, particularly regarding the processes at work, but it is necessary to make the attempt in order to understand the course of events that have shaped us. I have emphasized throughout this book, as well as in my other three books discussing the processes and outcomes of human evolution, that it is necessary to construct conceptual models, and then to evaluate those models using multiple sources of evidence. These different lines of evidence provide the convergence required to evaluate and refine models in order to arrive at more convincing explanations and to make better predictions.

There is general agreement that ritual cannibalism may have been widespread in the past, but that most of it has been eliminated under the onslaught of colonization, westernization, and Christian conversion. It should be kept in mind that even if this is the case, the savageries of cannibalism and torture have been replaced by more civilized savageries—

phosphorous grenades, chemical defoliants, nerve gases, napalm, land mines, and nuclear and biological bombs and weapons.

Although ritual cannibalism seems largely to have been eliminated, as far as we know, there have been numerous well-documented reports of survival cannibalism in the twentieth century. Among those to be discussed in this chapter are the Ukrainian famine of 1918–1922 and the second Russian famine in 1930–1932. This sequence of famines in Russia was replicated in China in 1949–1958 when the government enforced policies of agrarian reform during the Great Leap Forward; these policies were similar to those that had failed in Russia. In all three of these famines cannibalism was rampant, as it was again in the Cultural Revolution in China between 1958 and 1962.

The first of the famines in Russia and China were not due to natural disasters or fluctuations in environmental conditions, but to faulty economic and agricultural policies driven by a common political doctrine. Although the weather was intermittently bad during these periods, it was not bad enough to cause disaster. Rather, the famine was due primarily to crop requisitions, which took so much of the crops that the peasants were unable to survive, and to the fact that the peasants were not allowed to keep what they produced; these policies effectively removed incentives to produce. The second famine in Russia, and the cannibalism in China during the Cultural Revolution, were the result of policies introduced to serve the goals of political revenge and repression of dissent.

There were two famines that occurred in the nineteenth century that will not be discussed here—the Irish famine of 1845–1851 and the Indian famine of 1876–1878. These famines were primarily due to natural causes compounded by bureaucratic blundering and lack of concern. There were earlier instances of cannibalism in Europe—for example, in Sancerre, France in 1753 (Lestringant, 1997). In this case there was a long siege, and a family was found to have eaten their dead child. The Protestant missionary, Jean Léry (who had witnessed cannibalism among the Tupinamba), described the remains of the child in detail. He wrote (Lestringant, 1997, p. 74): "I was so afraid and taken aback, that my stomach heaved." Other instances of cannibalism occurred during this period in other "peaceful corners" of provincial France, such as Auxerre and Sens. I will not discuss these cases further, but will concentrate on the more recent, more extreme, and better documented cases in Russia and China.

I will discuss the aforementioned starvation (some accompanied by cannibalism) that took place in World War II in Russia, China, and in various prison camps throughout the world. These examples provide the strong evidence that some deny exists of cannibalism among civilized people in modern times.

RUSSIAN FAMINES

First, some general historical and political factors that preceded the two Russian famines will be discussed. Because political theory and history are far afield in terms of my professional training and competence, I will avoid going into details regarding aspects of political ideology in order to concentrate on the documented effects of social policies on food production. I will present enough background material to provide a fuller understanding of the dynamics causing the starvation that led to cannibalism.

I have relied on the writings of Robert Conquest (1986), whose book *Harvest of Sorrow* contains a wealth of statistical information, albeit embedded in a heavy context of anecdote, accounts drawn from fiction, and a strong antisoviet bias. Although Conquest presented a large number of anecdotes and newspaper reports, he defended this practice on the grounds that the sheer amount of evidence is enormous and it is all mutually confirmatory. In one passage he wrote (p. 9): "Almost every particular incident in the village recounted here could be matched by a dozen, sometimes even a hundred, more." I have considered his accounts of the Russian famines in light of accounts provided by others, in particular, Becker (1996), whose book *Hungry Ghosts* will be referred to in the discussion of the Chinese disasters that succeeded each of the Russian ones, and the book by Yang (1996), a political scientist who grew up in the Chinese countryside (Shandong province) just after the Great Leap Forward. I have also examined the three *Gulag Archipelago* volumes by Solzhenitsyn (1973, 1974, 1978), the account by Fisher (1927) of the relief efforts of the American Relief Administration, the general discussion of the effects of war and famine on human behavior by Sorokin (1942), and the discussion of life in Siberia by Bardach and Gleeson (1998)—as well as the descriptions of the Kolyma gulag in the Solzhenitsyn books. I present detailed information provided by the historian Fitzpatrick (1994) that supports the narratives presented by the others. She had access to official Soviet archives that were made available starting in 1988. These archives contained official records as well as letters and petitions to government officials by peasants throughout the time the Soviets were in power. These accounts confirm and elaborate the account presented by Conquest, and all weave a consistent pattern.

Sorokin (1942) enumerated a number of major famines in which cannibalism occurred in ancient Egypt, ancient Greece and Rome, Persia, India, China, and Japan. For Europe, he listed 11 such instances that took place between AD 793 and 1317. From all indications, it has not been at all unusual for cannibalism to take place under conditions of severe and prolonged starvation under a wide range of situations. Walford (1879), in his book *Famines of the World,* tabulated 350 famines that had occurred before 1878, in nine of which he indicated cannibalism had taken place. The countries in which cannibalism occurred included Italy, England, Ireland, Egypt, India, and North China. The events described for Russia and China could well be typical, rather than aberrant examples of human behavior under extreme circumstances.

At the conclusion of this chapter, when prison camp starvation is described, I will return to a discussion of Russia to consider the starvation in the Siberian mines and gulags of Kolyma. I will also discuss a few other instances of cannibalism during World War II.

Background
Russia has had a long history during which there was a class of peasants who were serfs, having what amounted to the standing of slaves or indentured servants, and required to work the land to provide food for the urban population. There were a number of different provinces in what became the Soviet Union, each with its unique ethnic identity and strong nationalistic loyalty. Fitzpatrick (1994) cited estimates indicating that Russia's population was about 140 million on the eve of the First World War, about four-fifths of which was rural and predominantly peasant at the time of the 1917 revolution. There was little in the way of modern agricultural technology available; only half of the peasant farms had iron plows, sickles were used for reaping, and flails were used for threshing. Conquest (1986) remarked that even in the 1920s, the wheat and rye yield in Russia was only slightly higher than for fourteenth-century English estates, and by 1921 only 20,000 tons of fertilizer was used, down from 700,000 tons in 1913.

Many of the disasters that befell the Russian people were due to political rivalries between different parties vying for control of the country following the revolution. Policies were announced because they sounded reasonable and effective, and were politically acceptable, but often they were not based on or actually defied reliable statistical estimates of production or realistic considerations of the possibility of achieving such estimates. They were presented primarily to enable those in power to gain political advantages—both to achieve political dominance and to justify revenge on the opposition.

Conquest (1986) identified two major political goals of the postrevolutionary government in Russia: One was "dekulakization" and the other was "collectivization." The kulak was described by Lenin as a rich exploitive peasant class that should be eliminated after all landlords had been removed. There was no consistent definition of what qualified a peasant to be designated as kulak: Sometimes it was owning livestock, sometimes employing laborers, sometimes possessing means of production of a certain value or giving credit to neighbors, and sometimes having a sizable sown area on a farm. The designation as kulak extended to the peasant's wife and children. Soviet statisticians estimated that at the end of the Civil War only 3% of peasant households were categorized as kulak, compared to 15% before the revolution (Fitzpatrick, 1994). Local Party leaders could label someone a kulak at their discretion. Although shifting criteria might appear to present a problem, they were useful, because any group or individual that officials wanted to characterize as a class enemy could be designated as kulak, which justified the confiscation of property, exile, or execution.

By 1918, a central aim of the government was to abolish the peasant's right to sell grain. To prevent such sales, the state declared that it had the authority to seize any grain surplus. A peasant who held grain back was categorized as a kulak, whose hoarded grain was forcibly collected by special food detachments of reliable urban workers. This myth that peasants were hoarding grain was used to justify setting even higher grain quotas for the villages. The amount of grain to be collected was determined by the needs of the state, with no concern for how much grain was left for the peasant. By 1929, the peasants' response was to bury grain, first on their own land and then in odd waste areas, haystacks, churches, and out in the countryside. Early in 1929 complete dekulakization was begun. Conquest quoted Stalin to the effect that dekulakization was now an essential element in forming and developing collective farms, asserting that it was wrong to admit the kulak into the collective farm because he is an accursed enemy of the collective farm movement. Stalin announced that he had moved from a policy of limiting the tendencies of the kulak to exploit to a policy of liquidating the kulak as a class. Stalin believed this to be an essential step in winning the struggle against the capitalist elements of the peasantry—the kulaks. To achieve this end hundreds of thousands of people were classified as kulak, their lands were expropriated, and they were deported.

Conquest (1986) claimed that in 1922, famine in the Ukraine was concealed, and the only information available was that provided by the official American Relief Administration Reports. This concealment was achieved by estimating the crop at levels that were almost twice the figure accepted by local authorities. The outcome was that almost all surplus grain was taken, leaving the peasants with an inadequate amount to survive, little seed grain, and little incentive to produce. The famine occurred because the central authorities set grain quotas far above possible levels of production, removed all surplus food, and at the outset displayed a reluctance to accept help from the outside to relieve the starving. These tendencies, plus the ability of authorities to control the dissemination of information, made it possible to conceal or confuse the facts—all of which led to a disastrous famine.

The other goal was collectivization—to force a transition from individual peasant farming to collective, socially conducted agriculture. Fitzpatrick (1994) noted that the drive to collectivize came from the central state, not from within the village, and that the main purpose was to increase state grain procurements and reduce the peasants' ability to withhold grain from the market. The new collective farms were organized by outside rural officials supplemented by tens of thousands of urban Communists who were not farmers, but workers and students sent out to the countryside. By introducing more efficient and scientific methods of collective farming, the problem of food shortages were to be eliminated, which would make it impossible for another class of kulaks to arise.

The results were mixed; dekulakization was eminently successful, in the sense that by the end of the first Five-Year Plan in 1933 (which Mao later copied as the plan for China) kulaks essentially had been eliminated, with millions killed or sent to labor camps. Conquest (1986) reported that in 1923, 67% of those shot by order of the courts were peasants. The problem was that these persecutions eliminated the most effective agricultural producers (who were by definition kulaks—the 3–5% of peasant households that produced around 20% of the grain), who were replaced with less effective elements of the peasantry or with inexperienced urban recruits. Conquest's analysis of Soviet data indicates that according to the original plan the number of kulak families to be put in camps or labor colonies was close to 1,065,000—about 5 to 6 million people. This estimate could be on the high side: Fitzpatrick noted that a Politburo commission headed by V. M. Molotov drew up guidelines to send about 60,000 kulaks to concentration camps, and to deport 150,000 households—the total goal being to dekulakize 3–5% of all peasant households. Even the lower estimate supports the conclusion that there was mass terror and destabilization of the peasant population.

The positive goal of collectivization was announced in the Five-Year Plan, which began in 1928. The plan was intended to double steel output and triple both pig-iron and tractor production within 5 years. The investment for industrialization was to come from the peasant sector, which was to be brought under control in collective farms (Becker, 1996). Stalin favored the creation of large grain factories of 50,000 to 100,000 hectares, a goal that was later cut to between 40,000 to 50,000, and by 1929 most small peasant holdings were merged into collectives (Conquest, 1986). The first step toward collectivization was to seize and remove the peasants' livestock (horses, cows, pigs, sheep, and even chickens in some cases) and make them the property of the collective farm (Fitzpatrick, 1994). The response of peasants was to slaughter and eat a significant proportion of their livestock.

One major problem was that the tractors required to meet the ambitious goals were not available, and wooden plows were not adequate to the task.

The lack of modernization required to develop large collective farms was a major factor leading to their failure to provide food for the large number of factory workers required to meet industrial goals. The lack of tractors was even more disastrous; because of a lack of food, combined with no incentive to produce what they could not keep, the peasants killed and ate their cattle and horses, leaving too few horses to pull plows in the absence of tractors. The number of horses in the Soviet Union dropped from 34 million in 1916 to only 15 million in 1934, and 37% of all peasant households in the Russian Republic lacked a draft animal of any kind (Fitzpatrick, 1994).

This disastrous state of affairs was compounded by reliance on the faulty views of agricultural science imposed by Lysenko, who ruled Soviet agricultural scientists as a dictator—those scientists who opposed him were either sent to labor camps or shot. Lysenko dismissed the science of genetics, relying instead on a theory emphasizing the primary role of environmental factors. This theory held that changes in plants acquired through manipulations of the environment would be transmitted to the next generation—implementation of the rejected Lamarckian notions of evolution. For example, he decided that winter wheat seeds could be turned into more productive spring seeds by soaking them in very cold water, which would produce a physiological change; unfortunately for the farmers this was not true. When the seedlings were sown they did not sprout at all. The frost-resistant wheat and rye seeds that Lysenko had had developed, the potatoes to be grown in summer, and the sugar beet planted in the hot plains of Central Asia all rotted. The Soviet press did not report these failures, but presented fanciful descriptions of the development of cows that produced only cream, barley transformed into oats, and lemon trees that blossomed in Siberia (Becker, 1986).

The agricultural authorities opposed using chemical fertilizers or planting hybrid corn developed in the United States—hybrids that had boosted U.S. yields by 30%. Furrows were to be plowed 4 or 5 feet deep to improve soil texture and obtain higher yields. Another innovation was to plant seeds and saplings close together to capitalize on Lysenko's law that individuals of the same species do not compete, but help one another to survive. These techniques led to disastrous crop failures in Russia, and (as will be discussed below) later in China.

Ukraine
Dekulakization

It has been estimated that 10% of the population in the Ukraine perished between 1917 and 1921 from hunger, and famine was raging in Kazakhastan by the spring of 1932. Solzhenitsyn (1973) remarked that shortly after the end of the revolution, famine existed to the point of cannibalism, with parents reduced to eating their own children. I will concentrate on only two of the several famines that have occurred in Russia in this century. The first is the Ukrainian famine, the result of the desire to rid the area of kulaks. The Soviets completely occupied the Ukraine by 1920, and set in motion policies, such as crop requisition, that caused the famine of 1921–1922, which took some 5 million lives (Conquest, 1986). Even though there was massive famine, Stalin had negotiated a treaty with Germany, and carloads of food supplies were being sent from the Ukraine to Germany.

The Soviet government finally admitted there was famine, and relief from abroad was actively encouraged for the first time. Fisher (1927) described the efforts of the American Relief Administration, which was active in the Volga region. The relief personnel encountered incredible bureaucratic chaos and corruption. It was difficult for relief personnel to accomplish anything without making bribes and giving tips for services to those in charge of warehouses and supply depots. It has been remarked by almost every observer that throughout all the political famines to be described, there was an elite who were always well supplied (Conquest called them the "priviligentsia"). These agents of the state and party were always allowed adequate rations throughout periods of famine. Another factor contributing to famine was that the most efficient tax collectors were rewarded, whereas those inclined to accept the peasants' lower (and more accurate) estimates of production were dismissed or punished (Fisher, 1927).

Starvation among villagers was extreme by the time American Relief workers arrived. Village clerks no longer kept death records, and those villagers still alive subsisted on food substitutes. If any grain was available it was mixed with chaff, or with ground-up weeds and acorns. If there was no grain, concoctions of weeds, tree bark, and even clay and manure were mixed and consumed. All domestic animals, including dogs and cats, had either died of starvation or been killed for food. As is usual in episodes of starvation, young children and the elderly died first, followed by men, with women tending to survive the longest.

Fisher (1927) claimed that in the more remote communities the "final degradation" of cannibalism took place. He remarked that peasants, crazed with hunger, had eaten the flesh of animals dug up from the ground, soon followed by the practice of eating the flesh of dead humans. Sorokin (1942) wrote that in many places the cemeteries had to be guarded to prevent the exhumation of recently buried corpses. Although no statistics are available, Sorokin believed that there may have been hundreds, if not thousands of cases of cannibalism, and mentioned that such reports became so common they could be found in almost any issue of Soviet newspapers at the end of 1921, and throughout 1922.

At the time some argued that eating human flesh was not a crime, because the living soul of the consumed person had departed—an argument we have encountered earlier when other cases of disaster were discussed. Because cannibalism was not covered in the criminal code, those accused of it were transferred to the Security Police. Conquest claimed that 325 cannibals from the Ukraine—75 men and 250 women—were serving life sentences in Baltic-White Sea Canal prison camps by the late 1930s. The pattern of events in this politically induced instance of cannibalism is similar to that observed in disasters: First foodstuffs and animals are consumed, then protein materials such as ground bone mixed with flour, then organic material that is not usually acceptable as food, and then dead humans; finally there is active killing for consumption, and in these famines, for sale.

Fisher reported a case in which only the head of a victim had been found. On investigation at the market where the head was discovered, it was found the murderer had cut up the victim's body and sold the flesh to a Persian, who sold it in the market. This case resulted in the issuance of an order by city authorities forbidding the sale of meatballs, cutlets, and all forms of hashed meats. One physician reported to the League of Nations that cannibalism was spreading rapidly—the result of 22 million people being directly endangered by starvation. Soviet officials continued, for a time, to tell the world that the famine had been conquered and Russia could take care of itself.

Fisher (1927, p. 436) reported that the Chief of the Department of Mental and Nervous Diseases of Kharkov University had run down all rumored cases of cannibalism, and was able to establish the authenticity of 26 case in which humans were killed and eaten by their murderers, along with seven cases in which murder was committed and the bodies were sold. In these latter cases the flesh was disguised in the form of sausage and sold on the open market. The practice of eating the dead was reported to be common in all districts.

Keys et al. (1950) cited a Russian source claiming that in one district there were hundreds of thousands of deaths from starvation, a few hundred cases of cannibalism, and dozens of instances of murder and cannibalism. Keys et al. (p. 792) concluded: "The resort to human flesh, often after months of ever-increasing hunger pangs, appeared to be an animal-like reaction without painful emotional overtones." So, again and again, the unthinkable occurs—what Sorokin (1942, p. 66) characterized as probably the strongest inhibition possessed by noncannibalistic people, "since the mere idea of such a practice fills them with loathing and disgust."

Famine and starvation persisted until the winter of 1921–1922 when authorities permitted American corn to reach the area. Admitting that there was famine and permitting relief aid signaled a retreat for the Soviets from assertions that there were only minor problems due to weather and distribution. The policies of 1922 were abandoned and unrealistically high grain quotas were eliminated, which allowed some of the productive peasantry to resume their agricultural practices for a time.

Political   By 1928, the state decided once again to confiscate
Repression and   grain produced in the Ukraine, and once again the
Collectivization   myth of hoarding was used to justify setting high
                                        grain quotas for villages. The peasants wanted the
collective farms to help them in bad years, and believed their needs should
be met before state procurements were taken. Managers of collective farms
objected to high quotas because they knew that meeting the quotas in one
year would only mean that the quotas would be higher next year. Higher
level officials would reject hard-luck stories, but pass them on to Moscow
to justify low quotas for their region, hopefully to excuse any shortfalls. All
of this resulted in wildly unrealistic grain production targets, leading to the
confiscation of even the seed grain required for the next year's sowing.
Once again, peasants began burying grain as conditions worsened, and urban party members were sent into the countryside to collect grain from
peasants. So much grain was confiscated that the peasants suffered, with
mass starvation and death beginning in early March 1933 (Conquest, 1986;
Fitzpatrick, 1994). It has been estimated that about 20–25% of the 20–25
million Ukrainian farm population died during this famine. Stalin had allowed relief grain to be given to drought-stricken areas in Russia in 1931,
but not to the Ukraine (Becker, 1996).

It was reported that peasants ate anything: they ate mice, rats, sparrows,
ants, and earthworms; bones, leather, and shoe soles were ground into
flour; old skins and furs were cut up to make "noodles," which were
cooked into glue and consumed; roots were dug up and anything that grew
in the spring was eaten. In Kharkov, in 1932, the police removed as many
as 250 corpses every morning from the railway station. Becker cited reports
by the Italian Consul in the Ukrainian capital of Kharkov that there was a
growing commerce in human meat.

Given the massive levels of starvation, grain collection in the Ukraine
was officially halted on March 15, 1933. People were given bread and the
starving were fed milk and buckwheat porridge, and by the end of May
deaths by famine on a mass scale virtually ended. As in the disasters described earlier, women and girls tended to recover better than did men and
boys.

By 1934, nine-tenths of the sown acreage was concentrated in 240,000
collective farms, which had replaced the 20 million family farms that existed in 1929 (Conquest, 1986). Fitzpatrick (1994) estimated that the total
transfer of population from village to town over the period from 1928 to
1932 was in the range of 12 million, with men (particularly the young,

strong, and energetic) leaving in greater numbers than women. The number of peasant households in the Soviet Union dropped from 26 million in 1929 to 19 million in 1937. This means that collective farms contained far fewer workers than previously. This mass exodus led to the introduction of internal passports to halt the exodus of peasants into towns, and the passport system remained in effect until the 1970s.

Given the flawed agricultural policies discussed above, the lack of tractors, and an inability to maintain those that were available, the farms were not able to produce a sufficient amount of grain. Many problems were caused by the farmers' lowered production, by export of grain from the Ukraine, and by accumulation of massive amounts of grain held in reserve in the famine area, but not released to the peasants—much of it left to rot as a result of inadequate storage conditions.

Conquest (1986, p. 329) summarized his allocation of the responsibility for these disasters:

> 1. the cause of the famine was the setting of highly excessive grain requisition targets. . . . 2. Ukrainian party leaders made it clear at the start to Stalin . . . that these targets were highly excessive. 3. the targets were nevertheless enforced until starvation began. 4. Ukrainian leaders pointed this out to Stalin. . . . 5. the requisitions nevertheless continued.

He also noted that the situation could have been alleviated if stored grain had been released to peasants. Orders were enforced to prevent peasants from entering towns and to expel them when they did; the authorities would not bring food from Russia to the Ukraine. Thus, dekulakization was successful, but collectivization was a colossal failure, and the combination of the two efforts was disastrous for peasants and the general welfare of the country. It is also clear that as conditions became worse, the patterns of consumption were similar to those described earlier, and that in the final stages of starvation, cannibalism began—first eating the dead, and finally killing people for consumption.

CHINESE FAMINES

An interesting aspect of the two Chinese disasters to be discussed is that they were created by Chinese leaders who had the same intentions as did the Russian leaders. The Chinese attempted the same types of agrarian reform that had failed so miserably in Russia, and later began a program to terrorize the peasantry, which had similar disastrous consequences for the people, the country, and particularly the peasants.

Zheng Yi (1996) and Becker (1996) agree that cannibalism has had a long history in China, particularly during periods of famine. Zheng Yi is a Chinese journalist, now living in the United States, who experienced some of the events, and is described as a leader of the 1989 Tiananmen Square protest. Becker is a journalist living in Beijing, who was the Beijing Bureau Chief for the *South China Morning Post* at the time he wrote the book. They provide descriptions of the frenzy that occurred during both Mao's Great Leap Forward, between 1959 and 1961, and the Cultural Revolution, beginning in 1968, and their narratives are at the level of experiences of the peasants. A quite different level of analysis is provided by Yang (1996), a political scientist who grew up in the Chinese countryside shortly after the Great Leap Forward. His analyses are in terms of policy, decision making, and economics, involve careful statistical treatment of production and population data, and profit from the availability of Chinese documents that were previously classified.

Background   Anderson (1988) noted that China was far ahead of any other civilization in agricultural productivity until relatively modern times. The soil in many parts of China is good, groups farmed regions to produce trade goods, and they also worked fields close to their homes, which made them able to maximally protect themselves from raiding. Throughout history, when famine and its accompanying problems occurred, it was usually caused by the state through taxes, wars, and legally maintained social inequalities. Anderson maintained there was no reliable evidence that the Chinese ate human flesh except during desperate famines, or in small quantities for medicine or revenge. This may have been the case until the Cultural Revolution.

Chong (1990), on the other hand, claimed that cannibalism has always existed in China, classifying it into two types: learned (which reflects cultural loves and hates—what I have been calling ritual) and survival (for the sake of biological existence). The cultural reasons he identified are those of loyalty, filial piety, and affection on the one hand, and hatred, resentment, and revenge on the other.

Waldron (1997) claimed that the long-standing famine culture of China led to the practice of exchanging babies to eat, although he cited no evidence to support that claim. Chong (1990) discussed several major accounts of survival cannibalism, one during a siege in 594 BC where it was recorded that children were exchanged with other families to be eaten. Chong remarked that many Chinese classics refer to people exchanging one another's children for food, and Sorokin (1942) mentioned that the exposure and abandonment of children, or their sale as slaves, attended almost all major famines in China. An account of a siege in 279 BC stated that starving soldiers were ordered to eat their companions, and in 259 BC children were exchanged and eaten, with finally several hundred imperial servants and concubines killed as food for soldiers in a besieged castle.

Chong (1990, pp. 56–62) compiled a list of 131 instances of survival cannibalism due to natural disasters (mainly droughts) taken from official dynastic chronicles between 205 BC and AD 1633. He also described a number of instances of survival cannibalism that were war-related between 205 BC and AD 1628, and listed numerous types of ritual cannibalism that had taken place through the centuries. These types included cannibalism for revenge, punishment, respect for the dead, to strike terror into enemies, and as medical treatment for loved ones. Although this listing might overemphasize the frequency of cannibalism, it supports the hypothesis that cannibalism of many types probably has taken place throughout Chinese history—especially in times of natural disaster and warfare.

The Great Leap Forward   Becker (1996) concentrated on the Henan province in his discussion of the agrarian reform that, beginning in 1949, Mao Zedong set in action in an effort to collectivize Chinese agriculture. During the period from 1949 to 1957, China adopted the Stalinist development model, emphasizing investment in industry, particularly heavy industry (Yang, 1996). Becker believes that Chinese Communists must have known of the dire consequences of the Russian attempts because many of them had studied and worked in the Soviet Union during the previous three decades. It seems reasonable to suppose they would have heard of the famine, and would even have experienced food shortages themselves. Mao insisted, against opposing views, that collectivization proceed at once in order to squeeze from the peasants the resources required to finance industrialization. This industrialization was necessary to make steel to build the tractors required to run the giant collectives that were to be established. [Yang (1996) noted that the term peasant was used to denote anyone who lived in the Chinese countryside.] In addition to revolutionizing the economic sphere, Mao wanted to renew efforts to increase literacy, raise the status of women (stopping foot-binding and forced marriage), improve public health and sanitation, and eliminate opium addiction.

All small-scale private enterprises in the villages of China were eliminated, leaving villagers dependent on the state to supply their needs. As had happened in Russia, priority was given to the needs of the urban population. Yang (1996) found that during the first Five-Year Plan (1953–1957), the rural sector produced more than 50% of the income and employed more that 80% of the labor force, yet it received less than 8% of total state investment, with more than 52% allotted to industry. When grain shortages were caused by collectivization, the peasants began killing farm animals to consume or sell for meat before the collective appropriated the animals—the same as had been done by Russian peasants. Although agricultural disaster was apparent, all opposition from political leaders and experts in agricultural science was silenced, and Mao set in motion the Great Leap Forward—an imitation of Stalin's collectivization campaign. According to Becker Mao's goal was for China to copy and outdo the methods used by Russian agriculturalists and scientists, including agriculture according to Lysenko; the result was a disaster that was as good, if not better than what Stalin had been able to achieve.

The chief Chinese Lysenkoist insisted on Soviet methods, and persecuted those who believed in genetics (Becker, 1996). When a potato virus struck large areas of China in the 1950s, nothing could be done, because political doctrine dictated that the incident had to be attributed to environmental factors, preventing the development of a new genetic viral strain. Becker (1996, p. 70) summarized the elements of Mao's eight-point Lysenkoist blueprint for Chinese agriculture: (1) the popularization of new breeds and seeds, (2) close planting, (3) deep plowing, (4) increased manure fertilization, (5) an innovation in farm tools, (6) improved field management, (7) pest control, and (8) increased irrigation.

Regarding point 1, there were claims of miraculous hybrids (such as cross-bred super plants, and crossed Yorkshire sows with Holstein Friesian cows) that were proclaimed immediate successes. However, there was no increase in production, and the hybrids were not made available to breeders or producers (if they ever existed). Close planting had the same results as in Russia—the seedlings died. Deep plowing was done even deeper than in Russia—if deep is good, then deeper is better still. Extravagant claims of increased productivity were made for deep plowing, and it was continued for 3 years in a few places—destroying the fertility of some fields for many years.

Given that Lysenkoism prohibited chemical fertilizers, the Chinese government instructed the peasants to mix 10% manure (augmented with household rubbish) with 90% earth and to spread this on the fields. Innovations in farm tools were not successful because they involved impractical designs, and used tractors and plows that were much too large for the terraces and paddy fields of southern China. The decision to reduce tilled land to one-third of that available had disastrous effects, because it let too much quality land lie fallow, and exhausted poor land that was planted with high-yield crops. Yang (1996) reported that as much as 30% of the spring crop in 1959 lacked base fertilizer, mainly because the peasants, hungry but not allowed to retain any surpluses they might produce, had no incentive to work. An interesting effect of the pest control policy, mentioned as point 7, was that birds were successfully exterminated, which resulted in an infestation of insects because there were no birds to eat them.

Irrigation plans required dams and water channels to be built; however, the engineering capacity of the country was not adequate to the task and most of the dams collapsed within 2 or 3 years. The dam on the Yellow River quickly filled with silt, and a dam in one province burst, killing 240,000 people. These massive projects took immense numbers of people away from agricultural pursuits in order to produce steel, work on dams, and construct irrigation systems. In fact, the movement of labor led to the neglect of agricultural work, sometimes leaving harvested grain to rot in the field (Yang, 1996). When the extent of the disaster began to be apparent, more than 10 million of the extra workers recruited for factory work from rural areas in 1958 were sent back to reduce urban demand for food, which further exacerbated the problems of feeding the rural population—the agricultural damage had already been done. Once again the Chinese surpassed the Russians in the rush to agricultural disaster.

Famine

As the winter of 1958 progressed, grain in collective granaries began to be exhausted, starvation set in, and the weak and elderly began to die. Becker reported that as reports of food shortages reached Mao, he concluded that peasants were hoarding grain in order to receive further supplies from the state. Mao had grown up in a farming family, and could not understand why the working class was not producing enough meat and poultry for them to eat. Those officials Yang (1996) called "Mao's sycophants" adopted special measures to improve the supply of these products to urban areas, which encouraged Mao to think that the problems had been solved. Yang calculated that because of the impossibly high grain-output forecasts, grain procurement accounted for as much as 39.7% of the estimated actual output for 1959 and 35.6% for 1960. The target for grain output in 1958 was 375 million tons, up 92% from the 1957 output of only 100.05 million tons, and the 1959 goal was 525 million tons (Yang, 1996).

The failure to meet these unrealistic goals prompted repression and dismissal of any bureaucrats who doubted there were abundant harvests. The unrealistically high grain quotas were imposed because of tremendous pressures put on directors of provincial statistical bureaus to report high levels of grain output, creating the aura of a make-believe world of abundance. Cadres were sent into the countryside to search for all the food that must be hidden there, and, according to Yang (1996, p. 39), militia commanders often turned predatory, "seizing grain, beating and cursing the people, raping their women, barring the roads and openly robbing the people." Again, shades of the Soviet's response.

Becker considered the famine of 1958–1961 to be unique in Chinese history, because every corner of the huge country experienced hunger. Yang (1996) estimated that this Great Leap Famine resulted in 30 million deaths (10 million in 1960 alone), making it the worst famine in human history;

ironically, most of the victims were the grain producers. In terms of precipitating reform in government policy, Yang likened the adverse effects of
the Great Leap Famine to those occasioned in Japan and Germany by their
defeat in war.

In previous Chinese famines some parts of the country were spared, because natural disasters are caused by local environmental conditions, making it possible to send food to famine regions from unaffected ones. The
tradition during the time of the imperial dynasties in China was to provide
famine relief. Now, instead of distributing food to peasants in the regions
of famine, grain reserves were used to feed the greatly expanded urban
population (Yang, 1996). In addition, China was a net exporter of grain:
1.88 million metric tons in 1957, 3.25 million in 1958, 4.74 million in 1959,
and 1 million in 1960, a year in which 10 million people are estimated to
have starved throughout the country (Yang, 1996). This export of grain was
necessary to secure more foreign currency to repay debts to the Soviet
Union and to purchase capital goods needed for industrialization. A study
by the U.S. Department of Agriculture, published in 1988, indicated that
Mao's Great Leap Forward caused overall grain yields to fall by 25%,
wheat yields by 41%, oil-seed production by 64%, cotton by 41%, and tex-
tiles by more than 50% (Becker, 1996). Yang (1996) noted that total agricultural productivity did not return to its 1952 levels until 1983.

As was the case in Russia, the Party cadres controlled substantial grain
stores, and only those who worked could eat, which left the sick, the old,
and the young to die. A major problem was that the communal mess halls
often provided nothing but watery gruel, which was insufficient to sustain
the hard-working peasants who were being forced to work longer hours to
meet production goals. In early stages of the famine, the elderly and those
men forced to do hard labor died, to be followed by women and children
as the famine continued. China's mortality rate increased from 12 per 1,000
in 1958 to 14.6 per 1,000 in 1959, and reached the astounding level of 25.4
per 1,000 in 1960; in the agriculture-rich Sichuan province the rate was 47
per 1,000 (Yang, 1996, p. 53).

The famine was broken in early 1961 when Mao ordered 30,000 men from
the army to distribute the grain in state granaries, distribute winter coats
and quilts, provide emergency accommodations, and arrest the local leaders—who were blamed for the catastrophe. Once again, this man-made
famine had been allowed to progress, even though granaries had abundant
stocks. The chief cause of famine was the state's excessive levy of grain in
accordance with imaginary high grain harvests. By the summer of 1961, the
Lysenkoists were replaced with scientists who began to develop agricultural sciences in such a way that sensible practical applications could be ac-
complished. In addition, the scale of waterworks was reduced and labor
was shifted to agriculture, with grain imported from abroad in 1961.

A common pattern within families seemed to be to allow the oldest and the youngest to die first, then young girls were not provided adequate rations, and when they died their bodies were exchanged with those of girl children from other families to be consumed. It was considered necessary to preserve sons. In some cases female babies were abandoned, and later even boys were left behind at hospitals in the hope they would be fed.

Cannibalism　　　　A unique characteristic of the Chinese famine is that people continued to live in their own homes, with standards of public health vigorously enforced by local authorities. As has been described repeatedly, people began preparing and eating shoes, boots, belts, and anything else made of leather. Compounds of earth and weeds were prepared; wild grass was made into a paste with broken grains of rice, then steamed and eaten in cake form.

With terminal starvation an everyday occurrence, cannibalism became widespread, beginning with eating the flesh of corpses, particularly those of children. Becker (1996) claimed that in his travels around the rural Henan province 30 years later, every peasant he met who was over 50 years old personally knew of a case of cannibalism. The pattern was for women to go out at night and cut flesh from human bodies buried in shallow graves, and this flesh would be eaten in secrecy. He reported that in one county, in 1960, authorities listed 200 cases of corpses being eaten; those arrested were charged with the crime of destroying corpses. Becker noted that it will never be known just how extensive cannibalism was, because the official policy was not to report the incidents.

Official party documents contain a record of cases of cannibalism: In one county, 200 cases of cannibalism were recorded in a population of 900,000 at the start of the famine; in another there were 63 cases in a population of 335,000 (Becker, 1996). There were enough reports from different parts of the country to convince Becker that the practice of cannibalism was not restricted to any one region, class, or ethnicity. He found that people ate the flesh of the dead, sold it, and killed and ate children, both their own and those of others. Becker concluded that the pattern of cannibalism closely paralleled that seen during the Ukrainian famine, and it would be repeated in the Chinese Great Leap Forward 30 years later. In both instances, the urban population received better rations than did rural peasants. Party members in the cities, as well as army and navy personnel, were the most protected social group.

As in Russia, peasants were prevented from moving to urban areas, and if they managed to do so they were sent back to the villages. These governmental decisions enhanced the severity of the man-made disasters, and made it impossible for peasants to cope, leading them to lose hope. And as in Russia, the peasants killed their domestic animals rather than surrender them. Becker accepted figures indicating that a slightly larger proportion of China's population died (4.6% of the total; 5.45% of the peasants) than was the case in Russia (4.11% of the total).

In spite of the desperate situation people were in, most observers agree that suicide was a very rare occurrence, just as has been found in the natural disasters I have discussed. Laycock (1944), a physician who observed hundreds of starving people in China for a year between 1942 and 1943, also remarked that he could not understand why more of these people did not take an easy way out through suicide.

The reform movement that resulted in decollectivization occurred primarily in rural areas. Yang believes that the Great Leap Famine changed the outlook of peasants and cadres at the basic level so greatly that institutional change was affected locally. A system of household farming was gradually and surreptitiously introduced, with peasants able to keep the surplus they produced beyond quotas. Although there was no landlord class to stubbornly defend its property rights, Mao, putting class struggle at the top of his agenda, considered household farming to be the nemesis of the collective economy, just as capitalism was to socialism.

Yang (1996) summarized matters quite well: Mao and his colleagues commanded enormous power and prestige among the people for their successful leadership in war. When famine shattered the economy, the central leadership retreated. Peasants lost any positive illusions they might have had about communes, and peasants and basic-level cadres widely adopted household farming. The more severely an area suffered from the Great Leap Famine, the more likely the peasants and cadres in that area were to adopt liberal practices, and the lower was membership in the Communist Party. Those who opposed household farming tended to be Communist Party and youth league members, activists, and households that lacked labor or skills—in Yang's words, people who would benefit from income sharing. All was not well, however, because Mao turned against household farming later, a move Yang considered to be due to Mao's need to emphasize that he was the ultimate political leader.

The Cultural Revolution
The most recent outburst of cannibalism was politically motivated during the Cultural Revolution launched by Mao in 1966, the purpose being to destroy members of the Party he declared were practicing capitalism. This was not a movement inspired in the rural areas; it was promulgated by the Red Guards who were sent from the cities against class enemies. Becker (1996) maintained that the purpose of the Cultural Revolution was to restore Mao's authority by purging those who had ended the famine, thereby weakening his invincible power. This move was

similar to that made by Stalin following the Ukraine famine. Becker also believes that the relatively well-educated and youthful Red Guards were employed because they knew little of what had happened in the countryside during the famine, and Mao wanted the young to distrust and betray the older generation, praising those who denounced and exposed their parents.

Zheng Yi (1996), undertook a trip in 1986 to document the events that had occurred during that time in the province of Guangxi, between 1966 and 1976, the year Mao died. His narrative is detailed and horrifying, and it is believable that the events described took place much as he and other reporters have indicated. He estimated that at least 10,000 people were killed and eaten in China during that period. The cannibalistic episodes usually began with the victim, who had been listed as an enemy in the class struggle, forced to parade through the streets and subjected to criticism. Each round of criticism was followed by a beating, and once the victim fell to the ground the crowd rushed forward and started cutting flesh, often while the victim was still breathing. Zheng Yi reported instances in which live victims had their hearts and livers cut out—"a rather skilled technique." When this occurred, the crowd scrambled for other parts, and sometimes there were communal village feasts.

At some villages there would be communal cooking and eating of stewed victims. Human flesh and pork were boiled together, and people would join in a collective act of cannibalism. Participation was made easier because the meats were dished up in no systematic way, so people never knew if they were eating human flesh or pork.

Often the property of the deceased was publicly displayed and divided among the militiamen who led the proceedings. The revolutionary regime in China finally stopped the killing, but very few of the identified participants were punished. In one county, those found guilty served prison sentences of between 2 and 14 years, with the average being 7–10 years.

Zheng Yi (1996, p. 103) summarized his findings:

An unprecedented frenzy of cannibalism in human history had occurred. Even uglier than the mere fact alone was that the frenzy was not caused by some uncontrollable defect in human nature. It was a violent act, caused directly by the very same class struggle advocated by Marxism-Leninism-Mao Zedong thought, armed by the theory of proletarian dictatorship, silently agreed upon and directly organized by the power organizations of the Chinese Communist Party.

He considered the events to be due partly to the fact that China, although known for its high level of morality, lacks the spirit of forgiveness that is revered by many Eastern and Western religions; revenge is reward-

ed using the policy of an eye for an eye. In his view, no matter how cruel
the means, acts of revenge are considered moral as long as the act is against
evil or against an enemy. Even though Zheng Yi is not a cultural anthropologist, as Arens would prefer, his writings convey an authenticity, particularly because they are consistent with independent reports by others.
The cannibalism that occurred here is different from other types I have described; it was not motivated by the necessity that characterizes survival
cannibalism, but was a clear instance of political cannibalism.

WARS, PRISONS, CONCENTRATION CAMPS, AND GULAGS

I will not discuss the many brutal instances in which political prisoners
were starved to the point where they engaged in cannibalism. I will consider only one of them in some depth, that occurring in Kolyma, and al-
lude to others only briefly. My purpose is to establish the fact that
cannibalism has taken place in the twentieth century when people are
driven beyond the limits of their endurance. Often the cruelties of those
responsible were calculated to cause the death of the victims, usually after having exacted productive labor from them throughout the process of
their extermination. It is easier for repressive governments to justify brutal incarceration during times of war by declaring prisoners to be enemies
of the state who constitute a threat to the welfare of the general public.
This is another instance of using the "Us–Them" distinction to justify barbaric acts on the grounds that "They" do not possess the degree of humanity that "We" do. This view enhances the likelihood that those in
charge will be permitted to treat victims harshly, and the prevailing harshness will quiet dissident views of those who might well become the next
victims.

The summary of Kolyma by Conquest (1978) draws heavily on the
Solzhenitsyn *Gulag* volumes, books and articles containing first-hand accounts by several other survivors of Kolyma, and a few major reports and
analyses published in the West or in the Soviet press. Conquest stated that
he relied on 17 first-hand accounts—16 from ex-prisoners and one from a
free employee. Solzhenitsyn (1974) made the ironic remark that Kolyma
was "fortunate" because several good writers survived there, and all of
them have written memoirs. A more recent book is based on Bardach's experience at Kolyma (Bardach & Gleeson, 1998); it adds little that is new, but
is yet another presentation of an individual's experiences. His book contains no references, but the accounts presented support those made by others, particularly those by Solzhenitsyn (1972, 1974), who acknowledged in
the Preface of his first volume that the material for the books was given to
him through reports, memoirs, and letters by 227 witnesses.

Kolyma

Throughout the earlier discussion of Russian famines, attention was focused on the peasant population of the country, particularly in the Ukraine. The urban population of Russia also suffered greatly during that time. People in cities were subjected to mass arrests, imprisonment, executions, and exile. The harshest and most deadly exile was to the mines in the region of Kolyma, which were located near the Arctic Circle, and where it is reasonable to accept the conclusion that millions died between 1932 and 1954. Initially, the purpose of the Kolyma operation was to produce badly needed gold; in the later period production of gold remained important, but the central aim was to kill prisoners in the process. Conquest (1978) estimated that at its full development, Kolyma had about 120 full-scale camps, about 80 of them mining camps, each with a probable average of about 5,000 inmates; the other camps supported fishing, lumbering, or agricultural activities. There probably was a total of about 400,000 people in the camps at a time, about 80% of them in the mines. He guessed that the death rate for miners was about 25% per year, leading him to conclude that a total of about three million would have died in Kolyma.

Prisoners were taken overland to Vladivostok, then by boat to the port of Magadan (the capital of the region), and finally to the camps and mines of the interior. The sea around Magadan is frozen for scores of miles beyond the shore for 5 months of the year (Conquest, 1978), and the temperature in the interior is as cold as is found in the Northern Hemisphere—reaching as low as −70°C. The brief Arctic summer melts the snow and the soil to a depth of about 6 feet, making it relatively easy to mine for about 100 days. Conditions were always harsh in the camps, not particularly intended to destroy the prisoners at first, but caused by a lack of sufficient resources—in terms of food, clothing, and shelter—to support them.

In 1937 Stalin attacked what he called the general practice of coddling prisoners, an attack that led to increasingly brutal treatment of prisoners. In 1938 prisoners at Kolyma were, for the first time, forced to work in the mines in winter, and Solzhenitsyn (1974) described mass executions of whole brigades of workers. At the outbreak of war, in 1941, the official 10-hour working day was raised to 12 hours, with no holidays, and the bread ration was reduced. When production norms were not fulfilled, it could be considered an act of sabotage, punishable by the death of any considered to be responsible.

Each worker had to achieve the norm or the bread ration was reduced; if the norm was exceeded, the ration was increased. The full ration was 800 g of bread per day, and if the norm was not reached the ration was reduced to 500 g—which is just above the starvation level. There was considerable falsification of production levels, because it looked bad if an administrator did not meet his quota, reducing the whole process to an exercise of imagination, and making it possible to apportion rations in any manner desired (Bardach & Gleeson, 1998). This process of manipulating quotas and over- or underestimating productivity is a familiar one that has been described in both the Russian and Chinese famines.

It should be remembered that these prisoners were engaged in hard labor in extremely cold temperatures. A 70-kg man working actively for 8 hours a day requires 3,000–4,500 calories a day, and those working extremely hard in inclement weather (New England bricklayers) require 8,600 calories. Temperature affects the number of calories required: at 0°C the voluntary intake of North American troops provided 4,700 calories; at −34°C the intake was 5,000 calories. Conquest estimated that the prisoners' diet provided only 2,600 calories, the punishment diet provided 2,100, and prisoners in punishment cells received only 1,300, with all of these diets deficient in vitamins and fat. Conquest reported that prisoners of war in Japanese camps on the River Kwai received about 3,400 calories daily.

When it was possible to avoid the attention of guards, who could summarily execute a prisoner for almost any reason, prisoners ate almost any conceivable item: the carcass of a horse which had been lying for more than a week and was crawling with flies and worms, grease found in a barrel, and moss. Those who were so weakened they were no longer able to work were referred to by the Russian word for "goner" and were put on starvation rations. They would growl and root about in the filthy garbage, looking for anything even remotely edible, and devour it on the spot. As reported for other starvation victims in many circumstances, there was a strong desire for tea, tobacco, and alcohol—even in the form of eau de cologne.

There are references to cannibalism in each of the sources I have discussed. Conquest (1978) described an escape in which prisoners overpowered their guards while being transported in a truck, with two of the men having taken a third with them to eat—an indictable offense. Bardach described an incident in which the "goners" were huddled around the stove in a tent, boiling and eating meat that he was told had been cut from the pile of cadavers outside the tent. Bardach and Gleeson (1998, p. 289) referred to the heap of cadavers that lay outside the mining camp, "their bones picked clean the very next day by scavengers—animal and human." Solzhenitzyn (1974, p. 398) described an incident in which an escaped prisoner was found with human flesh in his knapsack: "he had killed an unconvoyed artist . . . who had crossed his path, had cut his flesh off, and had not yet had the chance to cook it." He described another incident of cannibalism that took place in 1946–1947, when people were cut up into meat, cooked, and eaten.

As mentioned at the start of this section, about three million prisoners might have died in the Kolyma camps. Conquest (1978, p. 228) made the sensible conclusion that the actual number is not of much concern: "Kolyma still remains the 'pole of cold and cruelty' of the whole phenomenon, the illustration of its essence, and of the moral basis of the system which produced it."

Nazi   It should be no surprise that the German Nazis ex-
Concentration   celled in matters related to prison brutality, extermi-
Camps   nation, starvation, and related atrocities. The Nazis
had, from the beginning of Hitler's assumption of the Chancellorship of the Third Reich on 30 January 1933, begun to implement sterilizations that were intended to move Germany toward the ideal of racial purity, as outlined as early as 1924 in *Mein Kampf*. The plan was to achieve racial purification that would move from sterilization to extensive killing (Lifton, 1986). These policies required the development of an efficient bureaucracy, careful record keeping, and adequate facilities to exterminate all mental and physical defectives. In 1939, an article in a semi-official Nazi magazine contained an estimate that it would probably be desirable to exterminate one million people (Lifton, 1986). By 1939, the doctrine was being developed that it was necessary to eliminate every Jew—a doctrine that was the precursor to the Final Solution orders. The efficiency of the procedures and methods developed by the Nazis make the Russians and Chinese look like amateurs—both in the profitable employment of slave laborers who were exploited as long as they were possibly useful, and in the methods of starvation, mass gassing, and cremation when they were no longer of any use as workers.

Medical reports of the effects of mass starvation are available for the Belsen Concentration Camp, which was taken over by the British Army in April 1945. Mollison (1946) characterized this as a detention, not an extermination camp: In extermination camps people were not held long enough for starvation to be a problem; in detention camps organized extermination was not carried out. The Germans adopted the policy of depriving prisoners, who were mainly Jewish, of all care, allowing them to die of starvation and disease. At its peak Belsen contained 66,000 persons, but by the time of liberation there were only about 50,000 people alive, with some 10,000 lying dead in huts and around the camp. A report in *The Lancet* (1945) described the atrocious condition of the prisoners and the deplorable nature of the facilities, while noting that there was a magnificent barrack area with every possible facility for the German troops, including a beautiful German officers' mess and an excellently appointed military hospital. It was also noted that the standard of nutrition of German civilians in the surrounding area was very high, which means that the starvation was not due to a lack of available foodstuffs in the region.

An early medical report noted there was no running water or electricity; in fact the Germans had cut the water supply as a final gesture before the main body of troops left (Collis, 1945). Next to nothing had been done for the prisoners for months, and for a week they had had almost no water. Mollison (1946) observed that during the period prior to the arrival of the British, prisoners were fed almost nothing except large beets that are usually fed to cattle, and in the fortnight before rescue these were available only in the form of soup. He remarked that throughout the last weeks, a "gruesome form of the law of the survival of the fittest was in operation." The distribution of food was arbitrary, and those who still had some strength obtained more than their share. It was estimated that the average weight loss was about 39% (ranging between 29% and 57%) of the precamp weight. Mollison remarked that these figures probably do not represent the most severe cases; in these the prisoners would have died earlier or would have been too ill even to be weighed.

During the surrender of the German commanders to the British, prisoners attempted to take potatoes from a heap near the cookhouse and the SS began shooting them. The British stopped the killing by informing the German commander that one SS man would be shot for every prisoner shot. The SS guards were brought under control and were forced to bury the dead and to clean up the worst of the filth. A large number of medical units were brought in, and those prisoners capable of assisting were organized; due to extreme need, German medical personnel were also used. When German doctors and nurses attempted to give prisoners intravenous injections the patients would often cry out, begging not to be taken to the crematorium. This response was understandable because the Germans had often given intravenous injections of benzol and creosote to induce a paralysis that would justify sending prisoners to be gassed.

Collis reported that shortly after the camp was taken over 20,000 more prisoners died and had to be buried. A triage policy was adopted by the British medical personnel, who decided that the greatest number of lives would be saved by treating those who had the best chance of survival. These patients received controlled feeding and treatments to prevent further infections (Lipscomb, 1945).

Lipscomb's report noted that psychosis was less in evidence than in an ordinary community of the same size, which he thought was because only "the more extrovert and robust psychological types" had survived the ordeal. The most conspicuous psychological abnormality Lipscomb remarked on was a "degradation of moral standards characterized by increasing selfishness" that was proportional to the degree of undernutrition. Lipscomb (1945, p. 315) wrote: "In the first stage consideration for others was limited to personal friends, then the circle contracted to child or parent, and finally only the instinct to survive remained." This pattern is consistent with that observed in many instances of starvation considered throughout this book. He continued: "Eventually all self-respect disappeared and the only interest left was to obtain something which could be eaten, even human flesh." And again, when all appears to be lost, some of those who were able resorted to cannibalism to avoid death.

No point would be served by reviewing the numerous instances of wartime cannibalism. Even a cursory examination of the literature reveals instance after instance. For example, Markowski (1945), a Polish prisoner of war in Germany who served as a surgeon in prisoner of war camps and hospitals between 1939 and 1945, reported seeing bodies with pieces of flesh hacked out in a German prison camp housing Russian prisoners of war. He reported that this cannibalism was denounced by the Germans as proof of the bestiality of the prisoners, and commented that it was a proof of bestiality, but on the part of the Germans who engaged in such massive acts of sadistic cruelty. He also noted that this took place in the heart of Germany, where well-fed, fat Prussian peasants forced emaciated and starving prisoners to perform harsh physical labor.

The autobiography of Rudolf Hoess (1959) referred to cases of cannibalism that occurred in the Birkenau prison camp, one of which involved a Russian body that had been ripped open and the liver removed, and others in which his men often found the bodies of Russians who had been killed by their fellows and partly eaten. He wrote, with no evident emotion, that they were no longer human beings, having become animals, who sought only food. Of more than 10,000 Russian prisoners of war who were to provide the main labor force for building the camp at Birkenau, only a few hundred were still alive by the summer of 1942.

Chong (1990) quoted a report by a former British prisoner from the trial of the commandant of the Treblinka concentration camp in Poland. This prisoner was assigned to clear away dead bodies, and noted that he and his crew members observed that a piece of flesh was missing from as many as one in 10 cadavers. This same prisoner claims to have seen a prisoner in the mortuary take a knife, cut a portion of the leg of a dead body, and put it into his mouth.

Cannibalism was seen not only in German-run prison camps. In 1924, following World War I, there was a famous case of a shopkeeper in Münsterberg, Karl Denke (Friedrich, 1972). He was found to have several barrels filled with smoked human flesh, a case full of bones, and a number of pots of human lard. During the years of famine the villagers had grown accustomed to eating roasted dogs and cats, and Denke had done a brisk business in the sale of "smoked pork." His notebook was found and in it were recorded 30 murders, with the date of each killing and the weight of each victim. In another case, a man sold attractively packaged tinned meats labeled pork or veal on the Black Market, and after he confessed to one murder, the bones of between 24 and 26 victims were found. Friedrich chronicled several such examples, indicating that these were not isolated cases during this period of famine in Germany.

Both Solzhenitsyn (1973) and Craig (1973) reported the occurrence of widespread cannibalism during the siege of what was then called Stalingrad in the winter and spring of 1941–1942. After the German army was defeated, the Russians provided prisoners of war with little food, and many of them starved to death. Craig cited reports of physicians who found corpses without arms or legs, human heads with the brains scooped out, and torsos minus livers and kidneys. Although the cannibals were furtive at first, they soon searched for the newly dead who were just turning cold, and thus would be more tender. He remarked that they even helped the dying to die.

Japanese Cannibalism   There were several trials of Japanese military personnel for cannibalism committed at the end of World War II (Piccigallo, 1979). These included a Lt. General who had beheaded an American prisoner of war and then ate the flesh and viscera of the body. Interestingly enough, there was no precedent in modern international law to deal with cannibalism, and the United States naval authorities decided not to charge cannibalism as a "war crime." The Australians, however, did include a reference to cannibalism as a war crime in its supplemental list of war crimes, which enabled prosecution on that ground.

The Australians successfully prosecuted a Japanese officer for eating part of the body of an Australian prisoner of war, even though the officer explained that starvation had caused a temporary loss of his senses. The Philippine authorities tried 31 Japanese military personnel for eating local residents, and convicted them based on eyewitness testimony to the effect that the Japanese had enjoyed eating human flesh, well beyond what was required to keep them from starving.

An incident in World War II, in which Japanese soldiers ate Arapesh Indians of New Guinea, was discussed by Tuzin (1983). Japanese soldiers had been sent to the villages, where they foraged in the gardens for 6 months because their overseas supply lines had been cut. Tuzin spent 21 months in 1969–1972 doing field ethnographic research in the area, and believes the Japanese had resorted to cannibalism because of hunger. He had access to officers' battle diaries housed in the Australian war archives, physical evidence discovered in the packs of slain Japanese soldiers, and reliable eyewitness accounts secured in the field.

The Japanese soldiers had been living in the households of the Indians, and enjoyed good relations, some of them being virtually adopted into the families with which they were quartered. The Arapesh looked up to the Japanese as protectors and providers who had liberated them from Euro-

Australian tyranny. Tuzin remarked that this was not too far off base giv-
en the minimal and somewhat checkered history of outside contact. The
Japanese had put an end to intervillage warfare, and the area enjoyed unprecedented peace during the early phase of the occupation. The Japanese
introduced several new crops, including sweet potatoes, and taught improved methods of cultivation.

Cannibalism took place at a time when garden food was scarce, with the
population, as usual in that preharvest time of year, forced to subsist mainly on sago flour, which was difficult to produce and had minimal nutritional value. Hunger was more widespread than usual because several
hundred men had been garrisoned in the village Tuzin studied.

The soldiers were under considerable pressure; they were demoralized,
sick and weakened, and had little medicine. They had been ordered by the
Japanese command not to use their small supply of ammunition to hunt
animals, but to conserve it to fight Australian troops. Tuzin noted that by
official counts, the Australians had an almost trivial number of casualties,
whereas the killed-to-capture ratio among the Japanese was 33:1. By this
time some of the Arapesh (who saw that the Australians were going to win
the war and were experiencing increasing brutality at the hands of the
Japanese) had ceased being hospitable, and were beginning to harass and
ambush the soldiers when they ventured into the forest, making it increasingly difficult to forage away from the well-fortified village encamp-
ments.

Tuzin argued that the Japanese believed they were in critical need of
high-quality protein, particularly in anticipation of the severe physical demands of upcoming combat. They were right on that account, because they
put up a stiff, well-organized resistance, despite being greatly outnum-
bered. He considered the widespread cannibalism not to be the act of de-
mented, panic-stricken soldiers, but to have been an entirely rational act of
survival on the part of defeated, but fanatical soldiers.

The cruelty and viciousness of inhumanity induced by humans exceed
that caused by natural disasters. People have caused millions of innocent
people to suffer and die needlessly, often with almost cheerful disregard,
while they enjoyed comfortable lives. And this all occurred in the interest
of attaining political power and domination. In such circumstances, as well
as those involving disasters caused by wartime siege, noble, decent people
are driven to desperate measures in their attempts to survive. Once again,
the biological bias falls into place. First, favor your friends and neighbors,
then your family, next your immediate kin, then offspring or parents, and
finally save yourself at all costs. Seldom do people resort to suicide in these
circumstances. This pattern has been found to occur throughout the events
described in this book, and seems to reveal a deep aspect of basic human
nature that surfaces to enable survival.

9

The Literary Imagination

Sweeney: I'll carry you off
         To a cannibal isle
Doris: You'll be the cannibal!
Sweeney: You'll be the missionary!
         You'll be my little seven stone missionary?
         I'll gobble you up. I'll be the cannibal.
Doris: I'll be the missionary.
         I'll convert you!
Sweeney: I'll convert *you!*
         Into a stew
         A nice little, white little, missionary stew.
Doris: You wouln't eat me!
Sweeney: Yes, I'd eat you?
         In a nice little, white little, soft little, tender little,
         Juicy little, right little, missionary stew.

—T. S. Eliot, *Sweeney Agonistes* (1952)

After the unrelenting grim events discussed in the last chapter I believe it is appropriate to end on a whimsical note. Cannibalism has engaged writers, poets, and filmmakers for many years, and I will touch on a few of the better known (as well as some better forgotten) examples.

For something that is unthinkable and unmentionable, the practices of cannibalism have received considerable attention and discussion by social scientists, scholars in the humanities, journalists, and literary, theatrical, and cinematic practitioners. Dickens at various times labeled cannibalism the unpardonable sin—dreadful, horrible, wolfish, and a last resource that inspired loathing (Stone, 1994). He wrote that no well-bred Englishman, no matter what the extremity, would ever succumb to "that frightful feasting." The theme of Stone's (1994) book, *The Night Side of Dickens: Cannibalism, Passion, Necessity,* is that cannibalistic fantasies and themes were central to Dickens' life and writings—central to the point of obsession.

Malchow (1996) examined the concept of race in Gothic literature and the rhetorical manipulation of alien racial characteristics that involved cannibalism. He found that these manipulations provided a rich source of information about the social fears and cultural obsessions of Europeans. In that literature, cannibalism is described as barbarian, perverse, and degraded. He suggested it was a buried universal, and that the fascination with cannibalism (as with vampires) represented projections of nameless fears. Lestringant wrote (1997, p. 12): "The cannibal, nevertheless, continues to people our imagination and haunt our present day."

Rawson (1992, p. 349) made the amusing observation that Swift's friend, Thomas Sheridan, a clergyman, schoolteacher, man of letters, and grandfather of the playwright Richard Sheridan, considered cannibalism to be "a very horrible Fact; too horrible indeed to mention," which he then proceeds to mention at considerable length. As Rawson noted parenthetically, unmentionability is a common theme in the not inconsiderable literature dealing with cannibal behavior, and he found Sheridan's phrases to be "limp with a fussy sensationalizing speechlessness worthy of Poe."

MONTAIGNE'S ESSAYS

One of the most widely known discussions of cannibalism is Montaigne's essay "Of Cannibalism" (1580, Chapter XXXI, Book One), in which he discussed the cruelty, rapaciousness, and barbarity of Europeans, contrasting these characteristics with the more noble virtues of cannibals. In his essay "Of Coaches" (1580, Chapter VI, Book Three), he discussed the enormity of Spanish cruelties in Peru and Mexico, concentrating on the treachery and severe torture of people to exact payments of gold. He remarked in "Of Cannibalism" (p. 282): "We can, then, rightly call them [the cannibals] barbarians with respect to the rules of reason, but not with respect to ourselves, who surpass them in every sort of barbarism."

He characterized the warfare of cannibals as "wholly noble and honourable," and to have as much excuse and beauty as "that malady of mankind can have." Montaigne was familiar with the accounts of explorers and missionaries, and Lestringant (1997) noted that Montaigne met three Brazilian Tupinamba who had been brought to Rouen by the 12-year-old Charles IX in 1562. The Tupinamba found it remarkable that so many tall, bearded men, strong and well armed, should humble themselves to obey a beardless child rather than choose one of themselves to command them (Montaigne, 1580, Chapter XXXI, Book One). Their attitude was conditioned by the fact that a leader in Brazil gloried in marching at the head of his people during warfare, directly demonstrating his superiority.

Rawson (1992) agreed that "Of Cannibals" defends Amerindians from

charges of barbarism, and that Montaigne challenged the idea that cannibal customs are necessarily barbaric. Montaigne noted that there is more
barbarism in eating a living man than a dead one, or in rending by torture
and the rack, than roasting and eating a body after it is dead. Lestringant
(1997) stated that there can be no question that Montaigne admired the native virtue of the cannibal as Noble Savage, and also condemned the savagery of the French noble, what with the dueling and rivalries that
unleashed civil war, plunging the state into ruin. Montaigne, in the two essays discussed here, raised the Brazilian cannibal to the status of orator and
philosopher, emphasizing the importance of their words of defiance,
insults, and songs of death and revenge. They become free and fraternal
citizens of a "back-to-nature utopia" that no longer provoke horror. Lestringant (1997, p. 111) concluded: "He has successfully cleansed anthropophagy from the stigma of the flesh."

One reason Montaigne's essays were important is their influence on
subsequent writers of great stature. Rawson (1992) noted that Swift had
read Montaigne quite early, and cited him in letters as early as 1704 and as
late as 1732, and is known to have owned a copy of the essays in 1715. Rawson remarked, as did Craig (1961), on the close, almost word-for-word re-
semblance between Gonzalo's description of the ideal commonwealth in
Shakespeare's *The Tempest* (written in 1610) and Montaigne's description
of the culture of the Tupinamba in "Of Cannibalism." Norton (1946) stated that a 1603 translation of Montaigne's essays is the only book that is
known certainly to have belonged to Shakespeare; the British Museum has
a copy with Shakespeare's autograph on the flyleaf.

ROBINSON CRUSOE

DeFoe's *Robinson Crusoe* is an immensely popular story for both children
and adults, and cannibalism plays a strong role in its development. Daniel
Defoe was 60 years old when he published *Robinson Crusoe* (Defoe, 1719).
The cannibal savages that visited the island on which he was marooned are
described with considerable horror. Despite these dreadful cannibalistic
accounts, the book has been recommended regularly for children's reading since its publication—a tradition that continues unabated. The book
has been issued in at least 700 editions, translated into many languages,
and there have been numerous imitations of the story. Sheridan wrote a
pantomime based on *Robinson Crusoe* in the eighteenth century, Offenbach
composed music for an opera in the nineteenth, and Luis Buñuel made the
story into a movie in the twentieth. Perhaps the story's appeal is that it describes the trials and tribulations of a typical lower middle class Englishman, who survives, manages an adequate existence using only his wit

as a resource, outwits, defeats, and even befriends the dreadful cannibal savages, finally to be rescued to enjoy the benefits of civilization.

Lestringant (1997) remarked that the fear of being consumed haunts Crusoe throughout his time on the desert island: fear of being swallowed up by the sea after shipwreck, fear of being devoured by wild animals, and fear of being eaten by cannibals. When he first sees the tracks of a bare foot on the sand he knows, without doubt, that they were made by a cannibal. Later his suspicions are confirmed, and Defoe (1719, p. 163) describes the matter thus: "the horror of my mind at seeing the shore spread with skulls, hands, feet, and other bones of human bodies . . . and a circle dug in the earth . . . where it is supposed the savage wretches had sat down to their inhuman feastings upon the bodies of their fellow creatures."

Crusoe "gave God thanks that had cast my first lot in a part of the world where I was distinguished from such dreadful creatures as these," and "kept close within my own circle for almost two years after this." Defoe then adopts a perspective similar to that developed by Montaigne; the cannibals do not know that what they do is an offense, as we do, and do not consider it a crime to kill a captive in war any more than we do to kill an ox, nor to eat human flesh any more than we do to eat mutton. He contrasted this to the barbarous conduct the papist Spaniards practiced in the Americas, where they destroyed millions of people. Even though the customs of these Amerindians involved bloody and barbarous rites, they were innocent people.

Crusoe's suspicions are confirmed when the naked cannibals return and he observes them eating human flesh "with undeniable enjoyment." In the company of his rescued cannibal servant, his man Friday, he observes a group of cannibals eating the flesh of one of their prisoners, with another lying bound on the sand, who would undoubtedly be the next provender. This remaining victual was not one of the natives, but a white bearded man, and when the natives moved to butcher the unfortunate Christian, Crusoe and Friday attacked, killed several of them, "miserably wounded" most of them, and rescued the victim (who was a Spaniard)—with only 4 of the 21 cannibals escaping.

Lestringant (1997) considers Defoe's work to be an effective contribution to the black legends concerning cannibals, contributing to the tendency of the English to regard them as enemies to be avoided, to be reduced to slavery, or exterminated. Lestringant (1997, p. 142) sees Crusoe as representing "the type of new economic man, an implacable individualist, all the more ruthless towards others because of his belief that Providence supports him, inspires his smallest deeds and continually justifies the excesses of his conquering and civilizing progress." The notion of cannibalism as a characteristic of primitive peoples was enhanced by the story, where it was lodged in popular culture and recommended for the education of children (Malchow, 1996). In addition, it has been argued that the story had a profound influence on the young Dickens, and it, along with an early exposure to the *Arabian Nights* and *Gulliver's Travels*, shaped the cannibalistic imaginings that were central to much of Dickens' writing (Stone, 1994).

SWIFT AND A MODEST PROPOSAL

Swift is known to have owned a copy of the Montaigne *Essays* from at least 1715, and probably earlier (Rawson, 1992). Montaigne was a natural part of the reading of any educated person of Swift's time and cultural disposition, and Rawson cited repeated references to the influence of Montaigne on Swift's writings. Although in *Gulliver's Travels* Swift (1726) includes a scene in which the minuscule Gulliver is almost eaten by a child in Brobdingnag, Swift does no more than flirt with the theme of cannibalism in that instance. Stone (1996) considers the cannibalistic episodes in *Gulliver's Travels*, both in Brobdingnag and among the Yahoos, to have had a profound frightening effect on the young Dickens, however.

Cannibalism is the central concern of Swift's satirical *A Modest Proposal* (1729), which brings to mind the fact that some members of the Donner Party ate some of the babies who died, and that in times of famine some Chinese families exchanged children to be eaten. In *A Modest Proposal*, Swift suggested that one way to deal with the problems of the Irish famine would be to pay Irish mothers for their 1-year-old infants, who could be served as a delicacy at rich Englishmen's tables. There could also be a market in by-products such as "adorable gloves for ladies and summer boots for fine gentlemen." Swift (1729, p. 556) suggested that having such a profitable market would be a great inducement to marriage, put a stop to abortions, and "make men as fond of their wives during the time of their pregnancy as they are now of their mares in foal, their cows in calf, or sows when they are ready to farrow, nor offer to beat or kick them . . . for fear of a miscarriage." Swift assures us that a young, healthy, well-nursed child, when a year old, is a most delicious, nourishing, and wholesome food, whether stewed, roasted, baked, or boiled. He expressed the opinion that it would equally serve as a fricassee or ragout.

This misanthropic *A Modest Proposal* was suggested to help balance the Irish trade deficit, provide a solution to the poverty of survivors (who would be paid well for children), solve the population problem (the surplus children no longer existing), and give some pleasure to rich Englishmen. Swift's heading for the essay communicates the essence: "A modest proposal for preventing the children of poor people from being a burthen to their parents or country, and for making them beneficial to the public."

Rawson (1992, p. 353) construed Swift's proposal to be an uncomplimentary cannibal slur against the Irish, regarding them as a colony of savages near home; "just the kind of thing they can do by themselves and carry out successfully and profitably." The proposal also directs bitter sarcasm toward English habits, tastes, and morals.

Sanday (1986) discussed events similar to the tale spun by Swift that occurred in 1454 in the Valley of Mexico, at which time terrible drought-induced famine was experienced. It was reported that merchants came from other areas and bought children from their parents for a few handfuls of dried maize. These children were bought to sacrifice and probably were eaten.

DICKENS

One of the most respected and influential English writers of the nineteenth century was Charles Dickens. I have already mentioned that cannibalistic episodes play a central role in much of his writing, and that theme will be explored a bit more. Stone (1994, p. 15) advanced the thesis that during Dickens' infant days his nursemaid "used to tell him stories of a monstrous Captain Murderer, who married innocent young girls for the express purpose of cutting off their heads, chopping them up, baking them in giant meat pies, feasting on them, and picking their bones."

Dickens was familiar with the literature concerning shipwrecks and disasters at sea; his library contained many volumes about shipwrecks, and he used several of the famous sinkings discussed in Chapter 3 (such as the *Medusa, Nottingham Galley,* and *Peggy)* in various writings. Dickens made many references to Swift, and Stone believes his knowledge of Swift went back to his early days. Dickens was also familiar with DeFoe's *Robinson Crusoe,* and the Defoe images of savage cannibals appear in several of Dickens' writings and testimonials.

Stone believed stories such as those in the Brothers Grimm's fairy tales (Owens, 1981) had massive influence on the young Dickens, along with those of Ali Baba and his forty thieves, who quartered their opponents and hoisted their remains to the cavern ceiling. These, along with the stories of survivors of shipwrecks who butchered and ate one another, and ferocious cannibals who worked up an appetite while dancing around their prey, led Stone (1994, p. 27) to conclude they "enthralled and provoked him, and all this and much more registered indelibly on his consciousness."

Stone's conclusion is that many of Dickens' most famous writings are transformations of the anxieties of his early life. Stone (1994, p. 263) wrote:

> The unspeakable rites of cannibalism became a matrix of art, of bright humor, wild flights of fancy, great structuring metaphors, dark thematic undertones,

and penetrating social criticism. . . . But behind the humor, metaphors, and criticism . . . lurked profound uneasiness and at times profound dread.

He continued (p. 267):

> Humor allowed him to speak of impulses he hardly dared to think about. . . . He could now present cannibalism—that unspeakable crime, that unpardonable sin, that unexpungeable stain—as metaphor rather than a joke. He had transformed the raw fascination and horror of childhood—the anger and aggression too—into a powerful instrument for alerting and impeaching society.

In *Great Expectations* (Dickens, 1860–1861), one of the two major strands of action centers around the felon Abel Magwitch (Stoehr, 1965). The character of this escaped convict has been likened to a cannibalistic character Dickens read about as a child in a sensational weekly periodical called the *Terrific Register* (Stone, 1994). The character in this childhood image escaped from an island penal settlement with a group of fellow convicts. They stole a boat and reached the mainland, but the weaker members began to fail, and then to die, with the survivors being driven to feed on their former companions. Finally, the last survivors begin to murder one another, with only one "predator-convict" left, who eats his fill, lives to be recaptured, and is taken back to prison. This survivor, who developed "an inappeasable relish for this dreadful food," lures a fellow prisoner into an escape attempt, with the sole purpose of killing him and eating him— which he accomplishes.

Dickens recreates this scene in the initial chapters of *Great Expectations*, where the young boy, Pip, encounters Magwitch, who is in chains; Pip is threatened unless he brings food and a file to sustain and free Magwitch. This threat is in a cannibalistic form: "'You bring 'em both to me.' He tilted me again. 'Or I'll have your heart and liver out.'" This threat was embellished by the claim that Magwitch was not alone, but had a young man hid with him (which was not the case) "who has a secret way pecooliar to himself, of getting at a boy, and at his heart, and at his liver. . . . He will softly creep his way to him and tear him open. I am a keeping that young man from harming of you at the present moment, with great difficulty." And of course, Pip complies.

Stone (1994) related another invocation of cannibalism found in *Pickwick*, when the Fat Boy becomes enamored of Mary, and they go down to the "eating room" together. Fat Boy plunges his knife and fork into a meat pie, leans toward Mary, and exclaims slowly, "I say, how nice you do look," and Dickens adds, "there was enough of the cannibal in the young gentleman's eyes to render the compliment a doubtful one." Stone (1994, p. 189) noted that in *A Tale of Two Cities* there are ogres who exhibit strange cannibalistic appetites, and who seem to have a special relish for young mothers and their young children—"a favorite dish (a childhood-engendered dish) on the Dickens menu."

In *David Copperfield,* Dickens had David, who adores Dora, using cannibalistic terms to describe a dinner where David cannot remember who was there, except Dora. "I have not the least idea what we had for dinner, besides Dora. My impression is, that I dined off Dora, entirely, and sent away half-a-dozen plates untouched." And Dora later smiled at him and gave him her "delicious hand," with David later remarking that after meeting her, "I lived principally on Dora and coffee."

This scene is reminiscent of the playfulness of the epigram by T. S. Eliot from *Sweeney Agonistes,* with which this chapter opened: Doris would be "a nice little, white little, soft little, tender little,/ Juicy little, right little, missionary stew." The same, or similar expressions, often are used to refer to eating and making love (Lewis, 1986). One is "consumed with desire" and the lover "eagerly seeks to devour the object of his passion." Terms of endearment, likewise, regularly compare the love object to a tempting, dainty dish.

FLAUBERT

Although cannibalism has been seen by many writers as unspeakable, unthinkable, and unpardonable, it has occupied the attention of many great writers, particularly among the English and French. Flaubert (1862) wrote a particularly bloodthirsty and violent book, *Salammbo,* set in Carthage in the fourth century BC. The tale is full of erotic fantasy and gruesome details of slaughter, and raises siege cannibalism to what Lestringant (1997) called "epic heights." There is a minor reference to cannibalism early in the book when bodies were shamefully mutilated and hung up in bits in butchers' shops, with people sinking their teeth in them.

A climactic episode in the penultimate chapter has 40,000 soldiers trapped in a canyon with no exit, and the entrance blocked. On their ninth day with no food, three of them died, and meat was cut from these bodies by a few—who ate. By the middle of the night more joined, and soon many devoured the bodies "with delight." Flaubert (1862, p. 250) wrote: "They cooked bits on embers, on their swordpoints; they sprinkled them with dust and quarreled over the best morsels." Soon the available dead and dying were depleted and they delivered the wounded from their torment. The horror continues, with lions and jackals coming in to finish things off.

In the abstract, cannibalism is considered a horrible act, yet when it took place in survival incidents, such as those historical events described earlier, it was accepted by society as an understandable act necessary to survive. It was argued explicitly that not to have eaten human flesh would have constituted an act of suicide, an act that is not acceptable morally. Both governmental and religious institutions extended strong institutional support to survivors of disasters in which cannibalism occurred. The Roman Catholic Church considered cannibalism to be justified morally, provided no one is deliberately killed. The community at large, although sometimes expressing initial distress, does not disapprove or punish the survivors, nor in the Andean incident, did the relatives of those eaten condemn the survivors, after they recovered from a brief period of shock. The literature discussed to this point views cannibalism with horror, yet obsessive attention is devoted to the description of its disgusting details.

GOTHIC IMAGES

An interesting thesis was advanced by Malchow (1996) that in both the world of historical experience and the imagined world of literature, Gothic writers in the late-eighteenth and nineteenth century invoked images of cannibalism to demonize those who were different sexually, racially, and culturally. This demonization included the use of the vampire story, with its horrors of killing by drinking the blood of victims.

Malchow's (1996) thesis is that the savage cannibal and gothic vampire had much in common, with their sharp teeth and bloody mouths signifying an uncontrollable hunger infused with a deviant sexual sadism. Whereas the cannibal is in the savage outside world, the vampire is here among us in folk superstition and literary imagination. He considers both to be projections of nameless fears that informed an overarching gothic imagination.

I have remarked several times on the unfortunate (but perhaps evolutionarily understandable) tendency to view the world in terms of "Us" (our kin, friends, community, and race) and "Them" (strangers, foreigners, and those whose enslavement we want to justify). It is interesting that members of lighter skinned races, such as Asians and New Zealanders, were commonly thought by Europeans to be superior (although perverted and childlike) than the darker skinned New Guinea Highlanders and Fijian cannibals. Obviously, the former cannot be all bad because they are more similar to the white evaluators. Malchow characterized the "Us–Them" contrast in terms of victim and predator, innocent and depraved, sane and mad, white and black. In the case of cannibalism, he suggested that it was (p. 43) "not like eating like, but the victimization of an opposite: of one sex devouring the other, of age feasting on youth, of the young feeding on the old, of the living violating the dead and buried, of one 'tribe' or race consuming another." Throughout this book many historical examples of such consumption have been described and discussed.

As noted in Chapter 6, Lestringant (1997) discussed the Gothic demonization of other races as cannibals, maintaining that the motif of criminal cannibalism was commonly used in the English press to establish the depravity of domestic lower class subjects. I have discussed the tendency of white colonizers and invaders to characterize natives who inhabit a newly found country as cannibals, which enables the whites to treat them as less than human. There has been a tendency for natives to characterize whites as cannibals, what with the white's obsession with things cannibalistic, Eucharist rites, and the tendency to deport people as slaves—an activity that natives assumed meant that the people who disappeared had been eventually eaten. An interesting fact is that whites accused blacks of rampant cannibalism, but as described in Chapter 3, when it came time to eat people in shipwreck disasters, it was the whites who ate available blacks.

Malchow (1996) suggested cannibalism evokes an even deeper response than Western sexual taboos, indicating the depth of these fears and disgust. In folklore, murder, rape, and incest often involve victimization of the most innocent—children, boys, and young women. Stone (1994) developed the same theme, citing the story of *Jack the Giant Killer*, in which the giant Blunderboe led people home to stock his larder: "The giant declared / he'd devour / For breakfast who dared to come near." In the same tale the giant Thunderdel intoned: "Fee, fie, fo, fum, / I smell the blood of an Englishman. / Be he alive, or be he dead, / I'll grind his bones to make my bread."

The fairy tales of the Brothers Grimm (Owens, 1981) are exemplars of similar themes. For example, in *Little Red Riding-Hood*, the Wolf ate Little Red Riding-hood's grandmother, and then ate Red after she remarked, "But grandmother, what great teeth you have got!" The wolf remarked, just before he ate her, "The better to eat you!"

Another is *Hansel and Grethel*, in which their stepmother urged the father, who was unable to support the children, to take them to the forest and abandon them in its thickest part. The children heard the stepmother's urging, and Hansel defeated the plan by leaving a trail of white pebbles, which they were able to use to guide them home. The stepmother persevered in her attempts, and managed to abandon them in the forest. They were lost and hungry, and stumbled on the gingerbread house ornamented with sweet cakes and tarts, with a window formed of barley-sugar. They began eating, and were discovered by the wicked witch, who had constructed the house of gingerbread specifically to entrap children. Once they were in her power, she would feed them well until they became fat, and then kill and cook them for her feast-day. She remarked: "What nice tit-bits they will be!", grabbed Hansel and locked him in a cage, ordered Grethel to draw some water so she could boil up something good for Hansel, who was to remain locked up until he was fat, at which time she would cook and eat him. Every morning she had him stick out his finger to see if he was fat enough to eat, but he always stuck a bone out, and her eyesight was so bad she couldn't see the deception.

As weeks went on she grew tired of waiting and ordered the water boiled, telling Grethel that in the morning she would kill and eat Hansel. In the meantime, the witch kneaded bread dough and made the oven hot. She dragged Grethel up to the oven door and ordered her to "creep in there, and see if it is hot enough yet to bake the bread." Grethel tricked the witch, pushed her into the oven, shut the door, and fastened the bolt. "Oh! how the old witch did howl, it was quite horrible to hear her." She was left to burn and Grethel freed Hansel, crying "Hansel, Hansel, we are free; the old witch is dead." They found pearls and precious stones, were able to cross a river on the back of a white duck, found themselves in a familiar portion of the forest, and returned home. The father was overjoyed, the wicked stepmother was dead, they had the witch's pearls and precious stones, "and the father lived in happiness with his children till his death." The moral of the story seems to be that one should be neither a wicked witch nor an evil stepmother. In all, these are pretty scary tales for little children—as may have been the case for Charles Dickens.

Another story that compelled British imagination, and that enjoyed a musical renaissance in Stephen Sondheim's 1979 production, was that of Sweeney Todd, the demon barber of Fleet Street. The most familiar version was published in 1840, followed 2 years later by a London stage version, with "hack" variations appearing until at least the 1880s (Malchow, 1996). Sweeney turned his customers into meat for Mrs. Lovett's pies, a tale that could have been based on the story of a fourteenth-century Parisian baker accused of using the flesh of infants and a story of a revolutionary era Parisian who murdered his customers and served them as meat pies.

Malchow noted that Sweeney was Irish, and believes the purpose of the story was to demonize the barbarous Irish in the eyes of the English. Some English writers considered the poor rural Irish to be a species of "white chimpanzees" who were as good in the arts of forest warfare as the modern Maoris, "whom they so much resembled."

A similar story of cannibalism was used to support the eighteenth-century English anti-Scottish prejudice—that of Sawney Beane, the head of a cannibal clan toward the end of the fourteenth century. As the story goes, Sawney had his origins in poverty, ran off with a local girl, and settled in a cave in the southwest corner of Scotland. They began to murder and cannibalize innocent travelers; they carried them to their cave, quartered them, salted and pickled the parts, and dried them for food (Stone, 1974). The pair raised eight sons and six daughters, and as though that was not bad enough the family was sexually depraved, producing a "Bloodthirsty Clan" of 18 grandsons and 14 granddaughters through incestuous relations. The members of the clan hunted people together, but were finally caught in the act of dismembering a woman they had just killed, and their cave with its provisions and loot was discovered. The whole clan was captured and summarily and painfully executed in 1435: the "privy-members" of the men were thrown into the fire, their hands and legs were severed, and then they were permitted to bleed to death. The women witnessed this event, and they too were cast into separate fires and burned to ashes. Ah, civilization and justice triumph in the end.

OTHER LITERARY CANNIBALS

No point would be served by going into an extensive discussion of the massive literature that has cannibalism either as a main course or as a juicy side dish. Clearly, cannibalism has been a topic of central concern to many writers and readers through the centuries. There are some rather minor pieces by major writers; Poe (1838) published *The Narrative of Arthur Gordon Pym*, which contained an episode of shipwreck cannibalism in which lots were drawn among the four survivors (one of them the narrator, Pym), with the one who drew the shortest lot to be killed and eaten—as I noted in Chapter 3, a typical procedure among starving sailors. In the story, the evil sailor who had insisted on drawing lots lost, he was killed, his blood drunk, and he was consumed over the next 4 days after the hands, feet, head, and entrails were thrown into the sea. Subsequently the survivors found some stores, caught some tortoises, they survived, were rescued, and Pym sailed on to further adventures.

Mark Twain (1868) wrote a slight fantasy seen through the eyes of a narrator, a former Congressman, concerning cannibalism among 24 passengers in a snow-bound railroad car in Illinois. There was sufficient wood in the engine tender to keep the stoves going, but no provisions whatever. After 7 days with no food it was proposed to determine who should die to provide food for the rest. The story then moves to a parody of parliamentary procedures, with nominations, and election of a candidate for each meal. Twain spends several paragraphs commenting on the culinary merits of the various candidates, and the story breaks off when the Congressman reaches his destination. It is finally revealed that the story was only "the harmless vagaries of a madman instead of the genuine experiences of a bloodthirsty cannibal." The story parodies the nasty calculations of parliamentary debate more than it deals with bloodthirsty cannibalism.

Jules Verne (1862), in his first successful work of fiction, *Five Weeks in a Balloon*, threw in a rather tame scene involving cannibalism as observed from a balloon during an exploration of unplumbed regions of Africa. He dubs the natives observed engaging in warfare as the "Nyam Nyam," which he identifies as onomatopoeic, reproducing the sound of mastication—his characterization of the Niam Niam natives of the Bantu people who lived in Zandelande, Africa—discussed in Chapter 6.

Verne depicted the horror of witnessing the chief of the "savage army" throwing himself on a wounded enemy, cutting off his arm with a single blow, raising it to his mouth, and biting into it with his teeth. This is followed by a description of the victorious tribemen hurling themselves on the dead and wounded and fighting among themselves over the still warm flesh. One of the balloonists smugly concluded (p. 252): "Pah!. . . . How disgusting!" Lestringant (1994 described several later treatments of cannibalism in Verne's works, one of which he considers to be a gloss over the story of *The Medusa*—discussed in Chapter 3.

Typee (1844), an important work by Herman Melville, incorporated the cannibal theme as a major element. The practice of ritual cannibalism was used by Melville to characterize the behavior of neighboring enemies. Melville (1844, p. 195) wrote:

> Truth, who loves to be centrally located, is again found between the two extremes; for cannibalism to a certain moderate extent is practised among several of the primitive tribes in the Pacific, but it is upon the bodies of slain enemies alone; . . . still I assert that those who indulge in it are in other respects humane and virtuous.

Shortly before leaving the Polynesians of Typee (which in the local dialect means a lover of human flesh) the narrator remarked that most evidence of cannibalism had been derived second-hand from Europeans, or from the admissions of the savages themselves after they became civilized and were made aware of the detestation Europeans have of the custom (shades of Arens). In the final scene before escaping the Typee, the narrator, to his horror, discovers the remains of a cannibalistic feast, and concludes that the chiefs and priests frequently engaged in such feasts, and this conclusion strengthened his resolve to escape as soon as possible.

Joseph Conrad dealt with the topic of collecting heads as trophies in *Heart of Darkness* (1903), based on events that he had witnessed in Leopold's Belgian Congo—discussed in Chapter 6. There is an episode of cannibalism among starving, shipwrecked sailors in his short "reminiscence" *Falk* (1924), the central denouement of which involves an episode aboard a disabled ship. The lone survivor was the chief mate, Falk, who killed and ate several of the crew, and only he, "the best man," finally survived, with the weaker among the crew sequentially killed and eaten.

Finally, in his somewhat self-adulatory and at times factually suspect autobiography, Diego Rivera (1960) claims to have engaged in cannibalism as a dietary exercise in 1904 when he was in his late teens, while taking a course in human anatomy at the Medical School in Mexico City. It had been claimed that a French furrier fed his animals, cats, the meat of cats that had been skinned for their fur, and that they grew bigger with glossier and firmer fur. Rivera and his fellow students repeated the experiment by living on a diet of human meat. They purchased from the city morgue cadavers that had died of violence, were freshly killed, and not diseased or senile. He claimed that they lived on this cannibal diet for 2 months and that everyone's health improved. He remarked that he liked to eat women's legs, breasts, breaded ribs, and brains in vinaigrette—throughout the book he displayed a strong preference for women in many regards. His conclusion was that a human is probably the most assimilable food available to man, and that when man evolves a civilization higher than our currently primitive one, the eating of human flesh will be sanctioned because we will have thrown off all superstitions and irrational taboos.

SOME RECIPES

Now, for yet another change of pace; as I read I noted the various descriptions of how people were prepared for consumption. As discussed in Chapter 6, Levi-Strauss was not correct in his division of cannibalistic cooking methods into roasted (primitive) and boiled (cultured). People have been consumed in a number of different ways, including raw, roasted, boiled, dried, baked, smoked, salted, and pickled, and they have been made into sausage and meat pies in Europe. I hope the discussion of a few cooking methods will not prove to be too macabre. It should be remembered that many of these are the stuff of fantasy and legend, some are based on acceptable observational data, and some are intended to demonize the perpetrators as savages.

Among preferred cuts, savage persons are said to select from a sacrificed body those portions they intend to eat: particularly the liver, heart, and phallus—all of which are organs bearing a heavy symbolic load. In ritual cannibalism there is often a Lamarckian symbolic significance; for example, the heart of a brave warrior is eaten to acquire his courage, the leg muscle of a swift runner to gain his speed, the brain of a wise chief to attain his wisdom, and in some cultures women consumed the male genitalia to enhance the likelihood of giving birth to a boy. Lestringant (1997) remarked that the appetite thus satisfied becomes more metaphorical than bestial, and is an indirect expression of a passion driven by symbolic expression.

Malchow (1996, p. 109) noted: "Among the South Sea Islanders, the palm of the hand, especially of a young girl, was looked upon as the most dainty morsel; while New Zealanders gave a decided preference to the foot." Williams (1859) claimed Fijians considered the greatest dainties to be the heart, thigh, and arm above the elbow. Sahlins (1983) reported that Methodist missionaries generally agreed that the breasts of young women were considered the choicest repast. The Malekulans, according to Harrison (1937), considered the greater delicacies to be the inner part of the thighs and the head. Stone (1994) refers to the fact that those in South America and in the interior of Africa prefer the inside of the hand and the sole of the foot as the nicest parts of the human body. Stone cited Dickens' claim that Africans consider the head to be a tit-bit, and that they prefer the soles of the feet, and the fleshier part of the legs and back of young subjects.

Lestringant (1997, p. 24) remarked that many writers projected European culinary habits onto the American Cannibal: "because meat was regularly salted at home, their morbid imaginations produced lumps of salted human flesh hanging from the beams of cannibal huts; the familiar spit roast engendered the roasting of human victims over a small fire." One early account provided by Lestringant (1997, p. 195, note 6) is that "after splitting them [human corpses] down the middle, they take their steaming intestines and eat them; they do the same with the extremities; but they chop up the other limbs, salt them and keep them as we keep sausages and hams."

The Ache Indians of Paraguay were said to have built a grill, under which a big fire was lit. Clastres (1998, p. 327) wrote: "All the Atchei are roasted on the [grill], except very young children, who are boiled in earthen pots." A vegetable is eaten with the flesh, and the marrow or bud of a type of palm plant is boiled with the head and viscera, and then roasted on the grill with the meat. Leftovers are wrapped in palm leaves or ferns, to be eaten cold over the next few days.

Gero (1970) offered the following recipe of the African Zande: The flesh was cut to the size of a kettle, and it was stewed after taking care first to singe the hairs over the fire. The fat that collected on the surface of the boiling water was removed and kept in an earthen vessel, later used to season vegetables, as a cosmetic for the skin, or to prepare stalks of dried grass as torches. Harrison's (1936) description of the recipe used by the natives of New Hebrides was to hang the body and beat it until the bones are broken; then take it down, cut it into large pieces, wrap it in leaves, and cook it in a native oven, as would be done with other food. Davies (1984) reported that in Sumatra, condemned thieves and adulterers were eaten. Their relatives were obliged to be present at the ceremony and to provide salts and lemon with which to season their kin's body.

In general, arms and legs are favored in the initial round of meals on people, moving next to other meaty parts. Usually the liver and heart are then consumed, and finally brains and other innards, such as lungs and intestines. The Fiji considered the heart, thighs, and arm above the elbow to be the greatest dainties. In many of the maritime cases, sailors discarded the head, hands, and feet, but South American and African natives tended to prefer parts of hands and feet. These preferences might reflect the initial disgust at being driven by necessity in survival situations, as contrasted with the symbolic nature of ritual cannibalism.

Hogg (1958) described several recipes used by different peoples: When the Fijians baked a man he was referred to as "long pig," and herbs were nearly always cooked with the flesh, either to prevent indigestion or as a savory stuffing. The man-eating Hamatsa of the Kwakiutl Indians of North America were said to take down a corpse that had been smoked and lay it on a mat. Each, in strict order of tribal seniority, was invited to select the portion of the corpse that he would like to eat. When Nigerian warriors killed an enemy, they would often cut pieces off his body and eat them raw, in situ, without any formalities in order to absorb the courage of the slain warrior. Whatever the method of cooking, the cannibalistic practices take on a meaningful symbolic load, although there are a great variety of methods and meanings. These practices seem calculated to intimidate others, as well as to assume a ritual significance that lends a solemn dignity to what often was little more than an orgiastic ceremony.

TASTE TESTS

Throughout, I have presented descriptions of the taste of human flesh as contained in a number of narratives, and numerous preferences for various cuts have been stated. In the epigram heading Chapter 3, the wife of the ship's captain noted that brains were the most delicious thing she had ever tasted, and Lewis Keseberg of the Donner Party (discussed in Chapter 2) agreed, adding that human liver is better than lean beef. In the two airplane disasters described in Chapter 4, the meat was dried, and in both instances it was described as tasting like beef jerky.

As described in Chapter 6, Gero (1970) was told that human flesh is very sweet, even more so than monkey meat, which he tasted, and found it to be too sweet, much more so than pork. The Malekula described the taste as similar to tender pork, and rather sweet, and the Maori considered humans to be sumptuous food, also far sweeter than pork. Although, according to Nigerians, white men consider pork to be the tastiest of meat, the Nigerians did not find pork to have the fine taste of human flesh. Fore women described the meat of dead humans as tasty and sweet (Durham, 1991), and older women among their neighbors, the Gimi, remembered that human flesh had a uniquely delectable sweetness (Gillison, 1983).

Those in the Congo were said to have a preference for the meat of blacks over whites, because the Europeans used too much salt, giving their meat a strong taste. Stone (1994, p. 545) cited accounts in English periodicals that described the preferences of man-eating natives of the Marquesas Islands, who were described as "epicures in cannibalism [who] . . . do not think so much of white men as they do of black. Black men's flesh is greatly preferred to pork." And later (p. 560), he cited stories in the English periodical *All the Year Round* that stated that an African tribe "is said to come down to the shore to catch people living near the sea, whose flesh they suppose to have a brinier and choicer flavour." In yet another piece in *All the Year Round* (Stone, 1994, p. 561) a native was quoted: "'I no eat him, for my cook done spoil him; he no put nuff pepper on him,' meaning that the sauce had not been to his taste." On the other hand, "the Pangwe tribe . . . bury the dead bodies of their enemies for a week, to give them a gamy flavour before they are eaten." These stated preferences may not reflect real preferences, but probably are calculated to titillate and terrify the listeners.

Dickens wrote a series of straightforward articles on cooking, food, and dining, but included a concluding piece entitled "Pastry and an Entremet of Great Merit." The entremet consisted of *"The English sailor à la maitre d'hôtel, and the Sea captain au gratin,"* which was represented as having been obtained from the last chef of the King of the Sandwich Islands. Stone (1994, p. 562) quotes: "Take a shipwrecked sailor, not under three-and-forty, flour him and pepper him. Open him down the back, first carefully removing his head, then baste." The last of the five paragraph entremet contains other "secrets of cannibal cooking" (p. 563): "Tarry old boatswains are generally boiled down for soup. Captains, if under sixty, are treated with bread-crumbs, plum sauce, and lemon juice. Ship-boys are much relished scalloped, and a baby à la Metternich is said to require only legality to carry its fame to both the North and South Poles." The paragraph ends with a description of a custom in Sumatra to eat the elderly: "The chief mourner . . . shakes hands with the old party. . . . He is instantly clubbed, and eaten, with 'sauce piquante,' or 'sauce à la bonne femme.' Such is the remarkable custom of this very interesting people." Each of the series of 21 articles opens with the heading "CONDUCTED BY CHARLES DICKENS," and the final piece is an instance of what Stone has called Dickens' "attraction of repulsion" that was evident throughout his career.

Tannahill (1975) quoted a Frenchman who avowed that Caribs considered the flesh of the English the most delicate and desirable of any they had tasted, being far superior to that of Spaniards or French. However, another informant said Caribs thought French were delicious, English so-so, Dutch tasteless, and Spaniards so tough as to be virtually inedible. She also cited an English official who recited a joke about the local sharks; if they find an Englishman, a Frenchman, and a Spaniard in a boat or in the water, they will always attack the Englishman first. I guess it depends on whether you would rather be considered a delicacy, or something inedible, and that decision could well have to do with the particular circumstances in which you find yourself. If you might be an item for consumption, emphasize your stringiness and bad flavor; if not, feel free to celebrate your inherent superiority in all manner of things—including good taste.

To Serve Man   The above has served as the title of an episode of Rod Serling's "Twilight Zone" (1962) (based on a story by Damon Knight), as well as the title of a satirical cookbook that is in somewhat questionable taste. In the Serling episode, a spaceship lands on earth and its occupants announce their intent to bring peace and prosperity and to end famine through advanced farming methods, which they accomplish. They have with them a book in code, a copy of which someone obtains and gives to a decoding specialist (Chambers), who breaks the code for the title "To Serve Man," which seemed a noble and gracious goal of a generous people. The aliens induce Chambers to journey to their planet, promising one big holiday when he gets there. His lady partner keeps working on the book, and discovers that it is not a prescription for human salvation, but is a cookbook. The aliens insist that Chambers eat hearty because "we couldn't want you to lose weight." He doesn't eat at first, but decides that sooner or later all of us will be on the menu, and takes off with them. The moral is "dust to dessert."

The cookbook *To Serve Man: A Cookbook for People* (Würf, 1976) is organized in typical cookbook fashion, with headings such as "Old Standbys," "Variety Meats," and "Soups & Stews," complete with cartoon illustrations. In the foreword, a familiar sexual undertone is stated (Würf, 1976, p. 1): "There is no form of carnal knowledge so complete as that of knowing how somebody tastes." There follows a general discussion of who the best donor would be: Some argue that an athlete would be best and others that maximum tenderness and succulence would probably be found in a young healthy office worker. The former would be too tough and only passable for smoking, pickling, and long slow cooking, and the latter for steaks, oven roasts, or chops, because the fat would be marbled all through the meat.

To the question "Why eat Man?" the answer is that he is large, almost too plentiful, and is available. An array of standard recipes is presented with things such as "Person steaks" substituted for beef steaks, Boiled Leg of Man, Person Kebab, Minceman, Man-Loaf, Homme Bourguigon [sic], Mannerschnitzel, Sweet and Sour Man, Texas Chili with Cowboy, Chile Con Hombre, and recipes for most kinds of offal. There is no point to belabor the point any further; in all, the effort is a bit strained.

There have been humorous movie treatments of cannibalism as well.

The movie "Eating Raoul" has a Mr. Bland selling human bodies to La Fuente Taco House, and consigning the Raoul in question to Doggie King Dog Food.

In the movie version of *The Silence of the Lambs* (Harris, 1988), the cannibalistic psychopath, Hannibal Lecter (who had indulged in human sweetbreads), has escaped from confinement, and in a final phone conversation to Clarice Starling, the behavioral scientist handling him, mentions that he must go because he is having a friend for lunch—a delicious *double entendre*. This is a good point to end the literary and culinary journey into cannibalism. Once again, I note that this most abominable, unthinkable, and unmentionable topic seems to have stirred considerable interest through the ages, and it even is used to provide light entertainment. The food and sex metaphor run through many treatments, and there is always the oscillation between fascination and horror.

EPILOGUE

Several themes have been encountered in this trip through cannibal land. The major assumption was that aspects of basic human nature are the result of evolved tendencies that enhance the reproductive success of organisms. This principle has been shown to be of paramount importance when the life histories of various plant and animal species are examined. A great deal is known about the manner in which evolved processes work their way, and these basic principles can be applied profitably to help understand the human condition.

Of course, what we refer to as the human condition has a very pronounced cultural component that overlays evolved biological tendencies and that can modulate, and even override, these evolved tendencies. The developing organism, be it viewed at the individual or the community level, does not move along unvarying developmental paths, but develops in interaction with constant and varying experiential events throughout the course of existence. There is nothing resembling biological or genetic determinism in the process—there is a true interaction, particularly during the early stages of development.

Because there are such strong cultural influences that affect human behaviors, it is necessary to remove them in order to allow the underlying biological propensities to reveal themselves, unfettered by the rules, conventions, and ideologies imposed by society. One way we have taken to glimpse these underlying tendencies is to pose hypothetical dilemmas that no one would likely ever experience in real life. When such dilemmas are posed, and people must make decisions between different often unpalatable alternatives, we have revealed consistent and uniform patterns of choice that conform to expectations derived from evolutionary theory. People tend to operate using two basic dimensional systems: One is a positive component that includes cooperation and protection of kin and other members of the social community; the other is a negative component that increases the detection of violators of a basic social contract, enhancing the ability to detect cheaters and recognize potential threats to community well-being.

Another way to glimpse human nature is to examine the behavior of people who are in situations in which the rules that regulate normal societal behavior no longer are appropriate. Situations in which survival cannibalism occurs meet that specification: When people are starving to the point of death, and have abandoned hope of any relief, it is clear that a set of basic rules consistently comes into play. These rules are similar to those that regulate choices in the resolution of dilemmas, and they reflect the same two basic components. When it is determined who eats whom and when, a predictable pattern emerges, which favors kith and kin at the expense of other humans and any other class of animal, and which deals severely with any who violate the social contract.

Examination of the literature bearing on survival cannibalism indicates that not only are these patterns regular, but they are universal, and both of these characteristics are what would be expected if they reflect an underlying evolved reality. Throughout human history, people have from time to time experienced famine and starvation, and when they do, and no other resources are available, they begin eating any protein they can to sustain themselves, starting with those animals that typically are consumed and ending with the consumption of humans.

It is not surprising that survival cannibalism is found with great regularity for both humans and other animals under certain circumstances. What is more surprising is that ritual cannibalism has been found to characterize the practices of a great many societies. These rituals embody symbolic components intended to honor, vilify, terrify, and acquire the traits of the consumed. Such cannibalistic practices have been found throughout the world for as long as humans have been in existence. Now, they are encountered mainly in our folk tales, fiction, movies, and other avenues through which we express our imagination.

People have a deep fascination with the horrors of cannibalistic practices, which could well be the reflection of evolved traits that society has successfully controlled in the interest of establishing and maintaining a just society. Unfortunately, we still permit untold barbarisms to be perpetrated on humans by humans in the form of war, genocide, punishment, and impoverishment of those who are characterized as being different from us in some significant way, or who are considered to threaten our way of life. To paraphrase the line in the comic strip *Pogo* written by Walt Kelly, we have found the cannibals, and they are us.

References

Abler, T. S. (1980). Iroquois cannibalism: Fact not fiction. *Ethnohistory*, 27, 309–316.

Abler, T. S. (1992). Beavers and muskets: Iroquois military fortunes in the face of European colonization. In R. B. Ferguson & N. L. Whitehead (Eds.), *War in the tribal zone*. Santa Fe, NM: School of American Research Press, pp. 151–174.

Adams, W. H. D. (1877). *Great shipwrecks: A record of perils and disasters at sea, 1544–1877*. London: T. Nelson.

Almond, J., & Pattison, J. (1997). Human BSE. *Nature*, 389, 437–438.

Anderson, E. N. (1988). *The food of China*. New Haven, CT: Yale University Press.

Arens, W. (1979). *The man-eating myth*. Oxford: Oxford University Press.

Arens, W. (1986). *The original sin*. New York: Oxford University Press.

Bahn, P. G. (1992a). Ancestral cannibalism gives us food for thought. *New Scientist*, 134, 40–41.

Bahn, P. G. (1992b). Cannibalism or ritual dismemberment? In S. Jones, R. Martin, & D. Pilbeam (Eds.), *Cambridge encyclopedia of human evolution*. Cambridge, UK: Cambridge University Press, p. 330.

Balée, W. (1984). The ecology of ancient Tupi warfare. In R. B. Ferguson (Ed.), *Warfare, culture, and environment*. New York: Academic Press, pp. 241–265.

Bardach, J., & Gleeson, K. (1998). *Man is wolf to man*. Berkeley, CA: University of California Press.

Beatty, K. J. (1915). *Human leopards*. London: Hugh Rees, Ltd.

Becker, J. (1996). *Hungry ghosts*. New York: Free Press.

Bedau, H. A. (1997). *Making mortal choices*. Oxford: Oxford University Press.

Bell, G. (1997). *The basics of selection*. New York: Chapman & Hall.

Bettinger, R. L. (1991). *Hunter-gatherers: Archaeological and evolutionary theory*. New York: Plenum Press.

Bierce, A. (1911). *The devil's dictionary*. New York: Oxford University Press (edition published in 1999).

Bisset, J. (1958). *Sail Ho!* New York: Criterion Books.

Blakeslee, S. (1997). New evidence said to link mad cow disease to humans. *The New York Times*, September 30, A6.

Boswell, J. (1791). *Life of Johnson*. Oxford: Oxford University Press, 1970.

Bowden, R. (1984). Maori cannibalism: An interpretation. *Oceania*, 55, 81–99.

Brady, I. (1982). The myth-eating man. *American Anthropologist*, 84, 595–611.

Brodhead, M. (1997). The Donner Party and overland emigration, 1840–1860. In

D. L. Hardesty (Ed.), *The archaeology of the Donner Party*. Reno, NV: University of Nevada Press, pp. 19–29.

Brown, D. E. (1991). *Human Universals*. New York: McGraw-Hill.

Bullock, P. Y. (1991). A reappraisal of Anasazi cannibalism. *Kiva, 57*, 5–16.

Bullock, P. Y. (1992). A return to the question of cannibalism. *Kiva, 58*, 203–205.

Bullock, P. Y. (1998). Evidence of cannibalism? *Science, 277*, 1744–1745.

Burrows, G. (1903) *The curse of central Africa*. London: R. A. Everett & Co.

Buss, D.M. (1994). *The evolution of desire*. New York: Basic Books.

Carneiro, R. (1990). Chiefdom-level warfare as exemplified in Fiji and the Cauca Valley. In J. Haas (Ed.), *The anthropology of war*. Cambridge, UK: Cambridge University Press, pp. 190–211.

Chong, K. R. (1990). *Cannibalism in China*. Wakefield, NH: Longwood Academic.

Clastres, P. (1998). *Chronicle of the Guayaki Indians*. (Translation and Foreword by Paul Auster.) New York: Zone Books.

Colden, C. (1727). *The history of the five indian nations*. Ithaca, NY: Cornell University Press (1958 reprint).

Collis, W. R. F. (1945). Belsen Camp: A preliminary report. *British Medical Journal*, June 9, #4405, 814–815.

Conquest, R. (1978). *Kolyma*. London: Macmillan London Limited.

Conquest, R. (1986). *Harvest of sorrow*. New York: Oxford University Press.

Conrad, J. (1903). *Heart of darkness*. New York: McClure & Phillips..

Conrad, J. (1924). Falk. *The shorter tales of Joseph Conrad*. Garden City, NY: Doubleday, Page

Constable, A. C. (1812). *Constable's shipwrecks and disasters at sea*, Vols. I, II, and III. London: George Ramsay.

Cook, J. W. (1999). *Morality and cultural differences*. New York: Oxford University Press

Craig, H. (Ed.) (1961). *The complete works of Shakespeare*. Chicago, IL: Scott, Foresman.

Craig, W. (1973). *Enemy at the gates*. New York: E. P. Dutton.

Crapanzano, V. (1979). We're what we eat? *The New York Times Book Review*, July 29, p. 6.

Cronin, H. (1991). *The ant and the peacock*. Cambridge, UK: Cambridge University Press.

Culotta, E. (1999a). A new human ancestor? *Science, 284*, 572–573.

Culotta, E. (1999b). Neanderthals were cannibals, bones show. *Science, 286*, 18–19.

Cunningham, R. (1973). *The place where the world ends*. New York: Sheed and Ward.

Daly, M., & Wilson, M. (1988). *Homicide*. New York: Aldine de Gruyter.

Daly, M., & Wilson, M. (1990). Killing the competition. *Human Nature, 1*, 83–109.

Darwin, C. (1871). *The descent of man*. New York: D. Appleton.

Davies, N. (1984). Human sacrifice in the Old World and the New: Some similarities and differences. In E. H. Boone (Ed.), *Ritual human sacrifice in Mesoamerica*. Washington, DC: Dumbarton Oaks Research Library, pp. 211–226.

Dawkins, R. (1996). *Climbing mount improbable*. New York: W. W. Norton.

Deacon, A. B. (1934). *Malekula: A vanishing people in the New Hebrides*. London: George Routledge.

Defleur, A., White, T., Valensi, P., Slimak, L., & Crégut-Bonnoure, E. (1999). Neanderthal cannibalism at Moula-Guercy, Ardèche, France. *Science, 286*, 128–131.

Defoe, D. (1719). *Robinson Crusoe*. New York: New American Library. (Afterword by H. Swados, 1960.)

Degler, C. N. (1991). *In search of human nature*. New York: Oxford University Press.

Dennett, D. C. (1995) *Darwin's dangerous idea*. New York: Simon & Schuster.

Devine, P. E. (1978). *Ethics of homicide*. Notre Dame, IN: University of Notre Dame Press.

Diamond, J. (1997). *Guns, germs, and steel*. New York: W. W. Norton.

Dickens, C. (1860–1861). *Great expectations*. New York: Holt, Rinehart & Winston (1948).

Dong, Q., & Polis, G. A. (1992). The dynamics of cannibalistic populations: A foraging perspective. In M. A. Elgar & B. J. Crespi (Eds.), *Cannibalism: Ecology and evolution among diverse taxa*. Oxford: Oxford University Press, pp. 13–37.

Dorling, T. (1927). *Sea escapes and adventures*. New York: Frederick A. Stokes.

Dornstreich, M. D., & Morren, G. E. B. (1974). Does New Guinea cannibalism have nutritional value? *Human Ecology*, 2, 1–12.

Durán, F. D. (1994). *The history of the Indies of New Spain*. Norman, OK: University of Oklahoma Press.

Durham, W. H. (1991). *Coevolution*. Stanford, CA: Stanford University Press.

Edmonson, M. S. (1984). Human sacrifice in the books of Chilam Balam of Tizimin and Chumayel. In E. H. Boone (Ed.), *Ritual human sacrifice in Mesoamerica*. Washington, DC: Dumbarton Oaks Research Library.

Ehrenreich, B. (1997). *Blood rites*. New York: Henry Holt.

Elgar, M. A. (1992). Sexual cannibalism in spiders and other invertebrates. In M. A. Elgar & B. J. Crespi (Eds.), *Cannibalism: Ecology and evolution among diverse taxa*. Oxford: Oxford University Press, pp. 128–155.

Elgar, M. A., & Crespi, B. J. (1992a). *Cannibalism: Ecology and evolution among diverse taxa*. Oxford: Oxford University Press.

Elgar, M. A., & Crespi, B. J. (1992b). Ecology and evolution of cannibalism. In M. A. Elgar & B. J. Crespi (Eds.), *Cannibalism: Ecology and evolution among diverse taxa*. Oxford: Oxford University Press, pp. 1–12.

Eliot, T. S. (1952). *The complete poems and plays, 1909–1950*. New York: Harcourt, Brace & World.

Farnham, E. W. (1856). From California, in-doors and out. Reprinted in K. Johnson (Ed.), *Unfortunate emigrants*. Logan, UT: Utah State University Press, pp. 136–168.

Fisher, H. H. (1927). *The famine in soviet Russia 1919–1923*. New York: Macmillan.

Fitzpatrick, S. (1994). *Stalin's peasants*. New York: Oxford University Press.

Flaubert, G. (1862). *Salammbo*. London: Penguin Books, 1977.

Flinn, L., Turner, C. G. II, & Brew, A. (1976). Additional evidence for cannibalism in the southwest: The case of LA 4528. *American Antiquity*, 41, 308–318.

Ford, C. S., & Beach, F. A. (1951). *Patterns of sexual behavior*. New York: Harper & Row.

Forsyth, D. W. (1983). The beginning of Brazilian anthropology, Jesuits and Tupinamba cannibalism. *Journal of Anthropological Research*, 39, 147–178.

Forsyth, D. W. (1985). Three cheers for Hans Staden: The case for Brazilian cannibalism. *Ethnohistory*, 32, 17–36.

Freeman, D. (1983). *Margaret Mead and Samoa*. Cambridge, MA: Harvard University Press.

Friedrich, O. (1972). *Before the deluge.* New York: Harper & Row.

Garn, S. M. (1979). The noneconomic nature of eating people. *American Anthropologist,* 81, 902–903.

Garn, S. M., & Block, W. D. (1970). The limited nutritional value of cannibalism. *American Anthropologist,* 72, 106.

Gero, F. G. (1970). *Cannibalism in Zandeland.* Bologna, Italy: Editrice Missionaria Italiana.

Ghiselin, M. T. (1969). *The triumph of the Darwinian method.* Berkeley, CA: University of California Press.

Gibbons, A. (1997). Archaeologists rediscover cannibals. *Science,* 277, 635–637.

Gifford-Gonzalez, D. (1993). Review of prehistoric cannibalism at Mancos 5MTUMR-2346. *Journal of Human Evolution,* 25, 329–332.

Gillison, G. (1983). Cannibalism among women in the Eastern Highlands of Papua New Guinea. In P. Brown & D. Tuzin (Eds.), *The ethnography of cannibalism.* Washington, DC: Society for Psychological Anthropology, pp. 33–50.

Glasse, R. M. (1969). Marriage in South Fore. In R. M. Glasse & M. J. Meggitt (Eds.), *Pigs, pearlshells, and women.* Englewood Cliffs, NJ: Prentice-Hall, pp. 16–37.

Goodall, J. (1963). My life among wild chimpanzees. *National Geographic,* 124, 272–308.

Graulich, M. (1988). Double immolations in ancient Mexican sacrificial ritual. *History of Religions,* 27, 393–404.

Grayson, D. K. (1990). Donner Party deaths: A demographic assessment. *Journal of Anthropological Research,* 46, 222–242.

Grayson, D. K. (1993). Differential mortality and the Donner Party disaster. *Evolutionary Anthropology,* 2, 151–159.

Grayson, D. K. (1996). Human mortality in a natural disaster: The Willie Handcart Company. *Journal of Anthropological Research,* 52, 185–205.

Grayson, D. K. (1997). The timing of Donner Party deaths. In D. L. Hardesty (Ed.), *The archaeology of the Donner Party.* Reno, NV: University of Nevada Press, pp. 124–132.

Gregor, T. (1990). Uneasy peace: Intertribal relations in Brazil's Upper Xingu. In J. Haas (Ed.), Cambridge, UK: Cambridge University Press, pp. 105–124.

Griffith, W. B. (1915). Preface to Beatty, K. J., *Human leopards.* London: Hugh Rees, Ltd., pp. v—ix.

Gzowski, P. (1980). *The sacrament.* New York: Atheneum.

Harner, M. (1977). The ecological basis for Aztec sacrifice. *American Ethnologist,* 4, 117–135.

Harris, M. (1978). *Cannibals and kings.* New York: Random House.

Harris, M. (1979). 'Cannibals and Kings': An exchange. *New York Review of Books,* June 28.

Harris, M. (1985). *Good to eat.* New York: Simon & Schuster.

Harris, T. (1988). *The silence of the lambs.* New York: St. Martin's Press.

Harrison, T. (1936). Living with the people of Malekula. *The Geographical Journal,* 88, 97–127

Harrison, T. (1937). *Savage civilization.* New York: Alfred A. Knopf.

Hassig, R. (1992). Aztec and Spanish conquest in Mesoamerica. In R. B. Ferguson

& N. L. Whitehead (Eds.), *War in the tribal zone*. Santa Fe, NM: School of American Research Press, pp. 83–102.

Hausfater, G., & Hrdy, S. B. (1984). *Infanticide*. New York: Aldine.

Heinzelin, J. de, Clark, J. D., White, T., et al. (1999). Environment and behavior of 2.5-million-year-old Bouri Hominids. *Science, 284,* 625–629.

Helmuth, H. (1973). Cannibalism in paleoanthropology and ethnology. In A. Montagu (Ed.), *Man and agression* (2nd Ed.). New York: Oxford University Press, pp. 229–253.

Heyden, D. (1994). *Introduction to Durán, The History of the Indies of New Spain*. Norman, OK: University of Oklahoma Press, pp. xxv–xxxvi.

Hill, K., & Hurtado, A. M. (1996). *Ache life history*. New York: Aldine.

Hiraiwa-Hasegawa, M. (1992). Cannibalism among non-human primates. In M. A. Elgar & B. J. Crespi (Eds.), *Cannibalism: Ecology and evolution among diverse taxa*. Oxford: Oxford University Press, pp. 323–338.

Hochschild, A. (1998). *King Leopold's ghost*. New York: Houghton Mifflin.

Hoess, R. (1959). *Commandant of Auschwitz*. Cleveland, OH: The World Publishing Co. (English translation of the 1951 Polish version.)

Hogg, G. (1958). *Cannibalism and human sacrifice*. London: Hale.

Huntress, K. (1979). *A checklist of narratives of shipwrecks and disasters at sea to 1860*. Ames, IA: The Iowa State University Press.

Imperato, P. J., & Imperato, E. M. (1992). *They married adventure*. New Brunswick, NJ: Rutgers University Press.

Ingham, J. M. (1984). Human sacrifice at Tenochtitlan. *Comparative Studies in Society and History, 26,* 379–400.

Johnson, K. (1996). *"Unfortunate emigrants."* Logan, UT: Utah State University Press.

Johnson, M. (1922). *Cannibal-land*. Boston, MA: Houghton Mifflin.

Kalous, M. (1974). *Cannibals and Tongo Players of Sierra Leone*. Aukland: Wright and Carman Ltd.

Keeley, L. H. (1996). *War before civilization*. New York: Oxford University Press.

Kenrick, D.T., & Keefe, R.C. (1992). Age preferences in mates reflect sex differences in human reproductive strategies. *Behavioral and Brain Sciences, 15,* 75–133.

Keys, A., Brozek, J., Henschel, A., Mickelsen, O., & Taylor, H. L. (1950). *The biology of human starvation*, Vols. I and II. Minneapolis, MN: The University of Minnesota Press.

Kidd, J. S. (1988). Scholarly excess and journalistic restraint in the popular treatment of cannibalism. *Social Studies of Science, 18,* 749–754.

King, J. A. (1992). *Winter of entrapment*. Toronto, Canada: P. D. Meany.

Koch, J. (1993). 'Alive—the miracle of the Andes': In praise of the human spirit. *The Boston Globe*, January 30.

Kolata, G. (1986). Anthropologists suggest cannibalism is a myth. *Science, 232,* 1497–1500.

Krieger, M. (1994). *Conversations with the cannibals*. Hopewell, NJ: The Ecco Press.

Kurtz, D. V. (1978). The legitimation of the Aztec state. In H. J. M. Claessen & P. Skalnid (Eds.), *The early state*. The Hague: Mouton, pp. 169–189.

Lancet. (1945). Belsen concentration camp. *The Lancet*, May 12, #6350, 604–605.

Larson, G. (1998). The far side of science. *The New York Times*, December 22, D5.

Laycock, H. T. (1944). Some impressions of slow starvation in China. *British Medical Journal,* May 13, #4349, 667–668.

Leacock, E. (1992). Anthropologists in search of a culture: Margaret Mead, Derek Freeman, and all the rest of us. In L. Foerstel & A. Gilliam (Eds.), *Confronting the Margaret Mead legacy.* Philadelphia, PA: Temple University Press, pp. 3–30.

Lee, E. C. B., & Lee, K. (1971). *Safety and survival at sea.* London: Cassell.

Leslie, E. E. (1988). *Desperate journeys, abandoned souls.* Boston: Houghton Mifflin.

Lestringant, F. (1997). *Cannibals.* Berkeley, CA: University of California Press.

Lévi-Strauss, C. (1966). The culinary triangle. *Partisan Review, 33,* 586–595.

Lewis, I. M. (1986). *Religion in context.* Cambridge, UK: Cambridge University Press.

Lifton, R. J. (1986). *The Nazi doctors.* New York: Basic Books.

Lindenbaum, S. (1983). Cannibalism: Symbolic production and consumption. In P. Brown & D. Tuzin (Eds.), *The ethnography of cannibalism.* Washington, DC: Society for Psychological Anthropology, pp. 94–106.

Lipscomb, F. M. (1945). Medical aspects of Belsen concentration camp. *The Lancet,* 313–315.

Lopez, E. H. (1973). *The highest hell.* London: Sidgwick & Jackson.

MacCormack, C. P. (1983). Human leopards and crocodiles. In P. Brown & D. Tuzin (Eds.), *The ethnography of cannibalism.* Washington, DC: Society for Psychological Anthropology, pp. 51–60.

Malchow, H. L. (1996). *Gothic images of race in nineteenth-century Britain.* Stanford, CA: Stanford University Press.

Markowski, B. (1945). Some experiences of a medical prisoner of war. *British Medical Journal,* September 15, #4419, 361–363.

Mathews, J. D., Glasse, R., & Lindenbaum, S. (1968). Kuru and cannibalism. *The Lancet,* 2 (7565), 449–452.

Mayr, E. (1970). *Population, species, and evolution.* Cambridge, MA: Harvard University Press.

Mayr, E. (1982). *The growth of biological thought.* Cambridge, MA: Harvard University Press.

Mayr, E. (1991). *One long argument.* Cambridge, MA: Harvard University Press.

McCabe, J. (1983). FBD marriage: Further support for the Westermarck hypothesis of the incest taboo? *American Anthropologist, 85,* 50–69.

McGlashan, C. R. (1947). *History of the Donner Party.* Stanford, CA: Stanford University Press.

Mead, M. (1928). *Coming of age in Samoa.* New York: William Morrow.

Melville, H. (1844). *Typee: A peep at Polynesian life.* New York: Airmont Publishing Co. (1965 reprint).

Mollison, P. L. (1946). Observations of cases of starvation at Belsen. *British Medical Journal,* January 5, #4435, 4–8.

Montaigne, M. de. (1580). *The essays of Michel de Montaigne,* 3 Vols., Translated by G. B. Ives. New York: The Heritage Press (1946).

Needham, R. (1980). Chewing on the cannibals. *Times Literary Supplement,* January 25, 75–76.

Nisbett, R. E., & Cohen, D. (1996). *Culture of honor.* Boulder, CO: Westview Press.

Norton, G. (1946). *Comments upon the essays of Montaigne*, Vol. 3. New York: The Heritage Press.

O'Neill, P., & Petrinovich, L. (1998). A preliminary cross cultural study of moral intuitions. *Evolution and Human Behavior*, 19, 349–367.

Ortiz de Montellano, B. R. (1978). Aztec cannibalism: An ecological necessity? *Science*, 200, 611–617.

Ortiz de Montellano, B. R. (1990). *Aztec medicine, health, and nutrition*. New Brunswick, NJ: Rutgers University Press.

Osborne, L. (1997). Does man eat man? *Lingua Franca*, April/May, 28–38.

Owens, L. (1981). *The complete Brothers Grimm fairy tales*. New York: Avenal Books.

Pakenham, T. (1991). *The scramble for Africa: The white man's conquest of the dark continent from 1876 to 1912*. New York: Random House.

Paine, R. D. (1921). *Lost ships and lonely seas*. New York: The Century Co.

Parker, S. (1976). The precultural basis of the incest taboo: Toward a biosocial theory. *American Anthropologist*, 78, 285–305.

Petrinovich, L. (1995). *Human evolution, reproduction, and morality*. New York: Plenum Press.

Petrinovich, L. (1996). *Living and dying well*. New York: Plenum Press.

Petrinovich, L. (1999). *Darwinian dominion: Animal welfare and human interests*. Cambridge, MA: MIT Press.

Petrinovich, L., & O'Neill, P. (1996). Influence of wording and framing effects on moral intuitions. *Ethology and Sociobiology*, 17, 145–171.

Petrinovich, L., O'Neill, P., & Jorgensen, M. (1993). An empirical study of moral intuitions: Toward an evolutionary ethics. *Journal of Personality and Social Psychology*, 64, 467–478.

Pfennig, D. W., Ho, S. G., & Hoffman, E. A. (1998). Pathogen transmission as a selective force against cannibalism. *Animal Behaviour*, 55, 1255–1261.

Piccigallo, P. R. (1979). *The Japanese on trial*. Austin, TX: University of Texas Press.

Pinker, S. (1994). *The language instinct*. New York: William Morrow.

Poe, E. A. (1838). *The narrative of Arthur Gordon Pym*. New York: Hill and Wang (1960 reprint).

Polis, G. A., Myers, C. A., & Hess, W. R. (1984). A survey of intraspecific predation within the class Mammalia. *Mammal Review*, 14, 187–198.

Poole, F. J. P. (1983). Cannibals, tricksters, and witches. In P. Brown & D. Tuzin (Eds.), *The ethnography of cannibalism*. Washington, DC: Society for Psychological Anthropology, pp. 6–32.

Popper, K. R. (1979). The bucket and the searchlight: Two theories of knowledge. In *Objective knowledge: An evolutionary approach*, Rev. Ed. Oxford: Oxford University Press, pp. 341–361.

Rawson, C. (1992). "Indians" and Irish: Montaigne, Swift, and the cannibal question. *Modern Language Quarterly*, 53, 299–363.

Read, P. P. (1974). *Alive*. New York: Avon Books.

Rhodes, R. (1997). *Deadly feasts*. New York: Simon & Shuster.

Rivera, D. (1960). *My art, my life (with Gladys March)*. New York: Citadel Press.

Rivers, J. P. W. (1982). Women and children last: An essay on sex discrimination in disasters. *Disasters*, 6, 256–267.

Rivière, P. G. (1980). Review of Arens, W. *The man-eating myth*. *Man*, 15, 203–205.

Robicsek, J., & Hales, D. M. (1984). Maya heart sacrifice: Cultural perspective and surgical technique. In E. H. Boone (Ed.), *Ritual human sacrifice in Mesoamerica*. Washington, DC: Dumbarton Oaks Research Library, pp. 29–87.

Roper, M. K. (1969). A survey of the evidence for intrahuman killing in the Pleistocene. *Current Anthropology*, 10, 427–459.

Ross, J. B. (1984). Effects of contact on revenge hostilities among the Achuarä Jívaro. In R. B. Ferguson (Ed.), *Warfare, culture, and environment*. New York: Academic Press, pp. 83–109.

Sahagun, F. B. de. (1932). *A history of ancient Mexico 1547–1577*, Vol. 1. Nashville, TN: Fiske University Press.

Sahlins, M. (1978) Culture as protein and profit. *New York Review of Books*, November 23, 45–53.

Sahlins, M. (1979). Marshall Sahlins replies. *New York Review of Books*, June 28.

Sahlins, M. (1983). Raw women, cooked men, and other "great things" of the Fiji Islands. In P. Brown & D. Tuzin (Eds.), *The ethnography of cannibalism*. Washington, DC: Society for Psychological Anthropology, pp. 72–93.

Salmon, M. H. (1995). Standards of evidence in anthropological reasoning. *The Southern Journal of Philosophy*, 35 (supplement), 129–145.

Sanday, P. RS. (1986). *Divine hunger: Cannibalism as a cultural system*. Cambridge, UK: Cambridge University Press.

Saunders, A. (1827). Narrative of the shipwreck and sufferings of Miss Ann Saunders. In B. D. Smith (Ed.), *Terror at sea*. Cape Elizabeth, ME: The Provincial Press, pp. 93–106.

Scrimshaw, S. C. M. (1984). Infanticide in human populations: Societal and individual concerns. In G. Hausfater & S. B. Hrdy (Eds.), *Infanticide: Comparative and evolutionary perspectives*. New York: Aldine, pp. 439–462.

Seagrave, S. (1988). Foreword. In E. E. Leslie, *Desperate journeys, abandoned souls*. Boston, MA: Houghton Mifflin, pp. xi—xv.

Serling, R. (1962). *To Serve Man*. Episode of Twilight Zone, March 2.

Shankman, P. (1969). Le rôti et le bouilli: Lévi-Strauss' theory of cannibalism. *American Anthropologist*, 71, 54–69.

Shepher, J. (1983). *Incest*. New York: Academic Press.

Simpson, A. W. B. (1984). *Cannibalism and the common law*. Chicago, IL: University of Chicago Press.

Snow, D. R. (1994). *The Iroquois*. Oxford: Blackwell.

Sober, E. (1984). *The nature of selection*. Cambridge, MA: MIT Press.

Sober, E., & Wilson, D. S. (1998). *Unto others*. Cambridge, MA: Harvard University Press.

Solzhenitsyn, A. I. (1973). *The Gulag Archipelago 1918–1956*, Vol. 1. New York: Harper & Row.

Solzhenitsyn, A. I. (1974). *The Gulag Archipelago 1918–1956*, Vol. 2. New York: Harper & Row.

Solzhenitsyn, A. I. (1978). *The Gulag Archipelago 1918–1956*, Vol. 3. New York: Harper & Row.

Sorokin, P. A. (1942). *Man and society in calamity*. New York: E. P. Dutton.

Springer, J. W. (1980). Review of *The Man-Eating Myth* by William E. Arens. *Anthropological Quarterly*, 53, 148–150.

Stanback, M. T., & Koenig, W. D. (1992). Cannibalism in birds. In M. A. Elgar & B. J. Crespi (Eds.), *Cannibalism: Ecology and evolution among diverse taxa*. Oxford: Oxford University Press, pp. 277–298.

Steadman, L. B., & Merbs, C. F. (1982). Kuru and cannibalism? *American Anthropologist*, 84, 611–627.

Stegner, W. (1964). *The gathering of Zion*. New York: McGraw-Hill.

Steward, J. H., & Faron, L. C. (1959). *Native peoples of South America*. New York: McGraw-Hill.

Stewart, G. R. (1960). *Ordeal by hunger*. Lincoln, NB: University of Nebraska Press.

Stewart, G. R. (1962). *The California trail*. Lincoln, NB: University of Nebraska Press.

Stoehr, T. (1965). *Dickens: The dreamer's stance*. Ithaca, NY: Cornell University Press.

Stone, H. (1994). *The night side of Dickens: Cannibalism, passion, necessity*. Columbus, OH: Columbia University Press.

Sumner, W. G. (1940). *Folkways*. Boston, MA: Ginn & Co.

Swift, J. (1729). *A modest proposal*. Reprinted in 1948, *The portable Swift*. New York: The Viking Press, pp. 549–559.

Tannahill, R. (1975). *Flesh & Blood*. Boston, MA: Little, Brown.

Tattersall, I. (1995). *The fossil trail*. Oxford: Oxford University Press.

Thomas, R. (1835). *Interesting and authentic narratives of the most remarkable shipwrecks*. Freeport, NY: Books for Libraries Press (1970 reprint).

Thornton, J. Q. (1996). Oregon and California in 1848. In K. Johnson (Ed.), *"Unfortunate emigrants."* Reno, NV: Utah State University Press, pp. 14–120.

Todd, A. L. (1961). *Abandoned*. New York: McGraw-Hill.

Tuck, J. A. (1971a). The Iroquois confederacy. *Scientific American*, 224, #2, 32–49.

Tuck, J. A. (1971b). *Onondaga Iroquois prehistory*. Syracuse, NY: Syracuse University Press.

Turner, C. G., II, & Morris, N. (1970). A massacre at Hopi. *American Antiquity*, 35, 320–331.

Turner, C. G., II, & Turner, J. A. (1990). Perimortem damage to human skeletal remains from Wupatki National Monument, Northern Arizona. *Kiva*, 55, 187–212.

Turner, C. G., II, & Turner, J. A. (1992). On Peter Y. Bullock's "A reappraisal of Anasazi cannibalism." *Kiva*, 58, 189–201.

Turner, C. G., II, & Turner, J. A. (1999). *Man corn: Cannibalism and violence in the prehistoric American southwest*. Salt Lake City, UT: University of Utah Press.

Tuzin, D. (1983). Cannibalism and Arapesh cosmology. In P. Brown & D. Tuzin (Eds.), *The ethnography of cannibalism*. Washington, DC: Society for Psychological Anthropology, pp. 61–71.

Tversky, A., & Kahneman, D. (1981). The framing of decision and the psychology of choice. *Science*, 211, 453–463.

Twain, M. (1868). Cannibalism in the cars. *Mark Twain's sketches, new and old*. Hartford, CN: The American Publishing Company, 287–295.

Verne, J. (1862). *Five weeks in a balloon*. Ware, Herfordshire, UK: Wordsworth Editions Limited (1994 reprint).

Villa, P., Bouville, C., Courtin, J., et al. (1986). Cannibalism in the Neolithic. *Science*, 233, 431–437.

Viveiros de Castro, E. (1992). *From the enemy's point of view*. Chicago, IL: University of Chicago Press.

226 References

Wagner, U. (1979). Review of *The Man Eating Myth* by W. Arens. *Ethnos*, 44, 267–270.

Waldron, A. (1997). "Eat people"—A Chinese reckoning. *Commentary*, July 1997, 28–33.

Walford, C. (1879). *Famines of the world*. New York: Burt Franklin (1970 reprint).

Wang, X. T. (1996). Domain-specific rationality in human choices: Violations of utility axioms and social contexts. *Cognition*, 60, 31–63.

Wang, X. T., & Johnston, V. (1995). Changes in cognitive and emotional processing with reproductive status. *Brain, Behavior and Evolution*, 42, 39–47.

Westermarck, E. (1906). *The origin and development of the moral ideas*, Vol. I. London: Macmillan.

Westermarck, E. (1908). *The origin and development of the moral ideas*, Vol. II. London: Macmillan.

White, T. D. (1992). *Prehistoric cannibalism at Mancos 5MTUMR-2346*. Princeton, NJ: Princeton University Press.

Whitehead, N. (1990). The snake warriors—Sons of the tiger's teeth: A descriptive analysis of Carib warfare ca. 1500–1820. In J. Haas (Ed.), *The anthropology of war*. Cambridge, UK: Cambridge University Press, pp. 146–170.

Williams, G. W. (1966). *Adaptation and natural selection*. Princeton, NJ: Princeton University Press.

Williams, T. (1859). *Fiji and the Fijians*. New York: D. Appleton.

Wissler, C. (1932). Foreword. In F.B. de Sahagun, *A history of ancient Mexico 1547–1577*, Vol. 1. Nashville, TN: Fiske University Press.

Wolf, A. P. (1980). *Marriage and adoption in China, 1854–1945*. Stanford, CA: Stanford University Press.

Würf, K. (1976). *To serve man*. Philadelphia, PA: Owlswick Press.

Yang, D. L. (1996). *Calamity and reform in China*. Stanford, CA: Stanford University Press.

Zheng Yi. (1996). *Scarlet memorial*. Boulder, CO: Westview Press.

Name Index

Abler, T. S., 157–159, 163
Adams, W. H. D., 53
Alldridge, T. J., 124
Almond, J., 144
Anderson, E. N., 180
Arens, W., 13, 14, 18, 126, 141, 147–167, 188, 209

Bahn, P. G., 107, 148, 153
Balée, W., 127
Bardach, J., 171, 188, 190
Beach, F. A., 161
Beatty, K. J., 122–123
Becker, J., 171, 174, 175, 178–186
Bedau, H. A., 58, 59
Bell, G., 28, 30, 31, 165
Benedict, R., 163
Bettinger, R. L., 111, 112
Bierce, A., 117
Bisset, J., 50
Blakeslee, S., 144
Block, W. D., 98
Boas, F., 163
Boswell, J., 50
Bowden, R., 136
Brady, I., 153
Brew, A., 104
Brodhead, M., 22, 38.
Brown, D. E., 3
Brozek, J., 14
Bullock, P. Y., 108
Buñuel, L., 199
Burrows, G., 124
Buss. D. M., 9
Byron, G. G. (Lord), 52

Carneiro, R., 129, 135, 136
Chong, K. R., 180–181
Clastres, P., 129–134, 155, 211
Cohen, D., 111
Colden, C., 158
Collis, W. R. F., 192
Conquest, R., 171–174, 176–179, 188–190
Conrad, J., 209
Constable, A. C., 50, 52
Cook, J. W., 3, 13
Craig, H., 199
Craig, W., 194

Crapanzano, V., 152
Crespi, B. J., 85, 92
Cronin, H., 29
Cullotta, E., 102, 110
Cunningham, R., 67

Daly, M., 9, 19, 30
Darwin, C., 6, 19, 29, 160
Davies, N., 94, 211
Dawkins, R., 28, 29–31
Deacon, A. B., 138–190
Defleur, A., 102
Defoe, D., 4, 199–200, 202
Degler, C. N., 160, 161
Denke, K., 193
Dennett, D. C., 28, 29
Devine, P. E., 63
Diamond, J., 112–113
Dickens, C., 4, 197, 201–204, 207, 211, 213
Dong, Q., 86–87
Donner, G., 23, 27, 40
Dorling, T., 51
Dornstreich, M. D., 98, 144–145
Durán, F. D., 95
Durham, W. H., 140–142, 212

Edmonson, M. S., 7
Ehrenreich, B., 100, 114, 140, 164
Elgar, M. A., 85, 87, 88, 92
Eliot, T. S., 197, 204

Farnham, E. W., 38
Faron, L. C., 94, 118, 119, 128, 129
Figueredo, A. J., viii,
Fisher, H. H., 171, 176–177
Fitzpatrick, S., 171–175, 178
Flaubert, G., 204–205
Flinn, L., 104
Ford, C. S., 161
Forsyth, D. W., 126, 154–157
Freeman, D., 144, 164
Freud, S., 162
Friedrich, O., 193,

Gajdusek, C., 141–142, 144
Garn, S. M., 98
Gero, F. G., 120–122, 211, 212
Ghiselin, M. T., 28

227

Subject Index